THE RHETORIC OF ARISTOTLE

THE RHETORIC OF ARISTOTLE

AN EXPANDED TRANSLATION
WITH SUPPLEMENTARY EXAMPLES FOR STUDENTS
OF COMPOSITION AND PUBLIC SPEAKING

BY

LANE COOPER

LATE PROFESSOR OF THE ENGLISH LANGUAGE AND LITERATURE
IN CORNELL UNIVERSITY

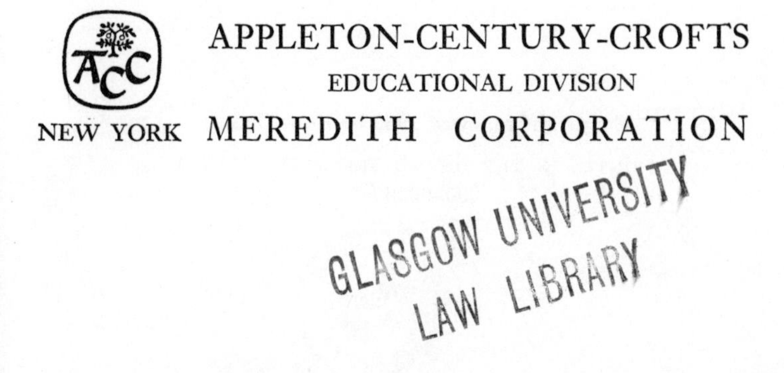

APPLETON-CENTURY-CROFTS
EDUCATIONAL DIVISION
NEW YORK MEREDITH CORPORATION

781–19

PRINTED IN THE UNITED STATES OF AMERICA
390–03590–4

TO

J. C. AND M. L. C.

IN LOVING MEMORY

PREFACE

Aristotle's treatise on Rhetoric is one of the world's best and wisest books. This may be gathered from the 'witnesses' who are later quoted (pp. xi–xiii), and I hope from the Introduction. When I began my translation of the work, there was room for a new one in English. Jebb's posthumously published rendering (1909) was not well edited by Sandys, who failed to supply phrases, and even clauses, that Jebb years before had skipped. I aimed at a version that should strike a mean between the baldness of Jebb's unpolished draft (while preserving some part of his admirable terseness) and the more expansive, usually readable, but sometimes prolix style of Welldon (1886). And I wished to provide a book that could be more easily obtained than either Welldon's or Jebb's in this country. More than that, I aimed to supply running explanations, and even examples, interlarded in the text itself, of what I thought the ordinary student of the *Rhetoric* might need light on as he went along. Sometimes the bare principle seems to need more illustration. Aristotle's citations of the Homeric poems, for instance, are commonly made with a line or the first words of it, when he has a longer passage in mind; his meaning often is not clear until more lines are given, sometimes preceding lines. I have done what I could to make his illustrations more intelligible to modern readers. Other of my interpolations may cause delay at the moment—but the *Rhetoric* was not meant to be read as a novel; it is a book to be chewed and digested. Sometimes sheer expansion of a condensed passage may lead the student to give adequate attention to what is said. Yet often I have avoided interruption, and have not put my added bits of connective tissue within the square brackets that indicate inserted matter; no one ever translated a scientific work of Aristotle without using more words than are found in the Greek text.

My book, then, is intended as a companion volume to my 'amplified' rendering of Aristotle *On the Art of Poetry* (now published by Harcourt, Brace and Company), as also to my *Aristotelian Theory of Comedy*, but is meant for more readers. The students of public speaking in this country far outnumber those who concern themselves with the principles of poetry; and it is for every serious student of public speaking, and of the art of prose, that I have tried to open the greatest of all books on the philosophy and technique of persuasion. So long as he cannot follow the original treatise in Greek, or wants access to the more costly volume containing the translation by Rhys Roberts, I hope that he will find a use for my volume.

My first draft was a little less than half done when Roberts' very excellent work appeared (1924). That admirable scholar himself encouraged me to complete my task, which, after all, has a different design from his. I have not kept much in mind the opinion finished scholars may entertain of my undertaking, though of course I desire their good will, and hope they may note some of the places (as 3. 10. 1411^a 18–20 and 3. 16. 1417^{b}16–20) in which my rendering or interlarded comment should alter hitherto accepted views of Aristotle's meaning. For the student of Greek I have indicated in the margin the pages and columns (but not the line-numbers) of the Berlin text. But the persons I have kept in mind are the undergraduate and the graduate student of public speaking in America, and the large body of teachers of this subject who have not studied Rhetoric in its sources, and otherwise lack a classical background. For them I have produced an inexpensive translation of the *Rhetoric*, adding every reasonable device I could think of that might assist them in reading it as a book in English. For such persons mainly I have done what is here done, and left undone what I have consciously omitted to do. Naturally I shall be glad if others find the translation useful, and of these particularly those readers who know my work on Aristotle's *Poetics*; I heartily wish that I myself had early seen the worth of the entire *Rhetoric* to the student of poetry.

That my purpose has met uniform success throughout is too much to hope. The translation of a difficult text has been carried on at intervals over nearly a decade of years, often for odd weeks in summer with the help of but a few books. Latterly, and the more I have consulted the work of Roberts, I have been less concerned to give precise reference to fragments, now almost or quite unintelligible, such as some that are listed (from the citations of Aristotle) by Baiter-Sauppe. Doubtless a lack of uniformity may be found in other small details, though I have labored to reduce errors, great and small, to a minimum.

I must not close without a few words of acknowledgment. Every one who gives himself seriously to Aristotle's *Rhetoric* must owe a heavy debt to the *Introduction* of Cope, and to his edition as issued by Sandys. Yet for the part of my translation that was done after the work of Roberts appeared, I believe my debt is even heavier to him. To me, Roberts' translation and notes are in effect the best commentary on the *Rhetoric* that has appeared in England. On occasion, however, I have found very real help in the translations and notes of Welldon and Jebb-Sandys. Last of all, let me heartily thank my colleagues, both of them my former pupils, Professor Harry Caplan and Professor James Hutton, for their generous help with my work in all its stages.

LANE COOPER

WITNESSES TO THE VALUE OF THE RHETORIC

If ever a writer labored more than another, in an age of sophistry and dogmatism, to establish the empire of common sense and reason, it was Aristotle.—EDWARD COPLESTON, *A Reply to the Calumnies of the Edinburgh Review against Oxford*, 1810, p. 20.

His chief characteristic is a resolute endeavor to get to the bottom of his subject, whatever it may be. In this resolution his firmness and intrepidity are beyond example. . . . He never rests satisfied with partial glimpses and imperfect demonstration, where the subject seems capable of closer handling.—COPLESTON, p. 21.

It is unfortunate for the fame of Aristotle that he should be known chiefly as the author of the Logical Treatises. The Treatise on Rhetoric is a magazine of intellectual riches. Under an arrangement the most accurate perhaps and the most luminous ever marked out, the diversified elements of thought, of feeling, and of taste, are presented in due order to the reader's mind. Nothing is arbitrary, nothing gratuitous. Long experience with mankind, attentive observation of human nature in public and in private life, the political history of past times, and the occurrences of his own age, furnished him with the materials of this great work. In the course of the inquiry, nothing is left untouched on which Rhetoric, in all its branches, has any bearing. His principles are the result of extensive original induction. He sought them, if ever man did seek them, in the living pattern of the human heart. All the recesses and windings of that hidden region he has explored; all its caprices and affections, whatever tends to excite, to ruffle, to amuse, to gratify, or to offend it, have been carefully examined. The reason of these phenomena is demonstrated, the method of creating them is explained. The Third Book contains a body of rules for good writing, traced to those natural principles out of which they all grow, and illustrated by examples which his own intimate acquaintance with the best poets and orators of Greece readily supplied. The whole is a textbook of human feeling; a storehouse of taste; an exemplar of condensed and accurate, but uniformly clear and candid, reasoning. —COPLESTON, pp. 26–7.

I do not believe there is a single refinement of the art that escapes him. . . . Nothing better proves the great sense and good taste of Aristotle than his having given each thing its place.—VOLTAIRE, *Dictionnaire Philosophique,* art. Aristotle (De sa Rhétorique), 1770, in *Œuvres Complètes de Voltaire* 17 (Paris, 1878).372, 374.

The science or, as Aristotle would call it, the art of Rhetoric has had a curious history. It was his creation; and whatever has been best in it from [his] time to the present is due to him. The definition of Rhetoric, its relation to Psychology, the distinction of its three kinds, the nature of its proofs, the use of enthymeme and example, the special and common topics, the style and arrangement of a speech, all are his. . . . Nor is there any rhetorical work of a later age which can be placed in comparison with his. . . .

The study of Rhetoric as an educational instrument . . . has at least in England been practically neglected since the beginning of the eighteenth century. . . . It is possible that the time will again come when the world will recognize that 'it is not enough to know what to say, but it is necessary also to know how to say it.' . . . Then the *Rhetoric* of Aristotle will, I think, be widely read, as being perhaps a solitary instance of a book which not only begins a science but completes it.—J. E. C. WELLDON, *The Rhetoric of Aristotle, Translated,* London, 1886, pp. vi, vii.

As in the *Politics,* . . . so here, he takes all due account of previous efforts and experience. . . . His repeated references either to 'the present-day writers on rhetoric' generally, or to specified teachers and theorists, are enough to show that he has faithfully reviewed the rhetorical field of his own and previous days. And in the light of current shortcomings he lays down the true philosophical principles of rhetoric, considered as a branch of the science of man, and writes a treatise which has never been superseded, and is never likely to be superseded. The *Rhetoric* has been described as an 'isolated' work. Its true distinction is that it does not stand alone without predecessors or successors, but that it stands apart and pre-eminent even where the predecessors and successors are so numerous; it is the most philosophical (or, scientific) work ever composed on the subject.—W. RHYS ROBERTS, *Greek Rhetoric and Literary Criticism,* 1928, pp. 34–5.

Through our rapid analysis it is easy to discern the philosophic value Aristotle has succeeded in giving to his theory of the art of speaking; and to see how, with his penetrating insight, he has duly allotted to every element the relative importance it has in the whole. What is hard to make the reader understand, in a few words, is the wealth of detail, the abundance of facts and ideas. —ALFRED CROISET, in CROISET, *Histoire de la Littérature Grecque* 4 (1900).735–6.

The goal of the orator is not debased; his eye is always fixed upon the good, under its various forms of the useful, the just, and the beautiful. . . . In giving Rhetoric this high mission—and the mission surely is his own—Aristotle does not mistake the rôle that technique plays in the art, but makes it subordinate; technique occupies less space perhaps than Ethics, Politics, and Psychology.

And thence, let us never doubt, has come the sovereign influence that the *Rhetoric* of Aristotle has exerted, and will always maintain, its power to satisfy alike the most practical reflections of statesmen and the studious labors of youth; albeit the work is not known in our days as it should be, not known as it was in the days of Philip and Alexander.—J. BARTHÉLEMY SAINT-HILAIRE, *Rhétorique d'Aristote, traduite,* 1 (1870). lxxiv-lxxv.

My task is completed if I have made the reader see that this Rhetoric, the oldest of all, nevertheless is the one that has aged the least, the one that to-day remains the most useful, because it is based upon principles higher and more universal than any other.—ERNEST HAVET, *Étude sur la Rhétorique d'Aristote,* Paris, 1846, p. 119.

We have been reading some of the *Rhetoric* in the Sixth Form this half-year, and its immense value struck me again so forcibly that I could not consent to send my son to [a] University where he would lose it altogether.—THOMAS ARNOLD (of Rugby), from a letter to Mr. Justice Coleridge, June 26, 1841.

CONTENTS

INTRODUCTION

A practical book

The *Rhetoric* of Aristotle is a practical psychology, and the most helpful book extant for writers of prose and for speakers of every sort. Every one whose business it is to persuade others—lawyers, legislators, statesmen, clergymen, editors, teachers—will find the book useful when it is read with attention. And the modern psychologist commonly will find that he has observed the behavior of human beings less carefully than did Aristotle, even though the author keeps reminding us that in the *Rhetoric* his analysis of thought and conduct is practical, not scientifically precise and complete. Such as it is, the treatise must be studied and assimilated, for, though full of life and interest, it is not an easy book; no more is the art of the finished writer or speaker an easy art. Yet the attentive student quickly finds that our treatise has the same value to-day as its author had in his day. Philip, says Plutarch, had observed that, however refractory the young Alexander might be, he could readily be led by speech to do what was right; and this was why he 'sent for Aristotle, the most famous of philosophers, and a master of speech.'[1] After the manuscripts of Aristotle were rediscovered, he, long dead, began to teach Rome, too. And, in effect, the Rhetoric not only of Cicero and Quintilian, but of the Middle Ages, of the Renaissance, and of modern times, is, in its best elements, essentially Aristotelian. There is no book on the subject since Aristotle's that is not at least indirectly indebted to his. Unfortunately the influence of his *Rhetoric* more often has not been direct; as a class, the latest text-books of rhetoric and composi-

[1] W. Rhys Roberts, *Greek Rhetoric and Literary Criticism,* 1928, p. 47.

tion, by authors who know little of the past, give, at fourth hand perhaps, only shreds of the rich thought that is compressed into Aristotle's treatise. The latest books also lack his perspective. He brought together all that was worth keeping in the earlier and current Greek text-books; rejecting their trivial novelties, he supplied the details they lacked; and taking what they gave and he added, he cast the whole into a pattern that has not yet been bettered. In detail and in perspective alike lie the reasons why his treatment of the art of persuasion seems so robust and 'modern,' when very recent, ostensibly modern, books are nerveless and trite. For permanent value, of course, it makes no difference when or where a book is produced, as a bare matter of date and place; some reader may like to think that the best Art of Persuasion will be produced in the year 1935, or 2935, and not on the Main Street of Athens; but if he has used or written text-books of composition, and is not yet acquainted with Aristotle, he does not yet know the most illuminating practical Rhetoric. In character it is different from the *Gorgias* and the *Phaedrus* of Plato, artistic dialogues with which it is eminently desirable that the modern speaker or writer should be acquainted. The *Phaedrus* also is unequaled, and the best thing in its class; but its type is so different from the extant works of Aristotle that we must not here enter into the suggested comparison.

Plato's *Phaedrus*

Relation of the *Rhetoric* to other works of Aristotle

The *Rhetoric* of Aristotle tells us how to frame a speech, just as his *Poetics* tells us how to construct and work out a dramatic action. In the *Poetics*, when he comes to the art of framing speeches, he naturally refers the poet to the *Rhetoric*. Looked at in one way, a narrative poem or a drama is entirely made up of speeches; in the act of composition, then, the epic or dramatic writer, or the novelist, must constantly use the art of rhetoric. Similarly, the *Rhetoric* refers us to the *Poetics* for a discussion of matters that are there more fully dealt with. The *Poetics* contains the first scientific sketch of grammar, a subject belonging almost equally to rhetoric; and it contains the more inclusive sketch, in outline, of diction and style to which the elaborate account in the *Rhetoric* is subordinate. Here poet and rhetorician must study both works. It seems, too, that the *Poetics* in its original shape contained a detailed analysis of comedy and the ludicrous; and to this lost section the speaker is now vainly referred by the *Rhetoric.* Yet light is thrown upon this reference, as I believe, and as Rutherford and Starkie believed, by the fragmentary or schematic *Tractatus Coislinianus*, which I have supplied with a translation and commentary in *An Aristotelian Theory of Comedy* (New York, 1922). The *Rhetoric* and the *Poetics* are further allied by their insistence upon order, natural or inevitable, in the parts of a composition; upon the pleasure all men take in learning; and hence upon a sequence of thought that constantly enables the hearer to draw his own inferences. And the two works are allied by their examples, since the *Rhetoric* illustrates so many of its points from the eloquence of Homer and the dramatists.

The *Rhetoric* and *Poetics* are intelligible by themselves

Readers who are mainly interested in these two works of Aristotle have no great need to go beyond them in order to understand them, unless it be to his writings on logic, in particular, the *Topics*, to which the *Rhetoric* more than once refers. It may, indeed, be misleading, when Butcher and his like tell us, on the authority of Goethe, that we must know something about Aristotle's philosophy outside of the *Poetics* in order to understand the *Poetics*; the same would have to be true of the *Rhetoric.* Of course it is a good thing to know the philosophy of Aristotle, and a knowledge of any one of his works helps to illuminate any other; that is a principle of interpretation, and one that is valid for all authors. But the main positions taken in the *Rhetoric*, as in the *Poetics*, are intelligible enough as soon as we grasp the literal meaning of the statements concerning them; when we need to go outside of either work for an understanding of it, we had best follow Aristotle's own hints and directions, going from the *Poetics* to the *Rhetoric* first of all, in order to see how Sophocles must construct appropriate speeches of Antigone and Haemon to Creon; and from the *Rhetoric* to the *Poetics* for supplementary information on Style. The other works that throw most light on these two are, after the logical treatises, the *Ethics* and *Politics*, which deal with the behavior of men as individuals and in groups. Still, Aristotle thinks that, for the ends of persuasion, the *Rhetoric* gives an adequate sketch of these and like matters. We have already called this treatise a practical psychology; how adequate it is, few psychologists, as we have intimated, and fewer theorists on education, in our day, alas! are aware.

Rhetoric a study of the human soul

The great merit of the treatise may be stated thus. It is a searching study of the audience, or, to use Aristotle's frequent term, of the 'judge,' the person (or persons) to whom your speech is directed. A speech is to be judged by its effect upon some one. Since discourse has its end in persuasion, the speaker or writer must know the nature of the soul he wishes to persuade. That is, he must know human nature, with its ways of reasoning, its habits, desires, and emotions, and must know the kind of argument that will persuade each kind of men, as also the emotional appeal that will gain their assent; every detail, the choice of the individual words and phrases, the arrangement of larger and smaller parts, each single item in the speech is to be determined by its effect upon the soul. Since every one is alternately listener and speaker, or reader and writer, the *Rhetoric* thus becomes a popular treatise on the interests of men in groups and as individuals, a popular logic, and a popular account of the emotions, the memory, the imagination in hope and fear, and the will.

Aristotle's emphasis is right but unexpected. The student who assumes Aristotle's position from the outset will escape some difficulties. He will waste no time upon the feeling of persuasion. Every one knows what it means to be persuaded. The emphasis is always upon the nature of the person to be persuaded, and the means by which it is possible, and just, to persuade him. The one legitimate means is reasonable argument; but since man is an emotional creature, and audiences are sure to be swayed by emotion, the speaker has to reckon with this side of his audience, and to deal with it.

Emphasis on the nature of the audience

The student must also bear in mind what Aristotle means by the 'judge.' When a speech is made, or a brief submitted, in a case at law, the judge is the person who decides the case. Or, when the decision rests with more than one person, as in a case submitted to a jury, then the jury are the judges. Here, then, 'judge' may mean what we mean by 'judge' or 'jury' or both. Whoever has the power of decision in the outcome of prosecution or defence is the judge of a forensic speech.

The 'judge'

In ceremonial discourse, in what Aristotle calls 'epideictic' speaking, or in such discourse when it is written to be read, the judges must still be those who have a power of decision. This kind of discourse has to do with praise or blame. Thus the 'judge' may be the reader of Antony's funeral oration over Caesar, or of Lincoln's speech at Gettysburg, or of Wordsworth's *Character of the Happy Warrior*. Or we may regard the actual auditors of Lincoln's speech as the 'judges.' More generally, the judge is any person of good education, sound sense, and complete human sympathy, who approves or disapproves of the speech.

In deliberative discourse the judge or judges must be the person or persons whom the speaker or writer tries to persuade to a course of action or to dissuade from it. A deliberative discourse gives advice. And hence, when one person counsels another in private, his speech falls under this head, and his judge is an audience of one. Or when a moral writer like Ruskin in *Unto this Last* counsels his readers, they, or the competent ones among them, the sound critics, are his judges. But deliberative oratory is more often thought of as the public speaking of statesmen, Senators, for example, when the future of the commonwealth is debated, and the audience is a legislative body or a group of voters. All voters are 'judges.' Of course the ideal judge is a great jurist, or literary critic, or a statesman like Pericles or Lincoln. Aristotle's word for 'judge'—κριτής—is related to our word 'critic.'

Hubris and other Greek words

Other difficulties in the *Rhetoric* are removed if we study other Greek words as they were commonly used, or as Aristotle uses them. A few, like *hubris* (ὕβρις), wanton insolence within, wanton violence without, are so common, full of meaning, and untranslatable, that it would be well if we took them over bodily into English; we could then denote both the mental state and its outward acts by the short and telling Greek word. Let us consider also the following: *ethos* (ἦθος), often translated as 'character,' but the translation is misleading when it suggests one of the persons in a story; ἐκ (ἐξ), a preposition meaning 'from' or 'out of'; and *topos* (τόπος), a 'place,' which must be rightly interpreted as 'region' or the like, if we are not to miss the true force of a 'common-place' in Rhetoric.

Ethos and *dianoia*

In the *Poetics* we find *ethos* distinguished from *dianoia*; there, if we take the two elements together, we have the personality of an epic or dramatic agent. The *ethos* of Achilles is his habit of choice, his disposition to act in one way, to refrain from acting in another. His *dianoia* is the way in which he argues. The poet gives Achilles a certain disposition, so that the choices of the hero give rise to an action. He also makes Achilles speak and argue in accordance with that disposition, and hence the *dianoia* of

Achilles is shown in his speeches. And hence it is, as we have seen, that for a study of *dianoia* we are referred to the *Rhetoric*. Since the art of speaking is fully treated in the *Rhetoric*, the subject of *dianoia* is only sketched in the *Poetics*.

In the *Rhetoric* we commonly find *ethos* in the sense of a *good* disposition or habit of choice. The *ethos* of the speaker as shown in his speech ought to be good, for the audience will not trust a speaker if they think him bad. But the speaker must know the whole range of human *ethos*, since he must understand all human motives and emotions, and their consequences. Thus, for example, speakers for the prosecution and the defence must know bad motives as well as good, and must be able to argue from both. And, again, a speaker should be dramatic; he must know how to act out a story before his audience, so that they may see the facts as they occurred or are likely to occur. Whether he be orator or poet, from such and such motives he reconstructs or constructs an episode, and with dramatic art supplies the arguments (*dianoia*) which a person of such and such a disposition (*ethos*) will use. People in actual life make their choices first, and then argue in accordance with those choices. Few argue a matter out so as then to make their choices from reasonable inference.

The notion of *from*, *out of*

But the sound rhetorician does draw one thing *from* another. Thus we come to the preposition ἐκ (or ἐξ), which is characteristic of Aristotle's thought, but often is hard or impossible to translate directly. The speaker is supposed to have resources, *from which* he draws his arguments and illustrations. He being well-educated, his studies supply him with premises, *from which* he derives his enthymemes. Time and again we translate Aristotle's active concept by some static notion such as that of *basis*; an argument, we say, is not *drawn from*, but *based upon*, a collection of facts. According to our way of looking, we do, indeed, draw conclusions from premises, but do not draw premises from our knowledge of the emotions. It will help the student to learn in advance that this way of looking at a fund of knowledge or of arguments, or of illustrations or maxims, or at previous conclusions, as sources to *draw from*, governs a good share of Aristotle's thought in the *Rhetoric*.

Topos or 'place'

Associated with this notion of *from*, or *whence*, is that of *topos* (τόπος) or *place where*. The common translation, 'topic,' suggests a rubric or category, a general heading under which specific details are collected or things are said. So to us 'topic' often comes to mean a theme, a subject under discussion, the matter of a paragraph or the like. To Aristotle *topos* means a place, and when with him it is a live metaphor, he thinks of a place in which the hunter will hunt for game. If you wish to hunt rabbits, you go to a place where rabbits are; and so with deer or with pheasants. Each kind of game has its haunt to which you go when you wish to fetch that sort of creature out. And similarly with arguments. They are of different kinds, and the different kinds are found in different places, from which they may be drawn. There are the commonplaces in which are found the universal forms of argument used by all men, and in every science. And, again, there are special places where you naturally seek a particular argument, or an argument on some point in a more special branch of knowledge. Obviously, if you are addressing the Senate about the tariff, you will need special knowledge about the production of hides, shoes, and the like. If that knowledge is in a book, or in a pigeon-hole, there is a place where you can find it. When the speaker has informed himself, there will be a place in his mind—'in the back of his head'—to which he can go for what he wants. *Topos*, then, may be regarded as a place or region in the whole realm of science, or as a pigeon-hole in the mind of the speaker. Sometimes the metaphor is not so lively; here and there in the long chapter (23) on the *topoi*, in Book 2, *topos* means one argument, not a place holding several or many. At other times the word is well translated by Roberts as 'line of argument.' But the metaphor is of value. A good writer or speaker, constantly learning, has a full, well-ordered mind; his memory is charged with living forms; and in it he usually can find what he needs. At all events, when he seeks for an argument he will know where to look in his own mind or in the mind of another.

Topos as meaning 'line of argument'

The foregoing paragraph anticipates an explanation that is later intercalated (p. 154) in my rendering of Aristotle. I risk the repetition partly because it may help some readers in an important matter that every reader of the treatise should grasp; but partly also because the notion of searching for what you wish to know where you are likely to find it, in its natural habitat, is a general characteristic of Aristotle's scientific method. The search bore fruit in his *Rhetoric*, and may bear fruit for us in our study of this work.

Enthymemes

How, for example, shall we know what our author means by the term Enthymeme? This question goes to the very heart of the *Rhetoric*, since Aristotle tells us that Enthymemes are the essential instrument of oratorical persuasion. He says, too, that they are a kind of syllogism. Yet many students of the *Rhetoric*, including learned men, and some professed logicians, do not seem to realize where Aristotle found his syllogisms or his enthymemes, or where, accordingly, we should look for them. Somewhere, of course, if they really exist as living forms, they must have each of them its natural habitat. Mr. F. C. S. Schiller seems to think that the habitat of the syllogism is the older works of formal logic only, where syllogisms dissected out are given as examples; but this is much like a hunt for animate bodies in a row of skeletons. It is right to look for skeletons in the anatomical museum; and there they have a scientific value. In the *Rhetoric*, again, the analysis of enthymemes is quite properly anatomical. Oddly enough, Mr. Schiller in his *Logic for Use* does not mention the enthymeme, nor show the least familiarity with the *Rhetoric*, a work on a similar subject. But, at all events, a writer as well-read as Aristotle in the history of philosophy would know that examples in a text-book are in an artificial habitat. It is unjust to Aristotle to consider the syllogism only in relation to the examples in his Logic; he did not find the thing itself there; he had discovered it, so to speak, in nature. Similarly it is a mistake to discuss Enthymemes as if they had no existence outside of his *Rhetoric*. It was this mistake that allowed another to grow up, the time-honored notion that an enthymeme was a syllogism with one of the three members taken for granted and suppressed—in other words, that an enthymeme consisted of two statements. Thus, supposedly, our syllogism would be:

All men are mortal;
Socrates is a man;
Socrates is mortal.

And the enthymeme, supposedly:

Socrates is a man;
He is mortal.

Or: All men are mortal, and Socrates is a man. Or: All men are mortal, and so is Socrates. Of course there are enthymemes that take such shape. Any popular syllogism is an enthymeme. But there is no reason why a public speaker should not use a syllogism of three terms.

All men are created equal;
Negroes are men;
Negroes and whites are equal.

And speakers on occasion do use complete syllogisms. But, again, an enthymeme may be a maxim of one term; so Lincoln's 'All men are created equal.' Or, again, it may be a maxim of two terms, yet not syllogistic; such are all the Beatitudes: 'Blessed are the pure in heart, for they shall see God.' The arguments good speakers actually use in persuasion are enthymemes.

Where to look for specimens

That, then, is the answer to our question, 'What is an enthymeme?' It is a thing one can find in a place; it is the kind of argument used by St. Paul or by Lincoln in a speech. The place in which to look for good enthymemes is a good speech, as the place in which to look for syllogisms is a tight scientific argument. To my mind, Aristotle makes the difference clear enough; and the difference between persuasion and scientific demonstration does not lie so much in the fashioning of the individual link in the chain; what counts for more is the formation of the chain. In a scientific treatise, such as the *Ethics* of Spinoza, or Dante's treatise *On Monarchy*, or any work on mathematics, the chain is long, beginning with an axiomatic first principle, the links are elaborately brought out (though not always as triplets), and the conclusion is rigorous. One may even double the chain, as does Descartes, working back by elimination to the basic principle, 'I think, therefore I exist' (in shape, an enthymeme!), and then working forward from that to a distant conclusion. In a narrow sense, an enthymeme is one link in a persuasive argument; more loosely, and commonly, it is a short chain. In a popular work for the general reader, in the *Convivio* of Dante, for example, the pattern of the argument is not very elaborate. You begin with an accepted or easily acceptable truth, and proceed by easily followed steps to an acceptable conclusion. If the process is clear and simple, it may be extended, but not too far.

Aristotle, writing compactly, gives examples when he thinks them needed, but does not give a complete example of the enthymematic process, though of course he refers to many single enthymemes. Perhaps it was too obvious a thing to say: 'If you wish to find a group of enthymemes, look at any speech in the *Iliad* or the *Odyssey.*' Or: 'Take this passage (*Odyssey* 1. 32–44), and observe the maxim, the enthymemes, and the example in it':

Enthymemes in a speech of Zeus

Lo you now, how vainly mortal men do blame the gods! For of us they say comes evil, whereas they even of themselves, through the blindness of their own hearts, have sorrows beyond that which is ordained. Even as of late Aegisthus, beyond that which was ordained, took to him the wedded wife of the son of Atreus and killed her lord on his return, and that with sheer doom before his eyes, since we had warned him by the embassy of Hermes the keen-sighted, the slayer of Argos, that he should neither kill the man nor woo his wife. For the son of Atreus shall be avenged at the hand of Orestes, so soon as he shall come to man's estate, and long for his own country. So spake Hermes, yet he prevailed not on the heart of Aegisthus, for all his good will.

Perhaps Aristotle knew that his students would look for enthymemes where they could be found. I, at all events, will add for the benefit of the modern reader, and perhaps of eminent logicians, some part of a speech (Acts 17. 22–29), from a well-known source, containing enthymemes so obvious that any one may see and recognize them in their natural state:

Enthymemes of Paul for the Athenians

Then Paul stood in the midst of Mars' Hill, and said, Ye men of Athens, I perceive that in all things ye are too superstitious; for as I passed by, and beheld your devotions, I found an altar with this inscription: *To the Unknown God.* Whom therefore ye ignorantly worship, him declare I unto you. God that made the world, and all things therein, seeing that he is Lord of heaven and earth, dwelleth not in temples made with hands; neither is worshipped with men's hands, as though he needed anything, seeing he giveth to all life, and breath, and all things; and hath made of one blood all nations of men for to dwell on all the face of the earth, and hath determined the times before appointed, and the bounds of their habitation; that they should seek the Lord, if haply they might feel after him, and find him, though he be not far from every one of us: for in him we live, and move, and have our being; as certain also of your own poets have said: 'For we are also his offspring.' Forasmuch, then, as we are the offspring of God, we ought not to think that the Godhead is like unto gold, or silver, or stone, graven by art and man's device.

There is the enthymematic process (we note also the use of a rhetorical 'sign,' and the telling appeal to the witness of the national poets): In all things you are too superstitious. For example, see your altar to the Unknown God. The inscription proves your ignorance, therefore I will enlighten you. Soon he counsels the Athenians to repent, and we see that the speech is a sermon, and belongs to the deliberative or hortatory branch of rhetoric.

Examples of the types of speaking

By seeking illustrations in the proper places, we get light on Aristotle's division of speeches into three types. Paul's speech on Mars' Hill is mainly one of advice; Antony's speech over the dead Caesar is ostensibly a ceremonial speech, as are funeral orations generally. Speeches in the law-courts obviously belong in general to the third type, that of accusation and defence. But the instructions a judge gives the jury may be regarded as a speech of advice. As we have seen, any counsel you may give, in speech or writing, whether to do or to forbear, belongs to this type of discourse. So any discourse of praise or blame belongs to the second type. And the accusation one child brings against another, like the latter's defence, belongs under the head of forensic eloquence.

The mixture of types

Examples show, too, that the types overlap and interpenetrate each other. Thus Lincoln's speech at Gettysburg is primarily a speech of praise, but ends in advice for the future. Shakespeare's Antony begins by saying that he comes to bury Caesar, not to praise him. With his tricky speech he does praise Caesar, but also accuses the murderers, and inflames the mob to violent measures against them. Primarily ceremonial, it is a speech of all three kinds. In Sophocles' *Antigone*, Haemon's longest speech to his father is a piece of counsel, in which, however, the people's praise of Antigone is quoted for her defence; and, before he has done, Haemon attacks his father's action. A speech of accusation or defence can hardly proceed without praise or blame, nor a speech of blame without advice, and so on. The three types, then, represent tendencies; we often have to decide the type to which a discourse belongs by noting its main tendency. Properly considered, the point should be determined by the end and aim of the speech, whether these are concealed or not. Sometimes the author may have two aims, as Plato in the *Apology* may intend both to vindicate Socrates and to praise the contemplative life.

Interrelated parts of Aristotle's treatise

This natural overlapping of the kinds of rhetoric brings about a difficulty in outlining the substance of Aristotle's treatise. Thus chapters 4, 5, 6, 7, and 8 of Book 1 are ostensibly concerned with deliberative speaking. Accordingly, they deal with men's interests, with happiness, and with goods positive, goods greater, and goods less. But virtue is a good, and it is virtue that the epideictic speaker praises; in fact, he is at liberty to praise anything that is good, as Pindar praises water and gold. Accordingly, chapter 9, which is ostensibly concerned with epideictic speaking, has a substance in common with earlier chapters; and the ceremonial speaker will draw arguments from those chapters. So also the forensic speaker in attacking and defending will argue that a man did right or wrong for the sake of a good or an apparent good, and, as we have seen, will distribute praise and blame. The interpenetration of the kinds of rhetoric could be further illustrated; but thus much will suffice for caution to the reader that page-headings such as 'Deliberative,' 'Epideictic,' and 'Forensic Rhetoric' are, in our translation, of service if their application is not pressed too hard. The overlapping of the parts of Aristotle's treatise is also illustrated by the practice of speakers. If a speech purports to be ceremonial, yet the speaker uses the occasion to counsel or to dissuade, then the speech really is deliberative. So President Lincoln actually used the occasion of November 19, 1863, in his *Address at the Dedication of the Gettysburg National Cemetery:*

Lincoln's speech at Gettysburg

Fourscore and seven years ago our fathers brought forth on this continent a new nation, conceived in liberty, and dedicated to the proposition that all men are created equal.

Now we are engaged in a great civil war, testing whether that nation, or any nation so conceived and so dedicated, can long endure. We are met on a great battle-field of that war. We have come to dedicate a portion of that field as a final resting-place for those who here gave their lives that that nation might live. It is altogether fitting and proper that we should do this.

But, in a larger sense, we cannot dedicate—we cannot consecrate—we cannot hallow—this ground. The brave men, living and dead, who struggled here, have consecrated it far above our poor power to add or detract. The world will little note nor long remember what we say here, but it can never forget what they did here. It is for us, the living, rather, to be dedicated here to the unfinished work which they who fought here have thus far so nobly advanced. It is rather for us to be here dedicated to the great task remaining before us—that from these honored dead we take increased devotion to that cause for which they gave the last full measure of devotion; that we here highly resolve that these dead shall not have died in vain; that this nation, under God, shall have a new birth of freedom; and that government of the people, by the people, for the people, shall not perish from the earth.

This celebrated speech is a good hunting-ground for illustrations of Aristotle's *Rhetoric*; so good, in fact, that a complete analysis of the speech by his principles would here be unwieldy. Reversing the order of the *Rhetoric*, let us briefly touch on salient points in the Arrangement (*Taxis*) and the Diction (*Lexis*) of the speech, and then on the Argument (*Dianoia*) and the *Ethos*; not much need be added on Emotion. Aristotle begins with the internal form of a speech, and does not take up the external form until Book 3. In examining a particular specimen, we begin from the outside, with the visible quantitative parts.

Lincoln's proem

Lincoln's proem is a bit of narration, 'Fourscore and seven years ago our fathers brought forth'; there is more room for narration in a ceremonial speech, which has to do with praise, than in a deliberative, which has to do with peace and war and with the future; yet you may recall the past in order to take counsel for the future, and so Lincoln does. His past comes down to the present, with which a ceremonial speech is concerned; the war thus far enables him to give good advice. The proem proper, in which he strikes the keynote of praise, is the first sentence, which is set off as one paragraph. The narrative praise of 'our fathers' rightly applies to the audience as well, gratifying them and securing their good will and attention; and it contains an abbreviated enthymeme, the maxim on the equality of men. Yet the Introductory part includes most of the second paragraph also, in which Lincoln states the subject of the *Address*: 'We have come to dedicate a portion of that field as a final resting-place for those.' Immediately, then, he begins his Argument with 'who here gave their lives that that nation might live,' from which words the inference is drawn, 'It is altogether fitting and proper that we should do this'—and therewith we have a true enthymeme. The body of the speech continues through the third and final paragraph. The first paragraph deals with the past; the second brings us to the present; the third, which is 'deliberative,' has mainly to do with the future. The Epilogue is a maxim in the form of an asyndeton (that is, it is without connectives)—'Government of the people, by the people, for the people, shall not perish from the earth'; from the shape of the statement you know that you have reached the end—though it is said that the audience was not prepared for so short a speech. Proem, body, and epilogue are naturally bound together by the successive concepts of birth, death, and rebirth.

His statement

His argument

His epilogue

His style

As for style or diction, the speech is characterized by

compactness, balance, and metaphor. The compactness is illustrated by two other cases of asyndeton: 'we are engaged,' 'we are met,' 'we have come'; and 'we cannot dedicate—we cannot consecrate—we cannot hallow—this ground.' It would seem, too, by this method of expression that many things have been said, more, in fact, than have been said, though the speech is full of meaning. The balance in thought and phrase is easily detected by both eye and ear, and the use of antithesis is obvious, as in the contrast between then and now, birth and death, the living and the dead. The language is neither metrical nor yet without rhythm, indefinite. The basic foot is the iamb (or, according to the point where one begins to count, the trochee) as it was in spoken Greek; so: 'shāll nŏt pērĭsh frōm thĕ eārth.' Variation from this may be seen in the use of dactyls (or anapaests) and spondees: 'Wē cănnŏt dēdĭcăte—wē cănnŏt cōnsĕcrăte—wē cănnŏt hāllōw—thīs grōund.' It is the variation of the English Bible: 'Though I speak with the tongues of men and of angels'; 'The Lord is my shepherd, I shall not want.' Compare also the language of Lincoln's *Second Inaugural Address*: 'With malice toward none; with charity for all.' There, too, the iambic basis and the dactylic variation from it are well-marked.

Rhythm

The metaphor of the dedication of a child runs through the speech, beginning with the violent figure of *sires* 'conceiving,' 'bringing forth,' and 'dedicating'—dedicating the newly-born to something like a proposition in Euclid. Still, the violent metaphor has thus far escaped the notice of most readers. And the language of the speech as a whole is clear and appropriate, and dignified, the clearness arising from the use of customary words, dignity and vividness from an archaic flavor (as in 'Fourscore and seven'), from the use of a special epithet like 'fathers' for the founders of the nation, and from active metaphors, as when 'brought forth' is echoed toward the close by

Metaphor

Clearness and dignity

'a new birth of freedom.' There are but two compound words, 'battle-field' and 'resting-place.'

The argument

The chief means of persuasion in a speech should be the enthymematic chain. Even in this brief speech Lincoln is able to interweave other matter between his enthymemes. His principal chain is in the third paragraph. Here he deftly proves the opposite of the enthymeme preceding, using the common topic of more and less: In a larger sense we cannot dedicate or hallow this ground; for the brave soldiers consecrated it through the power of their name and fame. Our power and fame are small. It therefore behoves us to be dedicated under God to the task of finishing the work the noble soldiers have advanced, that of saving the nation and this type of government. Enthymemes even when drawn from the common topics of the day are an 'artistic' means of persuasion; so are the maxims, and the example of the fathers. We note, besides, some 'non-artistic' means, in the suggested use of an ordeal—the 'test' of war; in the use of the oath—'under God'; even an appeal to an 'ancient witness,' the Euclidean maxim of the fathers that 'All men are created equal,' and to a more 'recent witness' through the maxim, 'Government of the people, by the people, for the people.' As maxims, these belong to the artistic means; as witnesses, to the non-artistic.

'Non-artistic' means

General and particular statements

The sequence of general statements and particular inferences is not very rigorous. But the student may see in the speech what he perhaps never before noted, that human discourse is always made up of more general and less general statements in succession; sometimes one or two general remarks followed by something more particular, sometimes one or two, or more, particulars followed by a general remark; or generals and particulars, positively or negatively stated, in some other order. Sometimes there are bad gaps in the order of thoughts, sometimes quick, intelligent leaps. In other words, human discourse, stumblingly it may be, always proceeds either by deduction or by induction; and it was through a study of actual human discourse, of the customary workings of the human mind, that Aristotle discovered the syllogism and the enthymeme. The syllogism he found in stricter reasoning, where scientific demonstration is attempted; and the enthymeme he found in everyday persuasion, in all popular attempts at persuasion, in public speeches, in poems, almost anywhere—wherever men are, or are represented as, discoursing. Lincoln's enthymemes, Aristotle would say, are concerned with what is advantageous to all, and that means with the common weal. It is easy to see that the speaker is concerned with the highest 'good.'

Lincoln's *ethos*

It was an emotional occasion, but the speech reveals no hard effort to stir the emotions; the speech is in this respect appropriate. The *Ethos* of the speech is more persuasive than the Argument. To the maxim, 'All men are created equal,' objection might be taken. It has not the certainty of a geometrical proposition. Nevertheless the maxims lend a good ethical quality to the speech. And still more is this ethical quality impressed upon the speech by the manly self-denial of the speaker, and by his suppression of blame, the absence of any condemnation of the enemy. The enemy could be included among 'the brave men who struggled here.' Even disaffected or irate listeners should be mollified by what is said. In fact, the *ethos* of the speaker is discovered through the speech itself to be that of a man with malice toward none, with charity for all.

ANALYSIS

BOOK I

CHAPTER 1 (p. 1). Rhetoric is the counterpart of Dialectic. Every one uses both. Rhetoric is an art; the efforts of successful speakers can be studied, and the principles of success methodized. The essence of persuasion lies in the arguments or proofs; these have been neglected by writers of text-books, who lay undue stress upon the emotions. But to excite emotion in the hearer is to warp his judgment. Would you warp a carpenter's rule? Law, not sentiment, should decide cases. The text-books also give undue attention to speaking in the law-courts, although the issues of political speaking are greater, being the interests of the commonwealth. It is easier to trick the judge in a case at law, where his own interests are not directly at stake; in a deliberative assembly he will protect himself against irrelevant pleading, and will demand proofs. Artistic speaking, then, consists in proofs, and the proof is a kind of demonstration which has the form of an Enthymeme; enthymemes are a kind of syllogism, the popular kind as distinguished from the rigorous syllogisms of scientific demonstration. Four uses of rhetoric. (1) By it truth and justice maintain their natural superiority. (2) It is suited to popular audiences, since they cannot follow scientific demonstration. (3) It teaches us to see both sides of a case, and to refute unfair arguments. (4) It is a means of self-defence. Its possible, and actual, abuse is no argument against its proper service in the cause of truth and right. To discover the genuine, and the spurious, means of persuasion is the office of one and the same art. There is no special name for the sham rhetorician.

CHAPTER 2 (p. 7). Definition: Rhetoric is the faculty of discovering in the particular case all the available means of persuasion. It has no special subject-matter. Certain forms of persuasion come from outside, do not belong to the art itself; thus witnesses, forced confessions, contracts, are external to the art of speaking; proofs such as these are 'non-artistic.' Other forms strictly appertain to this art, and must be supplied by the speaker's invention; and these 'artistic' means of persuasion are threefold. They consist in (1) evincing through the speech a personal character that will win the confidence of the listener; (2)

engaging the listener's emotions; (3) proving a truth, real or apparent, by argument. Mastery of the art, then, calls for (1) the power of logical reasoning; (2) a knowledge of character (*ethos*); (3) a knowledge of the emotions (*pathe*). Thus Rhetoric is an offshoot of Dialectic, and also of Ethics (the study of conduct, including the conduct of groups, which is the subject of Politics). Persuasion by argument is effected (1) by the example (which corresponds to the induction of Dialectic); (2) by the enthymeme (which corresponds to the syllogism of Dialectic); and (3) by the apparent enthymeme (corresponding to the apparent syllogism). The enthymeme is a rhetorical syllogism, the example a rhetorical induction. Rhetoric has a view to classes of men—there is no art or science of the individual; and this art has to do with matters that may turn out in more than one way (not those that can turn out in one way only). These matters are 'probabilities' in the sphere of action, the things about which men do deliberate and argue. Further, the audience with which Rhetoric is concerned is a popular one, untrained in rigorous thinking, and unable to follow a long, elaborate argument. The premises from which enthymemes are formed are 'probabilities' and 'signs'; and 'signs' are either infallible and conclusive, or not infallible, but only true as a rule. As for the 'example,' when two things fall under the same head, but one is the better-known, this one is the example. For enthymemes, there is a great distinction between those general ones that belong to rhetoric, and the special ones that have to do with more special arts and sciences. In other words, there are common *topoi*, or lines of argument, that concern many branches, and there are special *topoi* for special branches, such as physics, ethics, and so on. The speaker must be careful about entering special provinces of knowledge; otherwise he will overstep the bounds of rhetoric. Still he will derive most of his enthymemes from less general, while not too special, *topoi*.

CHAPTER 3 (p. 16). There are three kinds of rhetoric: (1) Deliberative (political, advisory); (2) Forensic (legal); (3) Epideictic (ceremonial). These may be distinguished by their (*a*) divisions, (*b*) times, and (*c*) ends and aims. The (*a*) divisions of deliberative speaking are exhortation and dissuasion; (*b*) its time is the future; (*c*) its ends are expediency and inexpediency. The (*a*) divisions of forensic speaking are accusation and defence; (*b*) its time is the past; (*c*) its ends are justice and injustice. The (*a*) divisions of epideictic speaking are praise and blame; (*b*) its time is the present; (*c*) its ends are honor and dishonor.

CHAPTER 4 (p. 20). Since deliberative speaking looks to expediency as its end, its subjects are good things and bad (expedient and inexpedient), yet not all such, but those that admit of more than one possibility in the outcome, and those that do not depend upon nature or chance. Its subjects are all such things, expedient or injurious, as depend upon free human action, for about these we may deliberate. The most important of them fall into five classes: (1) ways and means; (2) war and peace; (3) defence of the country; (4) exports and imports; (5) legislation. The speaker, then, must know (1) the sources of public revenue, how to increase it, and how to cut expenditure; must know (2) the actual and possible military forces of his own and other states, and the history of relations between states; must know (3) strategic geography, and the actual and necessary fortifications; must know (4) what his own state produces and needs, what other states may absorb or supply; and, under legislation, must know (5) the nature and history of the different types of government.

CHAPTER 5 (p. 24). Advice concerns happiness. All men, collectively and individually, aim at happiness; upon it, all exhortation and dissuasion turn. The orator must know the popular conceptions and main constituents of happiness. Four working definitions: Happiness is (1) prosperity conjoined with virtue; (2) a self-sufficient existence; (3) the pleasantest life, with security; (4) a thriving estate, with the ability to use and preserve it. Happiness involves the possession of internal goods (1) of the soul and (2) of the body, and of external goods. Various constituents of happiness; fourteen are enumerated: good birth, children (good, and many), wealth, reputation, honors, health, beauty, strength, size (with stature), a good old age, friends, good luck, virtue.

CHAPTER 6 (p. 29). Since advice concerns the interest of the audience, the orator must know the nature of means to 'the good.' Working definitions of 'the good.' It is 'desirable for its own sake'; or 'chosen for the sake of something else'; or 'what is sought after by all things,' or 'by all sentient beings'; or 'what reason prescribes for one'; or 'what brings a thing into good condition'; or 'what does these things, and works against their opposites.' The following are 'goods': happiness, virtues of the soul, virtues and graces of the body, wealth, friends, honor and reputation, power in speech and action, natural intelligence, the arts and sciences, life itself, and justice. These are admitted goods. There are also disputable goods, and arguments pro and con about them; a score of *topoi* are listed for arguments with which to prove that a thing in dispute *is* good.

CHAPTER 7 (p. 34). Comparison of goods. 'More' and 'less' in regard to the greater good and the expedient course. This brings us to consider the 'topic of degree' in many applications.

CHAPTER 8 (p. 44). The deliberative speaker should study the types of government (forms of political organization), since a knowledge of these will help him more than any other sort of learning. Each type is characterized by the nature of its supreme authority. There are four types. (1) In a democracy the offices are distributed by lot. (2) In an oligarchy they depend upon a property qualification. (3) In an aristocracy they go to the best-trained persons. (4) In a monarchy the power resides in one person; the power may be regulated, or it may be unrestricted. Each type of government has its end. That of (1) democracy is liberty; that of (2) oligarchy is wealth; of (3) aristocracy, discipline; of (4) tyranny, self-protection. The speaker must understand the customs and tendencies, the character, of each type.

CHAPTER 9 (p. 46). When a speaker is praising or blaming, his subjects are virtue and vice, the noble and the base. How his knowledge of these matters is related to his own speech, and to the person he praises or blames. Definition of the 'noble' in relation to virtue. A list of nine virtues, and a comparison of virtue as greater or less: the greatest are the most serviceable to our fellows. A speaker in praising a man will make the man's actual qualities look like the more serviceable virtues; in censure he will make them look like vices. He will also mark the qualities which his audience esteems; whatever is esteemed is to be treated as noble. And he will show that the deeds he praises or blames were deliberate; praising, in fact, is akin to urging a course of action. Further, you can intensify the praise or blame by all the ways of magnifying any action.

CHAPTER 10 (p. 55). With respect to accusation and defence, the speaker must understand wrong-doing, the incentives to it, the condition of the doers, the persons likely to be wronged, and their condition. Wrong-doing defined as voluntary harm done contrary to law. Law is particular (written), and universal (unwritten). The disposition to commit wrongs comes from vice and moral weakness. In general, there are seven causes of human actions: three are involuntary—chance, nature, compulsion; and four are voluntary—habit, reason, passion, desire. All voluntary actions are either good or apparently good, or else pleasant or apparently pleasant. The good or expedient has already been discussed.

CHAPTER 11 (p. 60). The pleasant. Pleasure defined as a motion of the soul, a settling of it into its own nature. Analysis of things pleasant and painful. Men will do wrong for the sake of pleasure, or to escape pain.

CHAPTER 12 (p. 67). The conditions of wrong-doing. Men will do wrong if they believe the thing possible, and possible for them; if they think to escape detection; or to escape punishment; or to lose less through the punishment than they gain through the deed. Conditions under which men are wronged: those will be wronged who have what others lack, or who are not vigilant, or who are easy-going; and crimes will be committed when concealment or escape is easy.

CHAPTER 13 (p. 73). Classification of just and unjust actions, in relation to (1) the law, (2) the persons affected. The law may be particular, that of a community or state; or it may be universal, the law of Nature. The persons affected may be the community, or the individual therein. The act of the wrong-doer must be done either in ignorance and unintentionally, or knowingly and with intention. If the act is conscious and intended, it must be either deliberate or the result of emotion. The motive must be made clear, and the crime properly described. Only deliberate purpose constitutes vice or crime. The unwritten law takes cognizance of exceptional goodness or badness. It also offers remedies when the written law fails; this justice which supplements the written law is Equity. Sometimes the lawmakers have observed no defect in their law; sometimes they are unable to render the law precise, and have framed a sweeping rule applicable only to a majority of cases. Illustrations of the nature and scope of equity.

CHAPTER 14 (p. 78). The comparison of wrongs. The degree of wrong is measured by the badness of disposition which prompts it. The little act may potentially contain greater ones. Sometimes, again, the wrong is to be measured by the actual damage. Other ways of measuring and comparing the badness of actions: the topic of 'degree.'

CHAPTER 15 (p. 80). The 'non-artistic' or non-technical means of persuasion, so far as they appertain to the art of rhetoric, belong especially to forensic speaking. They are five in number: laws, witnesses, contracts, tortures, oaths. (1) How to discredit or uphold the law, according as it makes against or for your argument. (2) Witnesses are 'ancient' or 'recent,' and the 'recent' are either involved, or not involved, in the risk of the action. 'Ancient' witnesses are poets, oracles, authors of maxims; 'recent' witnesses are living authorities, or persons who give evidence in court. The 'ancient' are the more persuasive. How to support or upset the evidence of a witness. (3) How to enhance or damage the credibility of contracts. (4) How to do the like with evidence extracted by torture. (5) Methods of dealing with the oath.

BOOK 2

CHAPTER 1 (p. 90). Rhetoric finds its end in judgment; an audience judges the counsels you give, a jury decides a case. Your speech, then, must not only convince through argument; it must evince the right character (*ethos* of the speaker), and also bring the judge or audience into the right state of feeling. Character is more important in deliberative speaking; inducing the right state of feeling, in forensic. For character, the speech should show the speaker to be a person of intelligence, virtue, and good will. Such a person wins the confidence of his hearers. The means of evincing intelligence and good character have been discussed in 1.9. Good will and a friendly disposition are to be discussed under the emotions. The emotions defined. In regard to each we must study (1) the circumstances (or frame of mind) in which it is felt; (2) the persons toward whom it is felt; (3) the things that arouse it.

CHAPTER 2 (p. 93). The first of the emotions to be treated is anger. The emotion is defined, and the three questions concerning it are settled. A similar analysis is followed in chapters 3–11, which deal with other emotions, and in which various hints are given for the speaker. Thus in the present chapter he learns how to arouse anger in his audience against his adversary.

CHAPTER 3 (p. 99). Mildness or placability, the opposite of anger.

CHAPTER 4 (p. 102). Love (friendship, friendliness) and hatred (enmity).

CHAPTER 5 (p. 107). Fear and confidence.

CHAPTER 6 (p. 112). Shame and shamelessness.

CHAPTER 7 (p. 117). Benevolence and the lack of it.

CHAPTER 8 (p. 119). Pity.

CHAPTER 9 (p. 123). Indignation.

CHAPTER 10 (p. 127). Envy.

CHAPTER 11 (p. 129). Emulation (and contempt).

CHAPTER 12 (p. 131). Types of character as related to emotions, virtues and vices, times of life, and states of fortune. The emotions have been discussed; so also the virtues and vices. The times of life are youth, the prime of life (maturity), and age.

Fortune means birth, wealth, power, and their opposites. A sketch, for the speaker, of the character of youth.

CHAPTER 13 (p. 134). The character of age is analyzed, similarly for the ends of the speaker.

CHAPTER 14 (p. 136). The character of men in their prime. This character shares the excellences of youth and age, and is free from the excesses and defects of both. The body is at its best from thirty to thirty-five, the mind about the age of forty-nine.

CHAPTER 15 (p. 137). Character as modified by fortune. Character of the well-born.

CHAPTER 16 (p. 138). Character of the wealthy.

CHAPTER 17 (p. 139). The character of men in power. The influence of good fortune. The character of the poor and the character of the powerless are evident from a study of opposites.

CHAPTER 18 (p. 141). Recapitulation. Plan of the treatise. The appliances common to all kinds of speaking will next be considered.

CHAPTER 19 (p. 143). The common *topoi* or general lines of argument are: (1) argument from the Possible or Impossible; (2) Past Fact; (3) Future Fact; (4) Degree (the topic of More and Less).

CHAPTER 20 (p. 147). The means of persuasion common to all three branches of rhetoric are the example and the enthymeme. The maxim is not a third means; it is included under the enthymeme. Examples may be historical, or invented, and invented examples may be parables of the speaker, or fables. Fables are suited to popular audiences, and rather easy to invent; it is harder to find your parallels in actual history.

CHAPTER 21 (p. 149). The nature and use of maxims. They are general statements about questions of human conduct, and are incomplete enthymemes. Maxims are of four kinds. (1) Some have no reason subjoined since they are generally accepted truths; (2) others because their truth is seen at first glance. Of those that do have a reason subjoined, (3) some are part of an enthymeme, and (4) others have the nature of an enthymeme, but are not part of one. Maxims are suited to men of experience, and to countering popular sayings. They please ordinary listeners by expressing as universal truths what individual persons know in special cases. They serve also to invest the speech with moral character.

CHAPTER 22 (p. 154). Enthymemes. The chain of argument must not begin too far back; nor may all the steps be put in before you reach your conclusion. But the speaker must know all the facts; without adequate knowledge you cannot argue at all.

There are two kinds of enthymemes, the demonstrative, drawing conclusions from consistent premises, and the refutative, drawing upon inconsistent premises. The special topics of enthymemes are derived from the facts of each branch of knowledge; there are also common topics that belong to all branches.

Chapter 23 (p. 159). A list of 28 *topoi* (lines of argument) for enthymemes whether demonstrative or refutative. Refutative enthymemes have more effect upon the audience; in brief compass the opposing arguments are worked out side by side, and the result is apparent. In general, we like those arguments, not too obvious, the end of which we can discern from the start, or those we can keep up with so as to see the point when the last word is uttered.

Chapter 24 (p. 172). As with syllogisms, so there are enthymemes that are but apparently true. A list of 9 *topoi* of apparent, or sham, enthymemes.

Chapter 25 (p. 177). Refutation. You may refute an argument either by a counter-syllogism or by bringing an objection. The *topoi* of counter-arguments are the same as those of the arguments. Objections may be brought in four ways: (1) by attacking your opponent's premise; (2) by bringing forward a premise like it; (3) by bringing one contrary to it; (4) by citing a previous decision. Illustrations of the four methods. Remarks on enthymemes depending upon probabilities; on fallible signs and on examples; on infallible signs. These last, if the alleged sign cannot be disproved, are irrefutable.

Chapter 26 (p. 180). Supplementary remarks. Two errors should be avoided. (1) Magnifying and minifying are not a mere element of enthymeme; they are a *kind* of enthymeme, the kind which tends to show that a thing is great or small. (2) Nor are destructive enthymemes a different species from constructive. Herewith we conclude the treatment of the Content of a speech. We have yet to take up two other main considerations, namely Style and Arrangement.

BOOK 3

Chapter 1 (p. 182). We have dealt with the means by which the hearer may be persuaded, namely, appeals to his emotions, the character impressed upon the speech, and argument. We have next to treat of Style, since it is not enough to know what to say; one must also know how to say it. And besides the content and the language, there is also the question of delivery, an art on which we have no systematic treatise, though it concerns rhetoric as much as it does poetry. In the drama the art of acting has been technically developed. It was the poets who gave the impulse toward the cultivation of style. But prose style is different from poetical. Here we have to consider only so much of the subject of style as concerns Rhetoric; the other kind of style is discussed in the *Poetics*.

CHAPTER 2 (p. 185). We may assume the general treatment of style in the *Poetics*. Style should be clear and appropriate. Clearness is gained through the use of the current idiom; freedom from meanness through limited deviations from ordinary usage. Rare, compound, and coined words should be sparingly used. Metaphors may be used more freely, for people do use them in conversation; they are a source of clarity, pleasure, and freshness. The best are proportional, are like good enigmas, and are derived from better things rather than worse. So epithets may be derived from the better side, as 'Orestes, the avenger of his sire'—not 'the matricide.' See, too, the formation of diminutives.

CHAPTER 3 (p. 190). Bad taste in style arises from the misuse of compound words; from the employment of queer words; from the unrestrained use of epithets; and from ridiculous or far-fetched metaphors.

CHAPTER 4 (p. 192). The relation of simile to metaphor. The implied comparison in metaphor. Simile, express comparison, is rather poetical. Examples of effective simile. Good similes are proportional: as *a* is to *b*, so is *c* to *d*. And the pairs of terms should be convertible.

CHAPTER 5 (p. 194). Stylistic purity is founded upon correct idiom. Purity of language depends upon five things: (1) the right use of connective particles; (2) the use of specific, rather than vague, words; (3) the avoidance of ambiguity; (4) attention to gender in conjoined words; (5) attention to number—singular, (?dual), and plural. A good style is easy to read and to punctuate. Avoid zeugma, and also long-suspended meanings.

CHAPTER 6 (p. 196). If you wish to be impressive and telling, (1) describe objects instead of merely naming them. (2) Use metaphors and epithets. (3) Use plurals for singulars. (4) Use the definite article rightly. (5) Use, or excise, connective particles, according to the proper and desirable effect. (6) Use negatives; say what a thing is *not*, what it does *not* do.

CHAPTER 7 (p. 197). Propriety. Language is appropriate when it expresses emotion and character, and is suited to our theme. For weighty matters use a corresponding diction. For emotion, on wanton outrage, use the language of anger; and so on. For character, let your words display the external signs of it; each class of men has its own language. But let your employment of all stylistic devices be seasonable; do not use all at once, or else apologize for any excess. Again, in moments of inspired feeling, carry your audience with you.

CHAPTER 8 (p. 199). Prose-rhythm. The pattern of the diction should not be metrical, nor yet devoid of rhythm, indefinite. The characteristic measure of the language is iambic. The ideal rhythm of prose, allied to the iambic, is allied to the heroic also; it is the paeon. Suitable paeons at the beginnings and ends of periods.

CHAPTER 9 (p. 202). The period and its members. Style is either loose (like the old style of Herodotus) or periodic, returning upon itself as in strophic verse. The periodic style is definite, satisfying, and memorable. The period may have several members, or be simple; the period, and the member, should be neither too short nor too long. Simple division, and antithesis. There are also parallel structure, and parallelism of sound.

CHAPTER 10 (p. 206). Lively sayings. Their relation to our pleasure in learning. Metaphor and simile are instructive and pleasing, metaphor more so. The secret of lively enthymemes is that they give us rapid information. Antithesis and balance contribute to this effect. And so does dramatic presentation. Metaphors are of four kinds (see *Poetics*, chapter 21), of which the best-liked are the proportional. Examples of this and other kinds.

CHAPTER 11 (p. 210). Liveliness, continued. How dramatic presentation—setting a thing before our eyes—is effected. Represent things as active: 'The bitter arrow *flew.*' Invest them with life and motion. For metaphor, the adept will see hidden resemblances between things superficially unlike. Thus we learn through surprise. Such is the effect of terse sayings. And so with 'novelties,' when the listener expects one thing, and hears another. The sayings should be concise and antithetical. Similes again. Proverbs, too, are metaphors, and likewise successful hyperboles.

CHAPTER 12 (p. 217). Concluding observations on style. Each kind of rhetoric has its appropriate style. That of written prose is not the same as that of controversial speaking, nor is the style of public oratory that of the law-court. The written style is more finished. The use of asyndeton and of varied repetition. The style of public speaking is like that of painted scenery. Forensic speaking is more elaborate. A speaker cannot shine in all styles at once. The epideictic style is the most literary. Further distinctions are needless. We turn to the last main subject, Arrangement.

CHAPTER 13 (p. 220). Order of the parts of a speech. A speech really has two parts; you state your case, and then you prove it. The text-books make confusing, even ridiculous, multiple distinctions among the parts. At most we may recognize four: Proem, Statement, Argument, Epilogue.

CHAPTER 14 (p. 221). The proem corresponds to the prologue of a poem, or the prelude of a flutist. So a ceremonial speaker will begin with an air that he likes, and from this will glide into his theme. The ordinary proem for such a speech is a bit of praise or blame. The proem of a forensic speech has the function of a dramatic or epic prologue. The function of any introduction is to make clear the end and object of your work. Other kinds of proem may serve as an antidote to prejudice against the defects of the speaker or the weakness of his case. An accuser will excite prejudice toward the close of his speech. Capturing or diverting the attention of the hearer by specious means is extraneous to the real function of the speech; such things come from the defects of the audience. The means of arousing the good will, or other emotions, of the hearer have been discussed (2. 1–11); friendship and pity are the emotions we should chiefly aim at. Praise at the opening of an epideictic speech should seem to include the hearer. There is less need of a proem in deliberative speaking.

CHAPTER 15 (p. 226). How to deal with prejudice. Nine possible methods for the defence. Three other methods, two of them for the accuser and accused, one of them for the accuser only.

CHAPTER 16 (p. 228). Narration. In ceremonial speeches it should be intermittent. If the subject is well-known, his deeds will not need to be detailed. Should the narration be 'rapid'? Make it *right*. In forensic speaking narrate what tends to your credit, and to your opponent's discredit. The defence needs less narration, but the story of what is past may be used to excite pity or indignation. Narration should depict character by the revelation of moral purpose. If the story contains something incredible, explain the difficulty. And give life to it by use of the familiar signs of emotion. Let the audience see that your *ethos* is good, but do this unobtrusively. In deliberative speaking there is least room for narration, but anything incredible in the narration must be explained.

CHAPTER 17 (p. 232). The arguments and their order as these severally appear in the three kinds of speaking. In forensic speaking the arguments should not appear in an unbroken string. Interweave other matter, or the chain will be tiresome. Avoid enthymemes when you would stir emotion. Maxims, however, have an ethical quality. Deliberative speaking is harder than forensic, since its argument concerns the unknown future. And it has less room for interweaving other matter than proofs. Still, the Athenian orators do indulge in attacks upon Sparta. In an epideictic speech interweave the argument with bits of eulogy. In general, if you have proofs, use them, and display a good *ethos*. If you have nothing for enthymemes, rely upon moral suasion alone, for good character is potent. Refutation of the opponent is not a separate thing, but belongs to the argument. In deliberative speaking, if you come first, present your arguments and then anticipate the opposing ones, unless the opposition has many. If your turn comes later, you must first deal with the opposing arguments, so as to make the audience receptive toward yours. *Ethos*: certain things about yourself you should quote from a third person; and similarly with certain things about your opponent. Again, present some of your arguments in ethical maxims.

Chapter 18 (p. 237). The argument, continued. Interrogation. Use this when you have worked your opponent to the brink of absurdity. Three other possible opportunities for it. How to meet the device yourself. The use of the ludicrous in rhetoric. Gorgias' advice on the subject.

Chapter 19 (p. 240). The epilogue has four elements. (1) You must make the audience well-disposed to you, ill-disposed to your opponent; (2) you must make your side look strong, and his weak; (3) must put the audience into the right state of emotion; (4) must refresh their memories. You may mark the close of your speech with an asyndeton.

[The following outline is taken from Rhys Roberts, *Greek Rhetoric and Literary Criticism*, p. 50:] If we consider the work as a whole, the first Book may perhaps be described as mainly logical and political, the second as mainly ethical or psychological, the third as mainly literary or stylistic. The speaker perhaps counts most in Book 1, the audience in Book 2, and the speech itself in Book 3. To the man who aspires to oratorical success, Book 1 seems to say: 'Be logical. Think clearly. Reason cogently. Remember that *argument* is the life and soul of persuasion.' Book 2: 'Study human nature. Observe the characters and emotions of your audience, as well as your own character and emotions.' Book 3: 'Attend to delivery. Use language rightly. Arrange your material well. End crisply.' And the whole treatise presupposes good wits and a fine general education.

THE RHETORIC OF ARISTOTLE

THE RHETORIC OF ARISTOTLE

BOOK 1

1. 1. [SCOPE AND PURPOSE OF THE ART.] Rhetoric is the counterpart of Dialectic [—that is, the art of public speaking and the art of logical discussion are co-ordinate, but contrasted, processes]; for both have to do with such things as fall, in a way, within the realm of common knowledge, things that do not belong to any one science. Accordingly, everybody to some extent makes use of both Dialectic and Rhetoric; for all make some attempt to sift or to support theses, and to defend or attack persons. Most people do so, of course, either quite at random, or else merely with a knack acquired from practice. Success in either way being possible, the random impulse and the acquired facility alike evince the feasibility of reducing the processes to a method; for when the practised and the spontaneous speaker gain their end, it is possible to investigate the cause of their success; and such an inquiry, we shall all admit, performs the function of an art.

1354a

Rhetoric and Dialectic

Rhetoric as an art

Now hitherto the authors of 'Arts of Speaking' have built up but a small portion of the art of Rhetoric truly considered; for this art consists of proofs [persuasions] alone—all else is but accessory. Yet these writers say nothing of enthymemes, the very body and substance of persuasion, and are concerned in the main with matters external to the direct issue. Thus the arousing of prejudice, of pity, of anger, and the like feelings in the soul, does not concern the facts, but has regard to those who decide. Consequently, if trials were everywhere conducted as at present they are in some cities—and espe-

Defects of current handbooks

cially in those that are best-governed—pleaders who were guided by the handbooks would have nothing to say; for by common consent the laws should forbid irrelevant speaking, and some courts, as that of the Areopagus, actually do forbid it. This certainly is right reason; the man who is to judge should not have his judgment warped by speakers arousing him to anger, jealousy, or compassion. One might just as well make a carpenter's rule crooked before using it as a measure. And obviously in a dispute there is nothing to do beyond showing that the alleged fact does or does not exist, has or has not occurred. The question whether it is important or trivial, the question whether there is justice or injustice, so far as the legislator has not defined these points, that is precisely what the judge is there to decide; he is not supposed to learn his lesson from the disputants.

Function of the judge

Naturally it is best that laws enacted on sound principles should, so far as may be, themselves determine everything, leaving as little as possible to the decision of those who judge; first, because it is easier to find one individual, or some few, with wisdom enough, and a capacity for legislative and judicial functions, than to find a large number with the like endowment; and secondly, because legislative acts are the fruit of long deliberation, whereas decisions must be given on short notice, so that it is hard for the judge or the assembly to satisfy the demands of private justice and public expediency. Most important of all, the decision of the legislator concerns no one actual case, but is prospective and general; whereas a member of the assembly or of the court must decide present and individual cases, in which their personal likes and dislikes, and their private interests, are often involved, so that they cannot adequately survey the truth, but have their judgment clouded by their own pleasure or pain.

Function of the law

1354b

On other points, then, we say the authority of the judge should be reduced as far as possible; but the decision whether a thing has or has not occurred, will or will not occur, is or is not so, must be left in the hands of those who judge, since for these matters the legislator cannot provide. Such being the case, it is clear that our authors of handbooks, in attempting to define the proper content of the Proem, the Narration, and the other divisions of the speech, and the like, are dwelling upon irrelevant matters, for their rules have to do, simply and solely, with the production of a certain mental attitude in the judge. These authors tell us nothing about artistic proofs —nothing, that is, about the way in which one is to become a master of the enthymeme. [By 'artistic' proofs or persuasions we are to understand systematic proofs by 'enthymeme' and 'example,' as opposed to 'non-artistic' proofs (1. 15, p. 80) such as 'laws, witnesses, compacts (=documents), tortures (=ordeals, inquisitions), and oaths,' as distinct also from the emotional appeals (already noted) to the judges, and as distinct from evidence drawn from character. Aristotle here anticipates his explanation (1. 2, p. 8) of 'artistic proofs.' By 'artistic' he means *appertaining to the art of Rhetoric proper*; by 'non-artistic,' what is external to the art—adventitious and adjunct means of persuasion that are not involved in the essential issue which is the subject of the speech. Similarly he anticipates his explanation (1. 2, p. 10) of 'enthymeme,' the rhetorical syllogism, drawn, not from the principles of the exact sciences, but from propositions, or probabilities, relating to everyday affairs. When he objects so vigorously to existing handbooks for their preoccupation with 'non-artistic proofs,' we are hardly prepared for Aristotle's own attention to them in the present treatise, which probably deals more systematically with the means of arousing emotion in the audience than did any of its predecessors. His extended treatment of the emotions is partly an inevitable concession to practice, for the orator must deal with an audience, and an audi-

The handbooks dwell on accessories

They neglect the enthymeme

ence necessarily is emotional; you may work on their emotions in a better way or a worse, but neglect them you cannot. Yet his method is also justified on grounds of perspective, since he does subordinate the 'non-artistic' to the 'artistic' proofs, the accessories to the main issue; whereas, he contends, his predecessors wholly neglected what was fundamental. Accordingly, though he owes some actual debt to them, his perspective is good, where theirs doubtless was bad.]

The handbooks have neglected deliberative speaking for the forensic or judicial branch

That is the reason why those authors have utterly neglected the deliberative branch of speaking, which is nobler and more statesmanlike than the branch that is concerned with the everyday relations between man and man, and treat only of the latter type, though the right method is the same for both. They all aim at a systematic treatment of the art of pleading, because the forensic type gives a better chance to introduce matters that are foreign to the issue. The deliberative branch, that of the statesman, since it deals rather with communal interests, affords less room for trickery [—that is, for biasing the judges (audience) by playing upon their emotions]. In a debate upon communal interests, the judges decide questions which really touch them as individuals, so that nothing more is needed than to prove that affairs are as the advocate of a given policy states [—since each can see what is advantageous to him, there is no need of arousing their passions]; but in forensic speaking this is not enough, [the judges have not the same interest in the outcome of a given case] and it pays to win the audience over [by working on their emotions]. Here the judges make award regarding interests that are not their own; if they view these in the light of their own feelings, and yield to the gratification of their ears, they lend themselves to the more plausible speaker, and so decide the case. They do not *judge* it. And hence in many places, as we said above, the law forbids irrelevant pleading. In deliberative assemblies, the judges themselves take care of that.

1355a

It is clear, then, that the artistic method has to do with proofs [persuasions] in the stricter sense. Now proof [persuasion] is a kind of demonstration; for we entertain the strongest conviction of a thing if we believe that it has been 'demonstrated.' Rhetorical proof, however, [is not scientific demonstration]; it takes the form of an enthymeme, this being, in general, the most effective among the various forms of persuasion. The enthymeme, again, is a kind of syllogism; now every kind of syllogism falls within the province of Dialectic, and must be examined under Dialectic as a whole, or under some branch of it. Consequently the person with the clearest insight into the nature of syllogisms, who knows from what premises and in what modes they may be constructed, will also be the most expert in regard to enthymemes, once he has mastered their special province [of things contingent and uncertain such as human actions and their consequences], and has learnt the differences between enthymemes and logical syllogisms. [The latter are complete, and yield an absolute demonstration.] Truth and likeness to truth are discerned by one and the same faculty; while human nature, let us add, has aptitude enough for discerning what is true, and men in most cases do arrive at the truth. Consequently one who is skilled in discerning the truth can do well in weighing probabilities [matters of opinion].

The true art of persuasion

The enthymeme; its relation to Dialectic

It is clear, then, that our handbooks have limited the art to extraneous matters; and it is clear, too, why they have leaned to forensic speaking.

But the art of Rhetoric has its value. It is valuable, first, because truth and justice are by nature more powerful than their opposites; so that, when decisions are not made as they should be, the speakers with the right on their side have only themselves to thank for the outcome. Their neglect of the art needs correction. [A proper knowledge and exercise of Rhetoric would prevent the triumph of fraud and injustice.] Secondly, [Rhetoric is

Four uses of Rhetoric

1. It prevents the triumph of fraud and injustice

2. It will serve to instruct when scientific instruction is of no avail

valuable as a means of instruction]. Even if our speaker had the most accurate scientific information, still there are persons whom he could not readily persuade with scientific arguments. True instruction, by the method of logic, is here impossible; the speaker must frame his proofs and arguments with the help of common knowledge and accepted opinions. This method has been noted in the *Topics*, in our remarks on popular discussion. [See Aristotle's *Topica* 1. 2.] Thirdly, in Rhetoric, as in Dialectic, we should be able to argue on either side of a question; not with a view to putting both sides into practice—we must not advocate evil—but in order that no aspect of the case may escape us, and that if our opponent makes unfair use of the arguments, we may be able in turn to refute them. In no other art do we draw opposite conclusions; it is characteristic of Rhetoric and Dialectic alone that, abstractly considered, they may indifferently prove opposite statements. Still, their basis, in the facts, is not a matter of indifference, for, speaking broadly, what is true and preferable is by nature always easier to prove, and more convincing. Lastly, if it is a disgrace to a man when he cannot defend himself in a bodily way, it would be odd not to think him disgraced when he cannot defend himself with reason [in a speech]. Reason is more distinctive of man than is bodily effort. If it is urged that an abuse of the rhetorical faculty can work great mischief, the same charge can be brought against all good things (save virtue itself), and especially against the most useful things such as strength, health, wealth, and military skill. Rightly employed, they work the greatest blessings; and wrongly employed, they work the utmost harm.

3. It makes us argue out both sides of a case

4. It is a means of defence

1355[b]

The abuse of a good thing is no argument against the proper use of it

Summary

We have seen that Rhetoric is not confined to any single and definite class of subjects, but in this respect is like Dialectic, and that the art has its uses; and we see that its function is not [absolutely] to persuade, but to discover the available means of persuasion in a given case.

The function of Rhetoric

[Not outward success, but a correct method, is the criterion of art; the correct method will bring success in proportion. An unwarranted appeal to the emotions might win an undesirable success.] Herein Rhetoric is like all other arts. Thus the aim of medicine is not, strictly speaking, to restore a sick man to perfect health, but to bring him as near to health as the case admits; people who never can be well may yet be properly treated. Further, we see that it is the office of one and the same art to discern the genuine means, and also the spurious means, of persuasion, just as it is the office of Dialectic to discern the true, and also the sham, syllogism; for sophistical dialectic, or sophistical speaking, is made so, not by the faculty, but by the moral purpose. [The faculty is the same in both arts.] There is this difference, however: we apply the term 'rhetorician' alike to describe a speaker's command of the art and a speaker's moral purpose; whereas, in the field of Dialectic, the term 'sophist' refers to the moral purpose, while 'dialectician' applies to the faculty [the normal function].

Double meaning of *rhetor*

[Having thus made clear that Rhetoric is an art, and when rightly practised an honest and useful art,] we must now proceed to discuss its method—the mode and the means that will enable us to attain to the proper ends. Accordingly, let us start afresh, as it were, first defining, and then going on to the rest.

1. 2. [DEFINITION OF RHETORIC. MODES AND MEANS OF PERSUASION.] So let Rhetoric be defined as the faculty [power] of discovering in the particular case what are the available means of persuasion. This is the function of no other art [save Dialectic]. The others are each instructive or persuasive with regard to some special subject-matter. Thus medicine informs us about the conditions of health and disease; geometry about the properties of magnitudes; arithmetic about numbers; and so

Rhetoric defined

with the rest of the arts and sciences. But Rhetoric, it would seem, has the function of discovering the means of persuasion for every case, so to speak, that is offered; and hence we say that the art as such has no special application to any distinct class of subjects.

Rhetorical proofs [persuasions]

Proofs [persuasions] are of two kinds, artistic and non-artistic. [Or we might call them 'scientific' and 'unscientific.' Aristotle distinguishes means of persuasion that inherently belong *in* the art, and those that, while associated with it, are really external and adventitious.] By 'non-artistic' proofs are meant all such as are not supplied by our own efforts, but existed beforehand, such as witnesses, admissions under torture, written contracts, and the like. By 'artistic' proofs [means of persuasion] are meant those that may be furnished by the method of Rhetoric through our own efforts. The first sort have only to be used; the second have to be found.

Non-artistic proofs

Artistic proofs

1356[a]

Means of persuasion *in* the speech

Of the means of persuasion supplied by the speech itself there are three kinds. The first kind reside in the character [*ethos*] of the speaker; the second consist in producing a certain [the right] attitude in the hearer; the third appertain to the argument proper, in so far as it actually or seemingly demonstrates. [Under all three heads, and explicitly under the third, Aristotle makes room, with the scientific branch of Rhetoric, for devices related to those of the sophistical branch. As in the *Poetics*, we see that the artist may use elements that are somewhat external to the art itself, in a more artistic way rather than a less.]

1. The *ethos* of the speaker

The character [*ethos*] of the speaker is a cause of persuasion when the speech is so uttered as to make him worthy of belief; for as a rule we trust men of probity more, and more quickly, about things in general, while on points outside the realm of exact knowledge, where opinion is divided, we trust them absolutely. This trust, however, should be created by the speech itself, and not left to depend upon an antecedent impression that the speaker is this or that kind of man. It is not true, as some writers on the art maintain, that the probity of the speaker contributes nothing to his persuasiveness; on the contrary, we might almost affirm that his character [*ethos*] is the most potent of all the means to persuasion.

2. Emotion in the hearers

Secondly, persuasion is effected through the audience, when they are brought by the speech into a state of emotion; for we give very different decisions under the sway of pain or joy, and liking or hatred. This, we contend, is the sole aspect of the art with which technical writers of the day have tried to deal. We shall elucidate it in detail when we come to discuss the emotions [2. 2–11, pp. 93–131].

3. Argument proper

Thirdly, persuasion is effected by the arguments, when we demonstrate the truth, real or apparent, by such means as inhere in particular cases.

What a mastery of Rhetoric calls for

Such being the instruments of persuasion, to master all three obviously calls for a man who can reason logically, can analyze the types of human character [*ethe*], along with the virtues, and, thirdly, can analyze the emotions—the nature and quality of each several emotion, with the means by which, and the manner in which, it is excited.

Relation of Rhetoric to (1) Dialectic and (2) Political Science

Thus it follows that Rhetoric is a kind of offshoot, on the one hand, of Dialectic, and, on the other, of that study of Ethics which may properly be called 'political.' [With Aristotle, Ethics, the science dealing with individual conduct, shades off into Politics (a broader subject), which deals with the conduct and activities of men in groups—of the State.] And hence it is that Rhetoric, and those who profess it, slip into the guise of Politics [and political experts], whether from defects of education, or through quackery [imposture], or from other human failings. As we said at the outset [1. 1, p. 1], Rhetoric is a branch of Dialectic, and resembles that. Neither of them is a *science*, with a definite subject-matter; both are *faculties* for providing arguments. On their function, and on their relation to each other, perhaps enough has now been said.

Persuasion by argument

1356[b]

[Let us turn to the instruments of persuasion.] As for real or apparent demonstration, there are in Rhetoric two modes, corresponding to the two modes in Dialectic. As in Dialectic we have, on the one hand, induction, and, on the other, the syllogism and apparent syllogism, so in Rhetoric: the example is a form of induction; while the enthymeme is a syllogism, and the apparent enthymeme an apparent syllogism. 'Enthymeme' is the name I give to a rhetorical syllogism, 'example' to a rhetorical induction. Whenever men in speaking effect persuasion through proofs, they do so either with examples or enthymemes; they use nothing else. Accordingly, since all demonstration (as we have shown in the *Analytics*) is effected either by syllogism [that is, deductively] or by induction, it follows that induction and syllogism [deduction] must be identified respectively with example and enthymeme. [See Aristotle's *Prior Analytics* 2. 23; *Posterior Analytics* 1. 1, 1. 18, 2. 19.] The difference between example and enthymeme may be inferred from the *Topics* [1. 1, 12]. There, with reference to syllogism [deduction] and induction, it has already been observed that to derive a general law from a number of like instances is in Dialectic induction, in Rhetoric example; whereas to conclude from certain assumptions that something else follows from those assumptions (something distinct from them, yet dependent upon their existing) either universally or as a rule—this in Dialectic is called a syllogism, and in Rhetoric an enthymeme. And of the corresponding two types of oratory it is plain that each has some advantage. What is said of Dialectic in our *Methodology* [a lost work of Aristotle] likewise holds true here; for, of the two kinds of speeches, in one the enthymeme predominates, in the other the example; and similarly some speakers are more

Inductive proof by example; deductive by enthymeme

Induction

Deduction

given to examples, and others to enthymemes. Arguments through examples are not less persuasive, yet arguments in the form of enthymeme are more applauded. The reason for this, and the right way of using both enthymemes and examples, will be discussed later [2. 20–24, pp. 147–77]. At present let us define the processes themselves more clearly.

'Persuasive' means persuasive to a person. To him, a statement may be persuasive and credible by itself, immediately, or it may become so when it seems to be proved from other statements that he believes. No art, however, has regard to the individual case. Thus medicine does not investigate the question what is a cure for Socrates or for Callias—for the individual as such—but asks what will cure a person or persons of such and such a type; the latter inquiry comes within the province of art, whereas, particulars being infinite, the individual fact cannot be scientifically known. And hence Rhetoric will consider, not what seems probable to the individual—to Socrates or to Hippias—but what seems probable to a given class; the same being true of Dialectic. [Conceivably, both Rhetoric and Dialectic might be used to argue any question or problem, but practically both are restricted.] Dialectic does not form its syllogisms out of any chance notions (such as the notions of crazy people), but takes problems that merit discussion; and similarly Rhetoric is applied to recognized subjects of deliberation. It has to do with things about which we commonly deliberate—things for which we have no special art or science; and with the sort of hearers who cannot grasp many points in a single view, or follow a long chain of reasoning. Now we deliberate about such things as appear to admit of two possibilities. [Is a course expedient or inexpedient, a deed just or unjust, a statement true or false?] On matters which admit of no alternative, which necessarily were, or will be, or are, certainties, no one deliberates, at least not

There is no science of the individual fact

So that Rhetoric is concerned with classes, not individuals

1357a

And the subjects are those in which the issue seems to be uncertain

No one deliberates about certainties

on that supposition—for nothing is to be gained by it.

Two faulty methods

It is possible to construct syllogisms and draw conclusions in a chain, working successively with the results of those that precede; or you may draw upon propositions that have not been thus proved, yet need proof because they are not commonly accepted. But, necessarily, the first of these processes will be hard to follow because of its length, for we assume the judge [audience] to be of but ordinary intelligence; and the second method will be unconvincing because the conclusions are drawn from premises that are not admitted nor commonly believed.

The deductions must be easy to follow

The process is simplified when the hearer supplies a link

Accordingly, the enthymeme, and likewise the example, must deal with matters which as a rule are variable (the example corresponding to an induction, and the enthymeme being a syllogism); and the links in the chain must be few—seldom as many as the links in a normal chain of deductions. Thus, if one of the premises is a matter of common knowledge, the speaker need not mention it, since the hearer will himself supply the link. For example, in showing that Dorieus was victor in a contest where the prize is a chaplet, it is enough to say, 'He has won a victory at the Olympic games.' The speaker need not add that the prize there was a chaplet, for every one knows it.

What a man will do cannot be predicted, though men are likely to act in one way or another

Let us grant that only a few of the premises of rhetorical deductions are necessarily admitted, and that the majority of cases on which we must decide, and into which we must inquire, may lie this way or that; for men deliberate and raise questions about the things they do, and human actions all belong to this class [of uncertainties or mere probabilities]; no human action, so to speak, is inevitable. And we see that, in Rhetoric, for the most part merely usual and contingent conclusions must be drawn from premises of the same sort; just as, in Logic, necessary conclusions must arise from premises that are determined—a matter that has been settled for us in the

Analytics [*Prior Analytics* 1. 8]. All this being granted, it is clear that the premises from which a speaker derives his enthymemes are sometimes necessarily true, but in the main only generally true. In fact, the materials of enthymemes are (1) probabilities [εἰκότα] and (2) signs [σημεῖα]; so these two terms must correspond respectively with the two terms of the foregoing division. ['Probabilities' correspond to propositions that are generally true (true as a rule), and 'signs' to propositions that are (or seem to be) certain.] A 'probability' is that which usually happens or follows [—as hatred usually attends envy], yet not (as some would define it) *anything* that so happens, for the thing must belong to the class of things that may turn out this way or that. The probable, then, bears the same relation to that of which it is probable as a universal statement to a particular. [Sons tend to love their mothers, is a general statement; it is probable, then, that Orestes will love his mother.]

Probabilities and signs

Probability defined

1357ᵇ

[A 'sign' (σημεῖον), as distinguished from a 'probable' generalization (one that is in itself likely), affects to be a proposition that is demonstrated by argument.] Signs are of two sorts: one bears, toward the statement it is to prove, the relation of a particular statement to a universal [—representing the inductive method], the other that of a universal to a particular [—representing the deductive method]. Of these, the second, the conclusive sign, is called τεκμήριον, the other, the non-conclusive sign, has no specific name. By conclusive signs I mean the statements from which a syllogism is derived. And hence it is that this sort of sign is called τεκμήριον, for when people take what they have said to be irrefutable, they think they proffer a τεκμήριον, as if the matter were now demonstrated and *concluded*; for in the old idiom τέκμαρ has the same meaning as πέρας [that is, 'limit'].

Signs

1. Particular or inductive

2. General or deductive

The sign having the relation of a particular to a universal would be illustrated by saying as an indication that wise men are just: 'Socrates was wise, and also just.' Of course this *is* a sign, yet it can be refuted, even though the statement be true, since the conclusion is not logically required. [You cannot argue: 'Socrates was wise and just; X is wise; therefore X is just.' The syllogism is faulty.] Take, however, either of the following. 'Here is a sign that the man is ailing: he has a fever.' Or, 'She has had a child, for she is in milk.' This kind of sign is infallible, and is the only one to be called *τεκμήριον*, for this alone, when the statement is true, is irrefutable. The kind having the relation of a universal to a particular would be illustrated if one were to say: 'This is a sign that he has a fever; his breathing is rapid.' Yet here again the point can be refuted, even if the statement [that his breathing is rapid] be true; for a patient may breathe hard without having a fever.

Summary

The nature of a probability, a sign, and a *τεκμήριον*, and the distinctions among them, have now been stated. A more detailed account of them may be found in the *Analytics* [*Prior Analytics* 2. 27], with an explanation of the reason why some of the forms are inconclusive, and others are reducible to valid syllogisms.

The example

As for the example, we have already stated that it is a kind of induction, and have noted the sort of materials with which, as an induction, it deals [1. 2, p. 10]. The example does not concern the relation of part to whole [particular to universal], nor of whole to part, but of part to part, of like to like. When two things fall under the same genus, but one of them is better known than the other, the better-known is the example, [and the less-known is the thing exemplified.] Thus, suppose one contends that Dionysius, in asking for a body-guard, aims to set up a tyranny. The speaker may urge that Pisistratus, with a similar aim, once asked for a body-guard, and, on getting it, established himself as tyrant; and that

Theagenes did the like at Megara. And so all the other cases that are known to the audience become each an example with reference to Dionysius, while hitherto we were unaware if he made the request with this design. All these cases [including that of Dionysius] fall under the same generic notion, that a man who aims at a tyranny asks for a body-guard.

1358[a]

Some enthymemes belong to Rhetoric, others to other, more special, arts

So much for the materials from which those proofs are constructed that pass for demonstration. But in the case of enthymemes there is a most important distinction that virtually every one has ignored—a distinction that holds also of the syllogisms employed by Dialectic: some enthymemes, or syllogisms, belong properly to Rhetoric, or to Dialectic; others to other arts and faculties—to disciplines already established, or yet to be formulated. Accordingly, the distinction is overlooked by speakers, who, the more they encroach upon some field of special knowledge, overstep the more the province of Rhetoric and Dialectic.

The universal *Topoi*

This point will be clearer if we discuss it at greater length. Let me say, then, that the proper subjects of dialectical and rhetorical syllogisms are those with which the so-called *Topoi* [Common-places, Lines of Argument] are concerned; and by these I mean arguments that are applicable in common to the study of justice and physics, to the study of politics—to a large number of inquiries of divers sorts. Take the topic of *more* and *less*: this is of no greater service when we make a syllogism or utter an enthymeme about matters of right and wrong than when we make one about physics, or about anything else, different though these things are in kind. [Arguments as to degree (*more* just and *less* just, *longer* and *shorter*, etc.) are equally applicable to all subjects.] On the other hand, there are particular arguments, those derived from the propositions relative to a particular species or class of things. Thus there are propositions in physics [natural science] from

For example, that of degree (*more* or *less*)

Particular *Topoi*

which it is impossible to form an enthymeme or a syllogism for ethics, and propositions in ethics from which it is impossible to do so for physics, and so on through all the special subjects. The universal *topoi*, since they are not restricted to any special subject, will not give a man intelligence in any one science. As for the particular *topoi*, the better our choice of propositions, the more we imperceptibly glide into some discipline other than Dialectic and Rhetoric; for if we light upon true scientific principles, the art is no longer Dialectic or Rhetoric, but is the discipline based upon those principles. [The rhetorician must not go too far in his use of special or technical knowledge.] However, enthymemes are mostly formed from these particular and special *topoi*; not so many come from the universal *topoi*. Accordingly, in Rhetoric, as in the *Topica*, we must distinguish between the special and the general *topoi* from which enthymemes are to be derived. [See Aristotle, *Topics* (*Sophistic Elenchi*) 9. 9, and compare *Topics* 1. 10, 14 and 3. 5.] By special topics I mean the propositions peculiar to any given discipline, by general topics those that are common to all. We shall begin with the special.

First, however, let us ascertain what are the several kinds of Rhetoric; their number once determined, we can then ascertain separately the elements and propositions of each.

Three species of Rhetoric

1. 3. [The Kinds of Oratory.] The kinds of Rhetoric are three in number, corresponding to the three kinds of hearers to which speeches are addressed; for, a speech being the joint result of three things—the speaker, his subject, and the person addressed—the end or object has

1358b

reference to this last, namely the hearer; and the hearer must be either (1) a mere observer [critic], or (2 and 3) a judge [decider], and, if the latter, then either (2) a judge of things past or (3) a judge of things to come.

One who (3) decides about the future is, for example, an ecclesiast [member of the Assembly]; one who (2) judges about the past is, say, the dicast [juror in a court of law]; while the person who (1) decides about the force and merit of the speech [the 'faculty' or art displayed in it] is the critic [observer, 'theorist']. It follows that there must be three kinds of speeches in Rhetoric, (1) deliberative, (2) forensic, and (3) epideictic. [That is, there are (1) speeches of counsel or advice (deliberation)—as political speeches addressed to an assembly or to the public on questions of State, but also, for example, a speech addressed to an individual (a ruler, or, indeed, any person who is to be advised); (2) judicial speeches, used in prosecution and defence (more generally, in any kind of attack or defence); and (3) panegyrical or declamatory speeches, in the nature of an exhibition or display, eulogies—in general, speeches of praise (or blame).]

Two distinctions under each of these three heads

(1) The elements of deliberation [counsel] are (*a*) exhortation [encouragement], (*b*) dissuasion; for, as advice given in private always has one or the other aspect, so is it with those who discuss matters of State in public—they either exhort or dissuade. (2) The elements of forensic speaking are (*a*) accusation, (*b*) defence, since the parties to a legal action will necessarily be engaged in either one or the other. (3) The elements of an epideictic speech are (*a*) praise and (*b*) blame. As for the divisions of time which severally belong to these several kinds of speakers, to the deliberative speaker belongs the future, for he gives advice about things to come, exhorting or dissuading; to the judicial pleader belongs the past, for it is always with regard to things already done that the one party accuses and the other defends; and to the epideictic speaker, above all, belongs the present, for every one praises or blames with regard to existing conditions [qualities], though a speaker often adds to his resources with reminiscences from the past and conjectures about the

future. [See, for example, the *Funeral Oration* by Pericles in the *History* of Thucydides; and compare Shakespeare's Antony in *Julius Caesar* 3. 2. 76–7.]

Three ends or aims of speaking

For these three kinds of Rhetoric there are also three several ends. (1) The aim of the deliberative speaker concerns advantage and injury; for the one who exhorts recommends a course of action as better, and the one who dissuades deters us from it as worse; other considerations —of justice and injustice, of honor and dishonor—he makes subsidiary to this end [of the expedient]. (2) The aim of judicial pleaders concerns justice and injustice, and they in like manner make the other considerations subsidiary to these. (3) The aim of those who praise and blame concerns honor and dishonor, and such speakers likewise subordinate the other considerations to these.

As a sign that the end or aim of each kind of Rhetoric is such as we have stated, we may note that a speaker sometimes does not care to contest the other points. Thus a man on trial may not deny that the act was committed, nor deny that it did some damage; but that he is guilty of injustice he never will admit—if he admitted this, there would be no need of a trial. Similarly, deliberative speakers will often concede the other points, but not that the course they recommend is inexpedient, or the one they deprecate advantageous; while they are often unconcerned about the question whether it is not unjust for one city to enslave another, a neighbor and quite inoffensive. So, too, in praising and blaming, the speakers do not ask *1359ᵃ* whether the deeds of a man were expedient or hurtful; nay, they often set it down to his praise that he performed some noble act at a sacrifice of his own advantage. Thus they praise Achilles for going to rescue his comrade Patroclus, when Achilles knew that it would lead to his own death, and that by refraining he might live on. For Achilles, death on such terms was nobler, while to live was expedient.

The ends of Rhetoric in relation to the means

From what has been said [cf. 1. 2, p. 16] it is clear that these [expediency, justice, honor, and their opposites] are the subjects, primarily, for which the orator must have a fund of propositions. And for Rhetoric the propositions consist of the demonstrations [τεκμήρια, complete proofs], and the probabilities, and the signs, already mentioned. Every kind of syllogism is composed of propositions, and the enthymeme is the kind that is composed of the propositions we have named.

[Rhetoric deals with human action, past, present, or future.] Now things which are impossible cannot have have been done in the past, or be done in the future, but only things which are possible; and things which have not occurred cannot have been done, and things which will not occur cannot be done hereafter. Consequently, the speaker, whether deliberative, forensic, or epideictic, must be supplied with propositions [in the general *topoi*] regarding the possible and impossible, and on the question whether a thing has or has not occurred, is or is not to occur. Further, all men in praising or blaming, in exhorting or dissuading, in accusing or defending, try to prove, not merely the facts just mentioned [possibility or occurrence, past or future], but also that the good or evil, the honor or disgrace, the justice or injustice, is great or small, whether absolutely or in comparison with other cases. Obviously, then, the speaker will need propositions [again in the general *topoi*] regarding magnitude and smallness, and the greater and the less, considered generally, and also in comparing individual cases—for example, in arguing which is the greater or less good, the greater or lesser act of injustice; and similarly with the other terms [bad (harmful), just, honorable, and disgraceful].

These, then, are the *topoi* [general and special] in which the speaker must be supplied with propositions [premises]. Next, we must analyze in detail each class of these subjects for each kind of Rhetoric. What are the subjects of deliberation, of epideictic speeches, and, thirdly, of lawsuits?

Deliberative Rhetoric: its subjects

1. 4. [The Subjects of Deliberative (Political) Speaking, under Five Heads.] First, then, we must ascertain the nature of the goods or evils about which the deliberative speaker gives his counsel; for he is not concerned with all goods and evils, but only with such as either may, or may not, come to pass [—only with contingencies]. On things that necessarily must be, now or in future, and such things as cannot possibly exist or come to pass, there is no room for counsel. Nor indeed is there room for it everywhere in the realm of the contingent; for there are some goods of the contingent class which are the gifts of nature or the results of chance [such as beauty and ugliness of person or lucky and unlucky strokes of fortune], and on which it is idle to offer advice. Clearly, the deliberative speaker is concerned with those things upon which advice is feasible; and these are all such as can be referred to ourselves as agents—all that we ourselves can originate and set in motion; for in deliberating we always carry back our inquiries to the point where we find that we have, or have not, the power to achieve our objects.

1359b

Now, accurately to enumerate and classify the usual subjects of public business and deliberation, and, further, to treat them in detail with all possible scientific precision, would be a task unsuited to our present undertaking; first, because this task is the affair, not of Rhetoric, but of some more scholarly and exact discipline; and next, because far more has hitherto been assigned to Rhetoric than its own legitimate subjects of investigation. To tell the truth, Rhetoric, as we said before [1. 2, p. 9] combines the science of logical analysis with the ethical branch of political science, and is akin partly to Dialectic, partly to sophistical argument. But the more one tries to build up either Dialectic or Rhetoric, not as a faculty, but as an exact science, the more will one be inadvertently destroying their nature, in the act of reconstruction, by encroaching upon sciences that deal each with its own subject, and do not deal simply with forms of argument. [Cope says (*Rhetoric* 1. 61): 'It may be as well here to sum up the characteristics of Rhetoric which respectively entitle it to the name of "art" and "faculty." In so far as it is systematic, and follows a method—a logical method—and can look forward to results (implying a knowledge of causes and effects) in *persuading* its hearers, it is an art; as a practical exercise, not admitting of absolute exactness, or universal conclusions, employing the propositions of all arts and sciences, and the axioms common to them all, only as probable and popular, and having itself no special subject-matter, taking opposite sides of the same question indifferently and arriving at opposite conclusions, . . . it is a *δύναμις*, a faculty, capable of development and to be exercised in practice.]

Nevertheless, so far as is needful in Rhetoric, and without the exhaustive scrutiny demanded by political science, let us proceed to analyze the affairs of public concern.

The five chief subjects of deliberation

Of the subjects upon which all men deliberate, and upon which deliberative orators speak, the chief ones, we may say, are five in number, to wit: (1) ways and means; and (2) war and peace; next, (3) national defence; and (4) imports and exports; finally, (5) legislation.

1. Ways and means

Accordingly, one who is to make recommendations on ways and means must know the sources of the public revenue, what they severally are, and their respective value; so that if any of them is being neglected, it may be added, and if any is too small, it may be increased; and he must know all the public expenses, so that any useless outlay may be cut off, and any excessive outlay reduced. Men become richer not merely by adding to their capital, but also by cutting down their expenditures. One cannot get a comprehensive view of these matters, however, from domestic experience alone; for the ends of deliberation, one needs insight also into devices of finance that have been tried abroad.

2. War and peace

With regard to war and peace, one must know the forces of the State, their actual strength, and the strength they can develop; also the kind of forces now existing, as well as any additional kind that can be brought into existence; further, what wars the State has waged, and how they have been conducted. Not only with respect to one's own State must one know these things, but with respect to bordering states also, or, more particularly, those states with which there is likelihood of war, so that one may cultivate peace with the stronger, and have the option of making war on the weaker. And one must know whether the alien forces are like or unlike ours; for in this point also we may have, or lack, the advantage. As regards these points, too, one must have studied the issue, not only of our own wars, but of the wars waged between alien states as well; for like conditions naturally lead to like results.

1360a

3. Defence of the country

Further, with regard to national defence, one must not be ignorant of details, but must know the extent and character of the protection, and the situation of the forts (a matter which calls for a practical knowledge of the country), so that an inadequate preparation may be increased, and any superfluous defence reduced, and special care given to strategic positions.

4. Exports and imports

Again, for the means of subsistence, one must know what total outlay will suffice for the State, the nature of the supplies produced at home or obtainable from without, which articles the citizens need to export, and which must be imported; these last, in order that treaties and agreements may be made with the proper states; for there are two sorts of alien powers with which we must see to it that our citizens maintain good relations—the stronger, and those that are useful for commerce.

For the stability of the commonwealth, the deliberative speaker must be an able student of these matters; but, above all, he must be competent in legislation, for the salvation of the State is in its laws. Accordingly, one must know how many types of government there are; what conditions are favorable to each type; and what things, inherent in the type itself, or antagonistic to it from without, naturally tend to destroy it. When I speak of destruction by causes inherent in the type itself, I mean that, save for the best type, they are all ruined by getting unstrung and by over-tension. [The figure is that of a stringed instrument.] Thus democracy grows weaker, not only by relaxation, until it ends in oligarchy, but also by excessive tension [intensification, exaggeration, ending in anarchy]; just as the aquiline or the snub nose, as its curve is relaxed, comes toward the intermediate type, but when the hook or the snub is violently intensified, it assumes such a shape as to lose all resemblance to a nose.

5. Legislation

For the ends of legislation, it is helpful to understand what type of government is desirable, and to learn this not only from the history of our own State, but also by studying the forms of government abroad, observing how the different forms are suited to different peoples. And hence, obviously, books of travel will be of use with respect to legislation, since from them one may learn the laws and customs of foreign nations; while histories [since they deal with human actions] should be read for their bearing upon counsels of state. All these inquiries, however, belong to Political Science, not to Rhetoric.

These, then, are the chief subjects upon which the intending deliberative speaker should be well-informed. Let us now start afresh, and state the premises from which he

1360b

must argue in exhorting or dissuading on these and other questions.

1. 5. [Advice Concerns Happiness. Happiness Defined. Its Constituents.] Both individually and collectively, we may say, men all have some object at which they aim in whatever they choose and whatever they avoid. This object may be summarily described as Happiness, with its constituent parts. So, for the sake of illustration, let us ascertain what, broadly considered, happiness is, and from what sources its parts are derived; for upon it, and the things that conduce to it, and the things that are adverse to it, all exhortations and dissuasions always turn. And whatever produces happiness or any of its parts, or makes any part greater instead of less, must needs be done; while whatever destroys or hinders happiness, or makes for its opposite, must needs be left undone.

The object of all human action is happiness

Happiness may be defined as prosperity conjoined with virtue; or as a self-sufficient existence; or as the pleasantest life, with secure enjoyment thereof; or as a thriving condition of property and persons, with the ability to take care and make use of them. Men would pretty generally admit happiness to be one or more of these things.

Happiness: working definitions

If happiness is so defined, then parts of happiness must be good birth, the possession of many friends, the possession of good friends, wealth, the possession of good children, the possession of many children, a happy old age; further, such physical excellences as health, beauty, strength, stature, athletic ability; also fame, honor, good luck, virtue. We see that a man would be most independent, if he possessed both the personal [internal] and the external goods—there being no additional kinds. Personal goods are partly mental, partly physical; external goods are birth, friends, wealth, and honor. We think,

Constituent parts of happiness

too, that the happy man should have various kinds of power, and also good luck, if his life is to be perfectly secure. Following the same method as before, let us ascertain what each of these constituents is.

Nobility (good birth)

Good birth, for a nation or a city, means that the people is indigenous or ancient; that its earliest leaders were men of eminence; and that many of their offspring have been eminent for such qualities and deeds as we admire. For the individual, good birth comes from his progenitors, either male or female, and means legitimacy [including pure citizenship] in both lines; as in the case of a state, it means that the founders of a line were notable for virtue, or for wealth, or for something else which men think honorable, and that many of the line, both men and women, in recent and in previous generations, have been persons of eminence.

1361[a] Children

What is meant by good offspring, and numerous offspring, is not hard to explain. The community has this when its body of youth is numerous and good—good physically, having excellences such as stature, beauty, strength, and athletic skill, and the moral excellences of a young man, which are self-command and courage. The individual has good offspring, and numerous offspring, when his own children are numerous and of the kind described, and include both sons and daughters. Feminine excellence of body means beauty and stature, while the feminine moral virtues are self-command and an industry that is not servile. Alike in private life and in public, and for women as well as men, we should promote the existence of each of the qualities described; for where the conditions governing women are poor, as in Lacedaemon, the people enjoy scarcely the half of happiness.

Wealth

The elements of wealth are plenty of coin; the possession of territory for the State, and, for the individual, lands of exceptional number, extent, and excellence; further, the possession of chattels, live stock, and laborers [slaves] of exceptional number and excellence—all these things to be secure, respectable, and useful. Under 'useful' belong rather such things as are productive; under 'respectable' [befitting a gentleman] those things that conduce to enjoyment. By 'productive' I mean those things from which we derive income; by 'conducing to enjoyment,' things that are in themselves desirable, and beyond this yield nothing worth comparison with it. [The distinction is that between property employed in business, yielding revenue, and luxuries perhaps, or perhaps science (for example), which is pursued for its own sake—not for any practical applications of it. The practical results of science are not worth mentioning in comparison with the satisfactions lying in the pursuit of science.] The definition of security [as regards ownership] is possession in such a place and in such a manner that the power of using a thing rests with the owner himself; the definition of ownership is the power of retaining a thing or alienating it; and by alienation I mean giving it away or selling it. In general, being wealthy is using means rather than merely possessing them; for wealth is the activity and employment of such things as we have noted.

Fame or good repute

Good repute [fame] consists in being universally respected, or in being thought to have some such thing as is desired by all, or by the majority, or by the good, or by the judicious.

Honor

Honor is the mark of a reputation for beneficence. It is rightly paid above all to those who have conferred actual benefits—not but that honor is paid to the man who simply has the power to confer them. A benefit may affect either the recipient's personal safety, and the various causes of his existing, or his wealth, or some one of the other goods which are not easily acquired, whether generally, or in a given place or at a given time; for one may gain honor through services that look small—but the place and the juncture account for it. [Thus, giving a cup of cold water looks like a small service, but as Sir Philip Sidney gave it at the battle of Zutphen, the act becomes renowned for its self-denial and heroism; cf. Mark 9.41.] The elements of honor are sacrifices; memorials, in verse or prose; special privileges; grants of land; seats in front; public burial; statues; maintenance at the public expense; Oriental [barbaric] homage such as obeisances and giving place; and such rewards as are given by this or that people. Since the reward is a gift of property and a mark of honor, it is an object of desire both to the avaricious and to the ambitious, offering each of them what they want. It is property, and that is what *1361*[b] the avaricious desire; it brings honor, and honor is the aim of the ambitious.

Health

Bodily excellence means health, and such health that the possessors, free from disease, can make due use of their energies; for many keep well in the fashion pursued, as the story goes, by Herodicus [a self-tormenting physician], and these persons no one would count happy for their health, since they abstain from all, or nearly all, the normal activities of mankind.

Beauty

Beauty is different for each several period of life. In a youth, beauty means a physique that is adapted to feats of racing and strength, the individual being pleasant to look at for mere enjoyment. Thus the contenders in the pentathlon are the most beautiful, being naturally formed at once for strength and for speed. For a man in his prime, beauty means a body fit for the toils of war, while his aspect inspires pleasure conjoined with fear. In an old man, beauty means a physique equal to the necessary toils of age, while his appearance causes no pain, the disfigurements of age being absent.

Strength

Strength is the power of moving another body at will, and necessarily means moving either by pulling, or pushing, or raising up, or pressing down, or squeezing together. Accordingly, a strong man will be strong either for all or for some of these movements.

Size

Excellence in size is superiority to the average in height, depth of chest, and breadth of shoulders, but only to the point where one's movements will not be retarded through the excess. Athletic excellence of body means a combination of size, strength, and speed—for the speedy man, in his way, is strong. One who can throw his legs in a certain style, taking long and rapid strides, is fit for running; one who can grip, and hold down, for wrestling; one who can drive with a blow, for boxing; one who can do both of the last two, for the pancration; one who can do all of them, for the pentathlon.

A good old age

A good old age means growing old slowly and without pain; for an old age that comes on quickly is not a good one, nor is an old age that comes on slowly indeed, but with pain. A good old age depends upon physical excellences and good fortune, both; for if a man is not free from ailments, and is not strong, he will not escape suffering, nor will he continue free from pain and live to a great age without good fortune. True, there is, apart from all this, a certain capacity for long life even in the absence of both strength and health, for many are long-lived who lack the physical excellences. A detailed examination of these matters, however, is not to the present purpose. [The subject of bodily excellences, and the like, as elements of happiness, has been sufficiently discussed for the ends of Rhetoric.]

Friends

What is meant by the possession of many friends, and of good friends, is readily understood once we have defined the term 'friend.' A friend is one who is ready to do for the sake of another what he thinks will be good for that other person. One who has many such well-wishers has many friends; one whose well-wishers are likewise excellent men has good friends.

1362a Good fortune (luck)

Good fortune means getting or possessing all, or most, or the most important, of those goods which are the result of chance. Some of the goods that come by luck may also be gained by the arts [by contrivance], but many gifts of fortune are independent of art—for example, gifts of nature; and, again, there may be gifts of fortune that are contrary to nature [are abnormal]. Thus health may be the result of art [is not always a mere gift of fortune], while beauty and stature are gifts of nature [—art has little, chance much, to do with them]. In general, the goods that come from fortune are such as excite envy. Fortune is also the cause of those goods which come contrary to normal expectation. For example, all his brothers are ugly, but M is handsome; or, all the others overlooked the treasure, but N found it; or, the arrow missed this man, and hit the next one to him; or, he who had always frequented the place stayed away, while the others who never had been there before were all killed. All such cases count for pieces of good fortune.

Virtue

As for virtue, it is so intimately related to the topic of praise that we shall postpone the discussion of it until we come to treat of this subject [1. 9, pp. 46–9].

1. 6. [The Good and Expedient as the Object of Deliberation.]

The aim of deliberative Rhetoric

We see, then, what points, future or actual, must be kept in view by one who is exhorting, and what points by one who is dissuading, the latter points being the opposite of the former. [We exhort with arguments relating to happiness and its elements; we dissuade with arguments relating to unhappiness and its elements.] Now the aim of one who gives counsel is utility [what is expedient]; for men deliberate, not about the ends to be attained, but about the means of attaining these; and the means are expedient things to do. Since this is so, and since anything expedient is a good, we must make sure of the elementary notions of 'good' and 'expedient' in general.

Good

Let good be defined as that which is chosen in and for itself; or as that for the sake of which we choose something else; or that which is desired by all beings, or by all sentient beings, or beings with intelligence, or that which would be desired by anything that acquired intelligence. Again, whatever universal intelligence would accord to each individual, or whatever would be accorded by the individual intelligence to each, that is, for each, good; or it is that which, if present, renders the individual in good case and self-sufficient. Or, again, good means self-sufficiency, whatever creates or preserves the like, whatever entails such things, and whatever prevents or destroys their opposites. One thing may 'entail' another in either of two ways—as a concomitant, or as a consequence. Thus knowledge follows learning as a consequence, while living attends health as a concomitant. And 'creative' [productive] must be understood in three senses: as being healthy (1) produces [active] health; or as food (2) produces health; or as exercise (3) produces health—since exercise as a rule does produce it.

These principles being laid down, it must follow that the taking of good things and the rejection of bad things are both good; the rejection of the bad entailing deliverance from the bad as a concomitant, and the taking of the good entailing possession of the good as a consequence. So, too, the taking of a greater good instead of a less, or of a lesser evil instead of a greater, is good; the

1362b

excess of the greater over the less is the measure of the good received or of the ill rejected. The virtues, too, are necessarily a good; for, in respect to them, their possessor is in a desirable state, and they are productive of good and effective for action. They are, however, to be severally named and described elsewhere [1. 9, pp. 47–8]. And pleasure must be a good; for all living creatures naturally pursue it. Consequently pleasant things and beautiful things must be good things; for pleasant things are productive of pleasure, while of beautiful things some are pleasant, and some are intrinsically desirable. [Beauty is here regarded as (1) physical, pleasing to the senses (a category including artistic pleasure), and hence desirable for its effect, and as (2) moral (honorable)—that is, *fair*—and thus desirable for its own sake.]

Goods, listed in detail

Listing things one by one, we see that the following must be goods. Happiness; for it is desirable in itself, and sufficient by itself, and is a thing for the sake of which we choose many others.

Justice, courage, temperance, magnanimity, magnificence, and all other like habits of mind; for they are excellences of the soul [virtues].

Health, beauty, and the like; for they are excellences of the body, and are productive of many things [that are good]. Thus health is productive both of pleasure and of life, and hence is thought to be the best of all good things, as being the source of two things which the generality of men most value, namely pleasure and life.

Wealth; for it is the excellence of possession, and is a good capable of producing many others.

A friend and friendship; for a friend is intrinsically desirable, and also productive of many advantages.

Honor, reputation; for they are pleasant, and also productive of much else that is good; and in general they are attended by the actual possession of the qualities and advantages which the honor or reputation implies.

Power in speaking, power of action; for all such qualities are capable of producing goods.

Further, natural ability, memory, aptness in learning, quickness of thought—all such qualities; for these faculties are productive of goods. Similarly all the sciences and arts.

And life; for even if no other good go with it, life is desired for itself.

And justice; for it promotes the communal interest. [It promotes that general good which is happiness.]

Lines of argument about the 'good'

That is a fairly adequate list of 'goods' as commonly admitted. About things, the goodness of which is disputed, we may draw arguments from the following. That is good of which the opposite is ill; and that of which the opposite is advantageous to our enemies. Thus, if it is a special advantage to our enemies that we should be cowards, then obviously courage is of special value to our citizens. And, in general, whatever our enemies desire, whatever they rejoice at, its opposite seems to be of advantage to us. That is the point in the speech [of Nestor (*Iliad* 1. 255–7), when he tries to reconcile Achilles and Agamemnon]:

> Of a truth would Priam exult, [and Priam's sons,
> And all the Trojans would have great joy of heart,
> If they should learn of all this strife between you twain].

It is not always so, however—that is only a general rule; for there is nothing to keep the interests of opponents from occasionally being at one. And hence the saying that 'Ills draw men together' (that is, when the same thing is hurting both parties).

1363a

Again, that which is not in excess is good, while that which is greater than it should be is bad. And that is good which has cost much toil or outlay; this cost argues that the thing appeared to be good; further, such a good is assumed to be an end, the goal of repeated efforts. Now an end is a good. And hence the speech [of Athena to Odysseus (*Iliad* 2. 174–8), dissuading the Greeks from a hasty return]:

> [Will ye indeed . . . flee homeward? . . .]
> Ye would leave to Priam and the Trojans their boast,
> [Even Helen of Argos, for whose sake many Achaeans
> Have perished at Troy].

And [again, the speech of Odysseus to the Greeks (*Iliad* 2. 298)]:

> Yet 'twere shame, after tarrying long, to go back empty-handed.

And hence, too, the proverb about 'breaking the pitcher at the door' [after the trouble and toil of filling and fetching it].

That is a good, too, which a multitude are pursuing, and which evidently is the object of competition; for, as we noted [1. 6, p. 30], whatever is aimed at by all is a good, and the 'many' will pass for 'all.' That which is praised is a good; for nobody praises what is not good. And what our enemies and worthless folk praise [in us is a good]; for the merit is as it were universally admitted, if even the ill-disposed grant it. They doubtless grant it because it is so manifest; as those whom their friends blame must be bad, so those whom their enemies praise must be good. That is why the Corinthians fancied they had been abused by Simonides in the verse:

> Ilium has no fault to find with Corinth.

[The allusion may possibly be thus explained: If Simonides had wished to compliment the Corinthians, he should have represented their enemy as praising them.] That is good, too, which has been preferred by some discerning person, or some good man or woman, as Athena chose Odysseus, as Theseus chose Helen, as the goddesses chose Paris Alexander, and as Homer chose Achilles. So in general the objects of deliberate choice are goods. Men voluntarily choose to do such things as we have mentioned, and such as are bad for their enemies and good for their friends—all these things, so far as they are possible [practicable]. Things are possible in two senses—as having been done, and as being easy to do. Easy things are those that may be done either without trouble or in a short time; for difficulty is measured either by the trouble a thing gives or the time it takes. Again, things are good if they turn out as we desire; but men desire, either no evil at all, or an evil less than the good that will ensue; and they will make this choice when the penalty escapes their notice, or when it is small. Those things are good, too, which are one's own, possessed by no one else, and exceptional [as personal gifts, graces, and accomplishments]; for here the credit to the individual is the greater. And things that specially suit us are goods—such things as befit our birth and influence. Also things in which we feel we are deficient, even little things; for not the less do we deliberately choose to attain them. Also things that we do readily, these being 'possible' in the sense of 'easy'; now things that are readily done are those in which the generality, or our equals or inferiors, have succeeded. And those things are goods which will gratify our friends or annoy our enemies. Also those which the people we admire deliberately choose to do. And those in which we are clever and experienced; for here we expect to succeed more easily. And those which a worthless person never chooses; for such things are more commendable. Those things are goods, too, which men actually desire; for such things appear to be, not only pleasant, but better. And, with each type of person, that counts for a good upon which each is especially bent. Thus the contentious like the prospect of victory; the ambitious, the prospect of honor; the avaricious, the prospect of money; and so with the rest.

1363b

With regard, then, to what is good, and what is expedient, our speaker must derive his proofs [persuasions] from the foregoing premises.

The good. More and less

1. 7. [GOODNESS AND EXPEDIENCY, CONTINUED. THE GREATER GOOD AND THE LESS.] But when two courses are possible, it often happens that people, while granting that both are expedient [that each has its advantages],

yet dispute as to which of them is the more expedient. Accordingly, we must next take up the subject of 'the greater good' and 'the more expedient.'

When one thing, x, exceeds another, y, x may be regarded as y plus something more; and the thing exceeded, y, may be regarded as that which is included in x. Also the terms 'greater' and 'more' are always relative to a 'less,' while 'great' and 'small,' 'much' and 'little,' are relative to the average magnitude of things—the 'great' being in excess of this average, the 'small' falling short of it, and similarly with 'many' and 'few.'

Now we are taking 'good' to mean that which is desirable for its own sake, and not on account of something else. We may call it the universal aim; what all things would choose if they could acquire intelligence and sagacity; and that which tends to produce or preserve such goods, or is always accompanied by them. Further, that on account of which things are done is the end; an end is that on account of which all else is done; and for the individual that is a good which fulfils these conditions for him.

[Returning to the topic of more and less,] it follows that the greater number of goods constitutes a greater good than a single good or the smaller number, when the single good or the smaller number is comprised within the larger; for then the larger number (x) exceeds, and the included number (y) is exceeded. [Thus virtue, health, wealth, strength, and beauty, are better than virtue alone (one thing), and are better than health, wealth, strength, and beauty (the smaller number); but the single thing, virtue, must be included, since virtue alone might exceed, or 'excel,' the other four put together.]

Again, if the largest member of one class exceeds [excels] the largest member of another, then the first class exceeds [excels] the second; on the other hand, if one class exceeds [excels] another, then the largest member of the first exceeds [excels] the largest member of the second. [These postulates, useful to the speaker, are open to question; and, indeed, Rhetoric should find the means of persuasion against as well as for them.] Thus, if the tallest man is taller than the tallest woman, then men as a class are taller than women; and conversely, if men as a class are taller than women, then the tallest man is taller than the tallest woman; the ratio of excess for class compared with class is the same as for largest member compared with largest member. Again, if B is attendant upon A, while A is not attendant upon B, then A is the greater good of the two (the attendance being either concomitant, or as a consequence, or potential); for the use [enjoyment] of the attendant B is included [involved] in the use of the A. Thus life (B) attends as a concomitant on (A) health, but health need not accompany life; knowledge (B) attends as a consequence on (A) learning; fraud (B) attends on (A) sacrilege potentially—for one who has robbed a temple would not hesitate at fraud. Again, of two things which exceed [excel] a third thing, that which exceeds [excels] by more is the greater [more excellent], because it must exceed the greater as well as the less. Again, those things which tend to produce the greater good are greater goods; this was involved in the assumption that they produce something greater [1.7, p. 35]. Similarly that which is produced by a greater good is a greater good; thus if the wholesome is preferable to the pleasant, and is a greater good, then health is greater [more excellent] than pleasure. Again, what is desirable for its own sake is a greater good than what is not, as strength is a greater good than is a wholesome regimen; for strength is, and a wholesome regimen is not, desirable in and for itself; and to be thus desirable was our definition of a good. Again, if one thing is an end, and another not, the first is the greater good, being desirable for its own sake, and not for the sake of

1364a

something else—as exercise is desirable for a good condition of the body. And of two things that which has less need of the other, or of other things, is the greater good, since it is more independent; and that is less in need of accessories which needs fewer of them or needs such as are more easily supplied. Or if B cannot exist or come to pass without A, while A can do so without B, then A appears to be the greater good, since that which requires nothing for its existence is the more independent. Again, if one thing is an orginating principle, and the other is not, the first is the greater good; and similarly if one thing is a cause, and the other not, for the same reason; for without a cause, or a first principle, it is impossible that anything should exist or come to pass. Again, if it is a case of two first principles, what proceeds from the greater principle is the greater result, and similarly if it is a case of two causes. Conversely, if it is a case of two results, the principle from which the greater result proceeds is the greater principle, the cause from which the greater result proceeds is the greater cause. From what has been said, it is clear that one thing may be shown to be greater [more important] than another in either of two ways. If A is an originating principle, while B is not, A will seem to be greater. And if A is not an originating principle, while B is, A will seem to be greater [that is, when A is shown to be an end]; for the end or aim is greater [than what is not an end] and is not an originating principle. Thus Leodamas in accusing Callistratus said that the plotter [the originator] was a greater criminal than the agent, since if he had not advised the thing, it would not have been done. But again, in accusing Chabrias [joint offender with Callistratus] he said that the agent [who accomplished the purpose or *end* of the conspiracy] was a greater criminal than the plotter, since the thing would not have come to pass if there had been no one to effect it; plots, he said, are laid to this end, that men may carry them out.

Again, what is rarer excels what is more abundant. So gold, though less useful than iron, is more precious; for the acquisition of gold is something more difficult, and hence greater. On the alternative side, the abundant is a greater good than the scarce, since there is more use of it; frequent use excels rare—whence the saying [of Pindar (*Olympian Odes* 1.1)]:

> Best of all is water, [but gold . . . shineth eminent].

In general, the more difficult of two things is a greater good than the easier, as being rarer. But, on the alternative side, the easier is a greater good than the more difficult, as conforming to our wishes. Again, one thing is greater than another when the opposite, or the loss, of the first is greater than the opposite, or the loss, of the second. Virtue and vice are greater than the absence of virtue and vice, for the positives are ends [objects of human aims], and the negatives are not ends. [The difference is one of magnitude for Rhetoric; the question here is not one of ethics.] And if the function of one thing is nobler or baser than the function of another, the first thing is greater than the second. Conversely, if the vice or excellence of one thing is greater than that of another, then the function of the first is greater than that of the second. That is, as the causes and first principles are to each other, so are the results to each other; and as the results are to each other, so are the causes and first principles to each other. [Cope thus elucidates: 'Virtues and vices, excellences and defects, stand to "works" in the relation of cause and origin to consequence and effect or result. Now as of the greater cause and origin, the one produces a greater effect, the other leads to a greater end, . . . and the less to a less, so in the case of excellence and defect the greater produces a greater work, the less a less, both in human action or comparative virtues, and in instruments of all kinds—in men and things.'] Again, those things are greater in which superiority is more desirable or nobler. Thus keen sight is more desirable than a keen sense of smell, since sight itself is more desirable than the sense of smell; and since it is nobler to surpass in loving one's friends than in loving money, love of one's friends is itself nobler than the love of money. [As the highest degrees are to each other, so are the positive degrees to each other.] Conversely, as the positive degrees excel one another, so the highest of the better things are better than the highest degrees of things not so good, and the highest degrees of more honorable things are more honorable than the highest degrees of things less honorable. Again, those things are more honorable or better, of which the desires are more honorable and better; for the stronger [or higher] impulses have the greater [higher or more important] objects. Conversely, the nobler and better the objects, the nobler and better the desires, for the same reason. Again, the higher and nobler the science, the higher and nobler its subject-matter; for as is the science, so is the kind of truth at which it aims, each science determining and governing its own field. For this reason, in proportion as the subject-matter is higher and nobler, the science is higher and nobler. Again, what would be judged, or has been judged, a good or the greater of two goods by the judicious, or by all men or the majority or the best of them, must be so; either absolutely, or in so far as the judgment was in keeping with good sense. The rule is a general one, and applies to all other things besides goods; for the nature, quantity, and quality of a thing are what science and good sense would pronounce them to be. Here, however, we have made the statement only with respect to goods; good having been defined as that which would be chosen by things as individuals, if they acquired sagacity [1. 7,

1364b

p. 35]. Obviously, then, that is a greater good which sound sense distinctly pronounces to be so. And that is the greater good which belongs to the superior class, either absolutely, or in so far as the class is superior; thus manly valor is a greater good than brute strength. So also that is the greater good which the superior man would choose, either absolutely, or in so far as the man is superior; thus to suffer a wrong is a greater good than to do it, since the first would be the choice of the juster man. And the pleasanter thing is a greater good than the less pleasant; for all things pursue pleasure, and desire the feeling for its own sake—and such are the terms in which the good and the end have been defined [1. 7, p. 35]. The more pleasant means the pleasure which involves less pain and which is more lasting. [Bodily pleasures, for example, are, in comparison with pleasures of the soul, more likely to bring pain, and to be fleeting.] And the nobler [fairer, more beautiful] is a greater good than the less noble [fair]; for the noble [fair] is either the pleasant, or what is desirable in itself. All those things are the greater goods, too, which men have more desire to effect [to be the causes of] for themselves or for their friends; and what they least desire in this way are the greater evils. Again, the more lasting goods are greater than the more transient, and the more secure than the less secure. The advantage of the more lasting is in respect to time; the advantage of the more secure is in respect to our voluntary control of them, for the use of what is secure is more in our power whenever we wish. Further, in accordance with the rule of co-ordinate terms, and of inflections of the same stem, what is true of one of the related words is true of all. [The 'co-ordinate' terms are logical concepts—for example, *just* and *justice*; and the 'inflections' are these same logical co-ordinates regarded in their grammatical aspects—are the changes which a root undergoes in passing into different parts of speech (as noun, adjective, adverb, verb), with the various grammatical forms of each.] Thus, if 'valiantly' is nobler and more desirable than 'temperately,' then 'valor' is more desirable than 'temperance,' and 'to be valiant' than 'to be temperate.' Again, what all men choose is a greater good than what is not chosen by all. And what the majority choose is a greater good than what is chosen by the minority; for 'good' was defined as that which *1365a* all desire; and hence that is the greater good which stirs desire in more. That, too, is the greater good which is so considered by our rivals or enemies, or by experts or judges whom the experts select; for an admission by our rivals and enemies is equivalent to universal consent, while the opinion of experts and judges means the verdict of authorities and men of special knowledge. Sometimes that in which all men share is the greater good, since not to share in it is a disgrace. But sometimes that is the greater good which one shares with none or few, since it is rarer. Again, the objects of higher praise are greater goods, since they are nobler [—virtue, for example]. So also, those things for which the honors are greater; for honor [an award] is, as it were, a measure of value. And those things are greater for which the penalties are greater. Also those things which are greater than things admittedly or obviously great. Again, the same things [facts, events] will seem greater when they are separately listed [than when summarily combined in one statement]; for then they will appear to exceed [excel] in a greater number of points. And hence the poet [Homer (cf. *Iliad* 9. 592–4)] says that [Cleopatra] persuaded [her husband] Meleager to arise [against the Curetes] by detailing

> All the woes that come to folk whose town is taken:
> The menfolk perish, fire consumes the city,
> Strangers lead away the children [and deep-girdled women].

So combination [accumulation] and climax [*gradatio*], as used by [the comic poet] Epicharmus, make things seem greater, for the same reason as the separate listing does (since the accumulation makes an impression of superiority), and also because you seem to have the origin and cause of great results. [An example of 'climax' (*gradatio*) is found in Epicharmus, fragment 148, Kaibel: 'From sacrificing comes feasting, from feasting drinking, . . . from drinking mockery, from mockery riot, from riot indictment, from indictment a sentence, from a sentence fetters, the stocks, and a fine.'] And since that which is more difficult and rarer is greater, critical junctures, or one's age, or places, or times, or one's powers, will make things great. Thus if one achieves things beyond one's normal power, beyond one's age, or beyond the power of one's fellows, or in some special way or place, or at a particular time, the acts will have magnitude among those that are noble or good or just or their opposites. And hence the inscription [? of Simonides] for the Olympic victor [—the inscription on his statue]:

> Of yore, with a rough yoke about my shoulders,
> I used to carry fish from Argos to Tegea.

[The honor of victory was accentuated by the previous circumstances of the victor.] So Iphicrates [the famous general] used to plume himself on having risen 'from a low estate to this.' [He was said to be the son of a cobbler.] Again, a natural gift is superior to an acquired talent, for it is harder to come by. That is why the poet [Homer] says [in the *Odyssey* 22. 347–9, where the minstrel pleads]:

> Self-taught am I, [and the god has put into my heart all manner of lays, and methinks I sing to thee as a god; wherefore be not eager to cut off my head.]

A thing is more precious, too, if it is the greatest part of something great. Thus Pericles in his *Funeral Oration* said that the loss of the youth from the City was as if the spring were taken out of the year. And those are greater goods which are useful in the greater need, as in old age or in times of sickness. And of two means that is the greater good which is nearer to the end or aim. Likewise what is good for the individual is for him a greater good than what is good abstractly considered. And the possible good is greater than the impossible, since the possible is good for the individual while the impossible is not. And those things which are involved in the end [object] of life are the greater goods; for those things are more like ends which appertain to the main object [—which is happiness]. And things that make for reality are greater *1365b* goods than what makes for reputation; the latter may be defined as that which a man will not choose if he is going to escape notice. For this reason, to receive benefits would seem to be more desirable than to confer them; since a man would choose to receive a benefit even if he were going to escape notice, but probably would not confer one unobserved. [That is the general rule; under it comes a particular case which follows.] Whatever men wish to be, rather than seem, is the greater good, since it is nearer reality. That is why they say justice is a small thing—because it is more desirable to seem just than to be so, while it is more desirable to be, rather than seem, healthy. And that is the greater good which is more useful in a number of ways—for example, what is conducive to life itself, to living well, to pleasure, and to honorable deeds. Accordingly, wealth and health are thought to be the greatest goods, since they carry all the aforesaid goods with them. Also the thing that has less pain, along with [positive] pleasure, is the greater good; for thus it has more than one excellence, and so we have both the pleasure, as a good, and likewise the absence of pain. [See 1. 6, p. 30, where we note that, of two things, the less painful is the greater good, the advantage being measured by the difference in the amount of pain.] Again, of two goods, that is the greater which when added to the same thing makes the greater total. And those goods which when present are perceived are greater than those which when present are unnoticed; for those that are perceived have a greater air of reality. Accordingly, wealth would appear to be a greater good through the display of it. Also that is a greater good which is a man's cherished possession, or which is all he has, while his fellows have more than one. Thus the damage is greater when you blind a one-eyed man than when you blind one eye of a man who has two, as the one-eyed man is bereft of a cherished possession.

The sources from which we must draw our arguments [persuasions] in exhorting and dissuading have thus been pretty exhaustively stated.

Forms of the commonwealth

1. 8. [DELIBERATIVE SPEAKERS SHOULD STUDY THE FORMS OF GOVERNMENT—DEMOCRACY, OLIGARCHY, ARISTOCRACY, AND MONARCHY.] The greatest help, the most effective of all in fitting a speaker to persuade his audience and counsel it well, is to have mastered all the forms of government. He should have analyzed the tendencies, institutions, and interests of each several form; for all men are ruled by their own interest, and their interest lies in whatever preserves the State. Further, [in each state] the sovereign utterance is the edict of the sovereign authority, and this authority [governing body] is different for each form of government; there are as many kinds of sovereign authority as there are forms of government. Now the forms of government are four—democracy, oligarchy, aristocracy, and monarchy; and hence the power that governs and decides in them is always some part or the whole of each.

Four types of state

Democracy

Democracy is a form of government in which all the citizens take part in distributing the offices by lot. Oligarchy is one in which there is a property qualification

Oligarchy

[that must be met before one can choose or be an officer.] Aristocracy is one in which the qualification is training [education, discipline]; and by training is meant the discipline established under the law; for in an aristocracy the offices go to those who have lived in constant obedience to the institutions of the State. Such persons are sure to be regarded as the best [ἄριστοι], and hence has come this name [aristocracy, the rule of the best]. Monarchy, as the name indicates, is a form of government in which one person is the ruler of all; but there are two sorts of monarchy, one the regulated kingdom [constitutional monarchy], the other the unrestricted tyranny [absolute monarchy].

Aristocracy

Monarchy

1366a

It is quite necessary to observe the end or aim of each form, for the citizens make their choices with reference to the end. The end of democracy is freedom; of oligarchy, wealth; of aristocracy, the promotion of discipline, and the institutions of the State; of tyranny, self-protection. [Some remark of Aristotle on the end of limited monarchy may have been lost; or, in the less precise treatment he gives to politics for Rhetoric, he may tacitly include self-protection (by means of a body-guard and the like) as the aim of a king as well as a tyrant.] Clearly, then, we must distinguish the tendencies, institutions, and interests which promote the end of each form of government, since it is with reference to this end that peoples make their choices. Now persuasions are effected not only by argumentative speaking, but also by ethical [by the moral quality evinced in the speech]; for we are persuaded when we think the speaker to be a man of a certain character—that is, when he seems to be good, or well-disposed or both. And hence as speakers we should have a command of the character [tendency] of each form of government; since for each form its own character [its political tone or tendency as evinced in a speech] will be most persuasive; and these political characters must

The aim of each form

be ascertained [for Rhetoric] by the same means [same kind of observation and comparison] as the character of individuals. Character is manifested in choice [in what men choose to do or avoid]; and choice is related to the end or aim.

We have now explained the objects, imminent or future, at which a speaker should aim in exhorting; and the sources from which he must draw his persuasions with regard to what is expedient. Further, the means and the method by which he will get information on the character and institutions of the several forms of government have been explained as far as befits the present occasion; the subject has been treated in detail in the *Politics* [3, 4].

Epideictic Rhetoric

1. 9. [THE OBJECTS OF PRAISE AND BLAME.] We have next to discuss virtue and vice, the noble and the base; for these are the objects of praise and blame. And our discussion will at the same time make plain the means by which a speaker may produce in his audience the impression that he is of such and such a character; this, as we noted [1. 2, p. 8], is our second method of persuasion. With regard to virtue, the same means will enable a man to make people accept either himself or another [the man about whom he speaks] as trustworthy. Now praise may be serious, or it may be trivial; nor does it always concern a human being or a god, for often enough it is applied to inanimate things, or to some insignificant animal. Whatever is praised, one must obtain the materials of argument in the same way. So we must include such things in our discussion, though for purposes of illustration only.

Working definitions of the 'noble'

The 'noble' is that which is desirable in and for itself, and also wins praise; or is that which is good, and also pleasant because good. If this definition is right, then it must follow that virtue is noble, since virtue is good, and is worthy of praise. Now virtue, in the popular conception, is a faculty tending to provide and preserve 'goods,' or a faculty tending to confer many great benefits—indeed, 'all manner of benefits on all occasions.' The elements of virtue are:

The virtues are noble

1366[b]

Justice	Magnificence	Gentleness
Courage	Magnanimity	Prudence
Temperance	Liberality	Wisdom

Now if we regard virtue as a faculty of beneficence, then the greatest virtues must be those that are most useful to other persons. And hence it is that none are so highly esteemed as the just and the brave; for courage is useful to one's fellows in war, and justice in peace as well as in war. Liberality comes next; for the liberal are open-handed, and do not join in the struggle for money, the principal object of other men's desire. Justice is the virtue whereby each and all have what belongs to them in accordance with the law; injustice is the opposite, whereby people have what belongs to others, and not as the law enjoins. Courage is the virtue which moves men to perform noble deeds in times of peril, as the law enjoins, and to uphold the law; cowardice is the opposite. Temperance [self-restraint] is the virtue through which men hold themselves as the law enjoins with regard to bodily pleasures; incontinence is the opposite. Liberality is the virtue tending to confer pecuniary benefits; illiberality is the opposite. Magnanimity is the virtue tending to produce great benefits, and magnificence the virtue productive of grandeur in outlay; the opposites are meanness of spirit and shabbiness. Prudence [sagacity] is an intellectual virtue which enables men to lay good plans for their happiness with regard to the goods and evils above-mentioned. [See 1. 6, pp. 29–34. The virtues are treated more fully and 'scientifically' in the *Nicomachean Ethics* 1, 2, 3. The curtailed account of them just given is in keeping with the more practical and popular aim of Rhetoric, a subject which naturally lays stress on the political and useful aspects of virtue. This emphasis may explain why we have here no definition of gentleness (placability), no allusion to its 'opposite,' or to the 'opposite' of prudence (an opposite easily supplied), and no definition of wisdom (*sophia*) or its opposite—*sophia* being the other, higher, intellectual virtue.]

For the present occasion, this is an adequate account of virtue and vice in general, and of their constituent parts.

The noble—other details

As to the other matters [including the noble and the base], they are not hard to discern. Obviously, whatever is productive of virtue (since it tends toward virtue) must be noble; as must also whatever results from virtue—and under this head come the signs of virtue and its works. And since these signs, and such deeds or experiences as belong to a good man, are noble, it follows that anything done by courage, any sign of courage, or anything done courageously, must be noble. Likewise just deeds, and deeds performed in a just way, must be noble (but not necessarily just sufferings, for, alone among the virtues, justice has this peculiarity, that 'justly' does not always mean nobly—in the case of punishment, it is more shameful to suffer justly than unjustly). And the same is true with regard to the other virtues [—things done by them, any signs of them, and things done in the manner of them, are noble]. And those things are noble, for which the rewards are honor [alone]; likewise those for which the reward is the honor more than the money. And any desirable thing one does in an unselfish spirit; and absolute [general] good deeds, all that any man did for his country, neglecting his own interest—these are noble. So also the gifts of nature [such as birth, personal beauty, intelligence, and the like]; and goods which are not such

1367a

merely for the possessor, since individual interests are selfish. Those things are noble, too, which may exist for the individual after death more than while he is alive; for what appertains to a man in his lifetime has more of a selfish interest. And things done on account of others are noble, as being less selfish; and all successful efforts for others which are of no benefit to the doer. What one does for one's benefactors is noble, since it is just; similarly benefits in general, as their object is unselfish. Again, the opposites of things that make one ashamed are noble; for people feel shame when they say or do, or meditate saying or doing, a shameful thing. Witness the lines of Sappho, in reply to the address of Alcaeus:

> [O violet-weaving, chaste, soft-smiling Sappho,]
> Something I would say, but shame prevents me.

[She answered:]

> Hadst thou desired to say aught good or fair,
> Had not thy tongue been meditating evil,
> Then shame would not have sat upon thine eyes,
> But thou wouldst speak about thy proper wish.

And those things are noble for which men are deeply concerned, without a sense of fear; for that is the way men feel about the goods that conduce to reputation. The virtues [excellences], and corresponding works, of a class that is naturally higher are more noble; those of a man, for example, are nobler than those of a woman. And the excellences which afford gratification to others rather than ourselves are noble; for that reason what is just and the virtue of justice are noble. It is noble to avenge oneself upon one's enemies, and not to come to terms with them; for requital is just, and the just is noble; and not to yield is a mark of courage. [The standard of Rhetoric in such matters is, of course, popular morality.] Victory and honor, too, are included among things noble, for they are desirable even when fruitless, and evince more than common excellence in a man. Also memorable things are noble—the more memorable they are, the more noble. Likewise things that continue after one's death [such as fame], things that are always attended by honor, and things that are exceptional. Unique possessions are noble, since they are more easily remembered. Also possessions that yield no profit, since they are more befitting a gentleman. The special characteristics of peoples are noble; also any distinctive marks of habits that are admired among a particular people. Thus in Lacedaemon it is noble to wear the hair long, as that indicates the gentleman; for with the hair worn long it is not easy to do any menial work. And it is noble not to ply any common trade; for it is the part of a gentleman not to live in dependence upon others.

Artifices in praise or blame

For the purposes of praise or blame, the speaker may identify a man's actual qualities with qualities bordering on them. Thus a cautious man may be represented as cold and designing, a simpleton as good-natured, a callous man as easy-going. And so [for the ends of eulogy] in each case we may substitute one of the collateral terms, always leaning toward the best; terming the choleric and passionate man, for instance, a plain-dealer, and the arrogant man superb and dignified. And men whose bad qualities are on the side of excess may be represented as possessed of the corresponding virtues. [In *Nicomachean Ethics* 2. 7 the virtues are seen to be intermediate states (for example, courage) between excess (for example, rashness) and defect (for example, cowardice).] Thus the rash man may be described as courageous, and the spendthrift as liberal; for so it will seem to the crowd, and meanwhile a false inference can be drawn from the man's motive. Thus if the rash man runs into danger when there is no need of it, much more (they can be made to think) would he do so when it was honorable; and if the spendthrift is lavish to chance-acquaintances, much more will he be generous to his friends; for it is the summit of virtue to do good to every one!

1367b

The audience

One must consider [not only the person praised, but] also the audience to whom the praise is addressed; for, as Socrates said [cf. Plato, *Menexenus* 235 D], it is not difficult to praise the Athenians to an audience of them. Whatever the quality an audience esteems, the speaker must attribute that quality to the object of his praise, whether the audience be Scythians, or Spartans, or scholars. [Thus: skill in hunting, or the like, among the Scythians; patience and fortitude among the Spartans; literary, scientific, artistic accomplishments at Athens.] The rule is, whatever is esteemed is to be treated as noble, since the two things are nearly one in the popular view.

Again, a thing is noble if it befits a man—for example, any deeds that are worthy of the man's lineage or of his own past achievements; for it is felicitous and noble to acquire additional honor. On the other hand, a thing is noble if it goes beyond what is natural to a man in the direction of what is better and more honorable—for example, if a man who while prosperous was of the common run becomes magnanimous in adversity, or if a man as he rises in the world becomes better and more conciliatory. Compare the saying of Iphicrates about his rise from lowly things 'to this.' Or take the inscription for the Olympic victor:

> Of yore, with a rough yoke about my shoulders,
> [I used to carry fish];

or the inscription by Simonides:

> Whose father, husband, brothers, [and her children,]
> all were princes.

['Yet she (Archedice) did not presumptuously lift up her mind' (cf. Thucydides 6. 59). This and the two examples which are repeated from 1. 7, p. 42, all illustrate in a general way the nobility of what goes beyond our expectations of a person (in view of his birth or previous circumstances) in the direction of the good and honorable; they do not illustrate the more specific statements under that head.]

Praise is given to acts done in accordance with moral choice

Since we praise men for what they have done, and since the mark of the virtuous person is that he acts after deliberate moral choice, our speaker must try to show that the subject of his praise is a man who does so act. To this end one will find it helpful to make it appear that the man has often acted with a moral purpose. Accordingly, [along with any cases in which he did so act] mere coincidences and the results of chance must be represented as the results of moral choice; for if many like cases are produced, they will give an impression [will appear to be a sign] of virtue and deliberate choice.

Definition of praise

Now praise is an utterance making manifest the greatness of a virtue. Therefore the speaker must show the actions of his man to be of such and such a quality. Encomium concerns the man's actual deeds; attendant circumstances such as his good birth and his training merely render his merit more credible; since it is likely that good men will spring from a good stock, and that a man who has been reared in a given way will be virtuous. Accordingly, we bestow encomium upon men after they have achieved something. Yet the deeds themselves do but indicate the moral habit, and we should praise a man even if he had not done a thing, if we were sure he was capable of doing it. As for felicitation [μακαρισμός] and congratulation [εὐδαιμονισμός], which are interchangeable terms, they are not identical with praise and encomium; still as happiness [εὐδαιμονία] includes virtue, so congratulation [εὐδαιμονισμός] includes praise and encomium.

Difference between praise and encomium

There is a specific interrelation between praise and advice; for anything you might suggest in a speech of advice can, by a shift in the expression, be turned into encomium. And so, when we know what should be done, and what a man ought to be, we must give to our utterance of these things as advice a shift around, and invert the expression. [In this way the statement becomes en-

1368ª

Relation of laudatory to deliberative speaking

comium.] Take, for example, the sentiment that a man should be proud, not of what fortune has done for him, but of what he owes to his own efforts [cf. Isocrates, *Panathenaicus* 32]. If you put it so, the statement has the force of a suggestion, [and hence belongs to deliberative speaking]. Put it thus, and it is praise: 'He [Evagoras] was proud, not of what fortune had done for him, but of what he owed to his own efforts' [cf. Isocrates, *Evagoras* 45]. So the rule is this: When you wish to praise, consider what you would suggest as advisable; and when you wish to advise, consider what you would praise a man for doing. The two modes of expression will be mutually opposed when a prohibitive element interchanges with a [permissive and] non-prohibitive. [That is, the 'suggestion' or advice and the 'praise' will contradict each other, if, for example, the advice is against pride, and the praise allows it.]

Heightening the praise

Again, the speaker should use various means of magnifying a deed. For example, he should make it clear if the man is the only one, or the first, to have done the deed, or if he has done it almost alone, or more than any one else; for all these things are noble. Then there are the circumstances of time and occasion, when a man's performances exceed what we might naturally expect. [It would be noble, for instance, if a man showed great liberality in a time of pecuniary stress; or take the action of Sir Philip Sidney at Zutphen (see above, p. 27), when the circumstances made his action seem the greater. In magnifying the deed, the speaker must make such circumstances clear.] Or it may be that the man has repeatedly succeeded in the same attempt; this in itself is great, and besides it looks like the result, not of fortune, but of the man's own efforts. Or it may be that special incentives to achievement, and honors for it, were devised and instituted on his account—as in the case of Hippolochus, who received the first public encomium, or in that of

Harmodius and Aristogeiton, the first persons to whom statues were erected in the market-place. And similarly in the opposite cases. [This seems to mean that the orator, in censuring any one, should use the opposite means in order to magnify the disgrace of a deed, noting, for example, if the man was alone, or the first, or almost alone, in committing it, or carried it to the highest degree, etc.] Further, if you are not supplied with means [of magnifying] as regards the man in and for himself, you must magnify him by comparing him with others, as Isocrates did for want of experience in forensic pleading. [Isocrates was practised rather in epideictic oratory, where such comparisons are more useful than in a trial. In a law-court the pleading has directly to do with your client or his adversary; comparison with others—with famous men, for example—will seldom help.] Such comparison must be with men of note; this will tend to magnify the subject of the speech, and if you make him seem better than men of worth, that will ennoble his deed. Magnifying naturally enters into laudatory speeches, since it has to do with superiority, and superiority belongs to noble things. And hence, if you cannot compare your hero with the men of note, you should at least compare him with the rest of the world, since any superiority is taken to reveal excellence.

Magnifying is best suited to epideictic rhetoric

The example to deliberative

The enthymeme to forensic

Considered generally, of the devices common to all speeches, magnifying is best suited to the epideictic, since the actions [to be praised] are taken for granted [are admitted], and it only remains to invest them with magnitude and beauty. Examples are best suited to deliberative speeches, since we judge of things to come by divining from things that have gone before. And enthymemes are best suited to forensic speeches, since the past, through its uncertainties, gives the greatest opportunity for explanation and demonstration.

Summary

Such, then, are the premises from which virtually all laudatory speeches, and speeches of censure, are derived;

and such are the things we must bear in mind when we praise or blame. Thus we have the materials from which encomiums are made, and the materials for reproaches as well. Having our materials on the one side, we at once see those on the other; for blame is derived from the premises directly opposite to those of praise.

Forensic rhetoric

1368b

1. 10. [ACCUSATION AND DEFENCE. WRONG-DOING, ITS AGENTS, AND ITS VICTIMS.] Passing to the subject of accusation and defence, we have next to enumerate and describe the premises from which the speaker should construct his syllogisms [enthymemes]. The points to be ascertained are three: first, the nature and number of the motives from which men do wrong; secondly, the states of mind in which they do it; and, thirdly, the kinds of persons who are wronged, and their situations. Let us first define wrong-doing, and then take up the other points in order.

Accusation and defence

The incentives to wrong-doing; the mental states of wrong-doers; characters and situations of the injured persons

We may define wrong-doing as doing voluntary harm contrary to law. And law is either special or universal. By 'special' I mean the written law by which a particular state is governed; by 'universal' the unwritten principles which are supposed to be acknowledged by all mankind. Now voluntary acts are such as are done knowingly and not under constraint. Not all voluntary acts are the result of deliberate choice; but all that are done by deliberate choice are done 'knowingly'—for nobody is ignorant of what he deliberately intends.

Two kinds of law

What makes men choose to do harmful and evil acts contrary to law? The causes are vice and moral weakness; for if people have bad qualities, one or more, then whatever the point of their failing, there is the point at which they will do wrong. Thus the illiberal man will do wrong with regard to money; the incontinent man with regard to bodily pleasure; the luxurious man with regard to comforts; the coward with regard to dangers, for cowards will

The causes and varieties of faulty choice

abandon their comrades in danger through fear. So the ambitious man will do wrong for the sake of honor; the passionate man through anger; the lover of victory for the sake of victory; the embittered man for revenge; the foolish man because he fails to distinguish right and wrong; the shameless man through disregard of public opinion. And similarly with the rest: each will do wrong with regard to the subject-matter of his vice.

All this will be clear, partly from what has been said on the virtues [1. 9, pp. 46–52], and partly from what we shall have to say on the emotions [2. 1–11, pp. 90–131]. We have now to discuss the motives of wrong-doers, the states of mind in which they act, and the persons who are wronged.

Let us first determine what things people want to get, and the sort of things they wish to shun, when they set about doing wrong; for obviously it is the accuser's [prosecutor's] business to find out how many of these universal incentives to injure one's neighbor, and precisely which of them, exist for [attach to] the adversary; as it is the business of the defence to find out which and how many do not exist for [attach to] him.

The causes of human action

All men do all their acts, either of themselves, or not of themselves. In the latter class of actions, some they do by chance, and others of necessity; and of those done of necessity, some they do under compulsion, and others by nature. Accordingly, all such actions as are not due to ourselves we perform either by chance, or by nature, or under compulsion. As for the things men do of themselves, the acts of which they themselves are the authors, some they do through habit, and others through impulse; and, of these last, some they do through (1) rational impulse, and others through (2) irrational impulse. Now (1) purposeful wish is an impulse towards [craving for] a good (for no one wishes a thing unless he conceives it to be a

1369[a]

good); (2) the irrational impulses are (*a*) anger and (*b*) desire [appetite].

Seven causes

Thus all the acts of men are necessarily done from seven causes: chance, nature, compulsion, habit, reason, passion, desire. [With regard to the causes of action] it is superfluous to make further distinctions according to periods of life, moral states, or other conditions [in which the acts are done]. Thus, [for one of the periods of life,] let us say it is incidental to youth to be quick-tempered and to have strong desires; yet the corresponding acts of young men have as their cause, not youth, but anger and desire. Nor, again, are wealth and poverty causes of action, but it is incidental to the condition of poor men that, lacking money, they desire it, and to the condition of the rich that, having the means for luxurious pleasures, they desire these; the corresponding acts are caused, not by wealth and poverty, but by desire. So is it, [in regard to moral states,] with the actions of the just and the unjust, and the rest [of the virtuous and vicious], who are said to act in accordance with moral states: they will act, [not because of these states, but] from the causes mentioned. The cause will be either reason or emotion, albeit some will act from good dispositions [habits] and emotions, and others from the reverse. Still it does happen that good moral states are attended by good impulses, and bad by bad. Thus the man of self-restraint, doubtless, is, through his self-restraint, at once attended by wholesome opinions and desires with regard to pleasures, and the licentious man by their opposites. Accordingly, while we may dismiss such distinctions [as superfluous, when we are dealing with the causes of human action,] still we must consider what kinds of actions and of people usually go together. A man may be fair or dark, tall or short, and there will be no regular connection between these attributes and his opinions and desires; but, [when we wish to know the motives of his actions,] it does make a difference whether he is young or old, just or unjust. In a word, we must consider any incidental state that makes the characters of men vary; thus the notion a man has that he is rich or poor, lucky or unlucky, will make such a difference. And so we shall discuss these points hereafter. At present let us finish with the matter in hand. [The subject of the varieties of character as related to emotions, moral states, periods of life, and fortune or misfortune, is discussed in 2. 12–17, pp. 131–40. These matters have but an incidental connection with the seven fundamental causes of human action, which are our present concern.]

The causes of human actions
1. Chance

The things [actions] that happen by chance are those for which no cause can be determined, which have no purpose, and which occur neither always, nor as a rule, nor in any orderly way. What they are will be clear from the definition of chance [cf. Aristotle, *Physica Auscultatio* 2. 5].

2. Nature
1369[b]

Those things [actions] are caused by nature, of which the cause is in themselves, and regular; for they always or usually issue in the same way. As for occurrences [actions] that are 'contrary to nature,' we need not narrowly inquire whether they really have some natural cause or other, since [in the popular view, and for the ends of Rhetoric,] the cause of such things would likewise be regarded as chance.

3. Compulsion

Those things [actions] are the result of compulsion, which are done through the instrumentality of the agents, contrary to their desire or calculations.

4. Habit

That is caused by habit, which men do as a result of having often done it before.

5. Reason

Actions are caused by reason [calculation], when, being among those things we have listed as 'goods' [1. 6, pp. 30–4], they are thought expedient as ends, or as means to an end, and are done on this account. The man who lacks self-restraint will, of course, do a certain number of expedient things, not, however, on this account, but for pleasure.

6. Passion

Passion and anger cause acts of retribution. And we must distinguish between retribution and chastisement: chastisement [correction] is inflicted for the sake of the one who receives it, retribution for the sake of the one who inflicts it—for his satisfaction. What anger is will appear in our treatment of the emotions [2. 2, pp. 93–9].

7. Desire or appetite

As for desire, it is the cause of all acts that seem pleasant. Among these are the acquired habit as well as the natural; for there is many an action, not naturally pleasant, which men do with pleasure when it has become a matter of habit.

Summary

Accordingly, we may sum up as follows. All actions which men do of themselves are either good or apparently good, or else pleasant or apparently pleasant. Again, the actions they themselves originate are voluntary, while involuntary actions are such as they do not originate; and hence, whatever acts they may do voluntarily, the objects they aim at will be either good or apparently good or else pleasant or apparently pleasant. And I reckon among goods [real or apparent] the release from evils or apparent evils, and the substitution of a lesser evil [real or apparent] for a greater—since these are, in their way, things to be desired. And, similarly, I reckon among pleasures the release from painful or apparently painful things, and the substitution of a lesser pain for a greater. We must ascertain, then, the number and nature of things expedient [useful or apparently so], and of things pleasant. As the expedient has already been treated [1. 6, pp. 29–34] in connection with deliberative speaking, let us now discuss the subject of the pleasant. Our definitions must be regarded as adequate [for Rhetoric] if, in each case, they are clear enough, without being extremely precise. [The definitions must be adequate and clear; but extreme precision, such as we demand of an exact science, would be out of place in Rhetoric—the resulting arguments would be drawn too fine for a general audience; compare 1. 2, p. 15.]

Definition of pleasure

1. 11. [PLEASURE. ANALYSIS OF THINGS PLEASANT.] We may lay it down that pleasure is a certain motion of the soul [of the vital, sensitive system], a perceptible settling of it, all at once, into its rightful nature; and that pain is the reverse. If that is the way to describe pleasure, then the pleasant manifestly is what tends to produce the condition described; and whatever tends to destroy it, or to produce the opposite of this settling, is painful. Therefore any passage to a natural [normal] state must, as a rule, be pleasant; and especially when anything coming into a natural state [generally considered] conforms to its own [individual] nature. Habits also must be pleasant, since the acquired custom has come to be like a natural instinct, habit being, as it were, a second nature; for 'often' is not far from 'always,' and, as the sphere of nature is the invariable, so the sphere of habit is the frequent. That is pleasant, too, which is not compulsory, for compulsion goes against nature. Accordingly, constraint is painful, and rightly has it been said [by Evenus of Paros]:

1370ᵃ

Pleasures and pains

Everything done by constraint is grievous.

Concentration, hard study, and intense effort are painful, since they involve constraint and compulsion—unless they have become habitual, in which case it is habit that makes them pleasant. Their opposites, again, are pleasant; and hence ease and comfort, intervals of release from toil and attention, amusements, repose, and sleep are in the class of things pleasant, none of them being related to constraint. Everything is pleasant, too, of which the desire exists within us; for desire is an impulse towards the pleasant. Now desires are either irrational or conjoined with reason. By irrational desires I mean those that are experienced with no preconception [of ulterior advantage].

Irrational and rational desires

Such are all that are called 'natural'; so the desires that exist for us through the body—the desire of nourishment, for instance, namely thirst and hunger. And similarly with each kind of bodily desire; desires of taste and sex—of touch in general—of smell [fragrance], hearing, and sight. Desires conjoined with reason are those we have from conviction; for there are many things that we desire to see and possess after hearing of them and being persuaded [of their excellence]. Now to be pleased consists in experiencing a certain feeling, and imagination is a kind of faint perception; and so the man who remembers or anticipates must carry with him some mental image of the object he remembers or anticipates. This being granted, it is clear that there are pleasures (since there is sensation) accompanying both memory and anticipation. Consequently all pleasures must consist in the perception of things present, or in the memory of things past, or in the anticipation of things to come; for men perceive the present, remember the past, and expect the future. Now remembered things are pleasant—not only those that were pleasant when they happened, but some that were not pleasant at the time, provided that the sequel has been noble and good. And hence the sentiment [in Euripides' *Andromeda*]:

Pleasures of memory and anticipation

1370b

> But sweet are toils remembered when survived.

So [cf. *Odyssey* 15. 398–401] also:

> [But let us twain within the hut both drink and feast,
> And in our grievous woes take mutual delight,
> Rehearsing them;] for afterwards a man takes joy even
> in griefs,
> When he recalls much suffering and much toil.

The reason is that there is pleasure even in the mere absence of evil. Again, everything is pleasant in anticipation, which, if present, would seem to give great delight or profit —profit without pain. In general, whatever gives delight when present will as a rule be pleasant both in anticipation and in memory. And hence there is pleasure in being angry, as we may see from Homer's description of wrath [*Iliad* 18. 109]:

> That sweeter far than dripping honey
> [Waxeth like smoke in the breasts of men];

for no one is angry with another when the second seems beyond the reach of vengeance, nor are we angry with those who are far above us in power—or if angry at all, we are less angry. [Where vengeance seems possible, there is room for anger; and the prospect of vengeance is pleasant.] And so most of the desires are accompanied by a certain pleasure, since there is some glow of pleasure either in the memory of past, or in the anticipation of future enjoyment. Thus a patient with a fever gets some pleasure in his thirst from the recollection of the previous drink and the anticipation of the drink to come. So, too, lovers delight in talking or writing about the beloved one, or in somehow busying themselves about him; for in all such doings the recollection seems to them like actually perceiving the beloved with the senses. Indeed, this always marks the beginning of love, when they have joy not only in the presence of the beloved, but also in remembering him if he is away. Accordingly, even when the loss of his presence gives us pain, still a certain pleasure arises in our mourning and lamentation; for pain is felt at the loss of the beloved, but pleasure in remembering him and, as it were, seeing him as he lived and moved. And hence the propriety of the passage [in the *Iliad* 23. 108, where Achilles relates his vision of the dead Patroclus:

> 'And wondrous like his living self it seemed.']
> So spake he, and in them all he stirred the yearning for
> lament.

[The line quoted by Aristotle occurs also in *Odyssey* 4. 183.]

And revenge is sweet; since where failure is painful, success must be pleasant; and while angry men are pained above measure at not being revenged, they have joy in the prospect of vengeance. And to conquer is pleasant, not only to the [class of] persons who love victory [hate to be beaten], but to all men; for winning gives a man an impression of superiority, and to be superior is the desire of every one, more or less. And since to conquer is pleasant, it follows that sportive contests, whether bodily or mental, are pleasant—for in these there are many opportunities of winning; and so with games—knuckle-bones, ball, dice, draughts. And the same principle holds in the case of more serious amusements—some of which become pleasant only when we have gained proficiency in them, while others are pleasant from the start, as the chase and all other kinds of hunting. That is, wherever there is competition, there is also victory. And hence legal contests and debating are pleasant to those who have the requisite practice and ability.

Other pleasures: revenge

Victory

Games

1371[a]

Debate

Again, honor and reputation are among the most pleasant of things, since every one who has them gains the impression that he must be such a person as the excellent man [to whom honor and reputation are due], and especially when those people say so who in his opinion tell the truth. Such people are one's neighbors rather than those who live far away, associates and fellow-citizens rather than strangers, contemporaries rather than a coming generation, judicious men rather than foolish, and a number of persons rather than a few; for the classes specified are more likely to form a true opinion than the ones contrasted with them. When the class is one for which the man has very little regard, as children or animals, he cares not at all for their respect or good opinion; or if he does care, it will not be on account of the opinion itself, but for some other reason.

Honor

Again, a friend is among pleasant things, since to love

Friendship

[like, be fond of] is pleasant (as no one loves wine who does not find pleasure in it), and to be loved is pleasant; for here we have an impression of possessing some good which all who perceive it desire, and to be loved means to be esteemed for one's own sake. And, again, to be admired is pleasant, simply on account of the [implied] honor. Flattery, too, and a flatterer are pleasant, the flatterer being ostensibly an admirer and ostensibly a friend.

Repetition

And repetition of the same acts is pleasant, since, as we saw [1. 10, p. 59], the habitual is pleasant. And to change [not to go on repeating an act] is pleasant, as change means a return to nature; for an unceasing repetition of the same thing will make a vicious excess of the [artificially] settled state. [We must distinguish between the natural state, a return to which constitutes pleasure (see the definition above, p. 60), and the state produced by habit—as it were, a second nature. When the habitual action is done to excess (and in general all excess is vicious and hurtful), then change is a return to our original nature, and hence, by definition, pleasant.] And hence the saying [in Euripides' *Orestes* 234, where Electra first lays her well-nigh helpless brother on the couch, and then induces him 'to take one step']:

Change

In all things change is sweet.

That is why occasional visitors, and things that come at intervals, are pleasant; they are a change from the existing condition, and furthermore the occasional is rare. [The rare thing is preferred to the usual (1.7, pp. 38, 41, 42), and, being preferable, is pleasant.]

Learning

Learning, too, and wonder, as a rule, are pleasant; for wonder implies the desire to learn, so that the wonderful is something desired, [and desire is always for the pleasant (1.11, p. 60)]; while learning implies a settlement into our normal state. [All men desire to know; complete knowledge is the settled state to which we tend; and by definition pleasure is a settling into our normal nature.] Again, to confer benefits [favors], and to receive them, are among pleasant things. To receive them means getting what we desire; to confer them implies possession and superiority, and both these things are objects of human ambition. And since beneficence is pleasant, men find it pleasant to set their neighbors straight again and to complete deficiencies. [This may mean, to restore one's fellows to a normal condition after a mistake or fall, and to supply their pecuniary, mental, and moral deficiencies. But the second part of the statement may mean, to complete imperfect things; this interpretation would readily lead on to the next thought.] Again, since learning and wonder [admiration] are pleasant, such things as artistic imitation must be pleasant; for example, painting, sculpture, and poetry—indeed, every successful imitation of an object, even though the object which is imitated is not in itself pleasing. Our delight is not in the original; rather, there is an inference: *This* [the artistic imitation] is *that* [the object represented]; and so an act of learning takes place. [A fuller account of our pleasure in art—a pleasure derived from our noting the resemblance, say, between a portrait and its original (some person already known to us)—is found in *Poetics* 4; even when the object reproduced, as a dead body or a toad, is repulsive, we delight in seeing a faithful picture of it.] So also reversals of fortune [as in dramas] and hairbreadth escapes from danger are pleasant, for all such things excite our wonder.

1371 b

Art

And since what is natural is pleasant, and kindred things are natural to each other, all things that are akin and like to one are pleasant, as a rule—as man to man, horse to horse, youth to youth; whence the proverbial sayings, 'Mates of like age delight,' 'Ever like to like,' 'A beast knows his fellow,' 'Jackdaw to jackdaw,' and all the rest. But since everything like and akin to oneself is pleasant, and since each of us bears this relation above all to

Congeners are pleasant

Likeness and liking

The standard is likeness to oneself

himself, it follows that all men are lovers of self in greater measure or less; the main standard of reference for all such resemblances is yourself. Since, then, all are self-lovers, it follows that what is one's own is pleasant—as, for example, our own deeds and words. Hence, also, all men are fond of their flatterers, fond of honor, and fond of their children—for our children are our own work. Further, to complete imperfect things is pleasant, since the whole work then becomes our own [cf. 1.11, p. 65].

Wisdom and authority are pleasant

And since it is very pleasant to exercise authority, it is pleasant to be thought wise; for practical wisdom gives one power over others. Speculative wisdom is pleasant, since it means the knowledge of many wonderful things. Further, since men as a rule are ambitious [fond of honor], it follows that to censure one's neighbors is pleasant; [like governing them, censuring them implies superiority in ourselves, and hence the pleasure.] Also it is pleasant to spend one's time in the occupation where one appears at one's best, just as the poet [Euripides in *Antiope*] says:

> And to that he speeds,
> To that devotes great part of every day—
> To the work in which he shines most brightly.

The ludicrous.

Similarly, too, since sport and every form of relaxation are among pleasant things, and since laughter is among them, it follows that the objects of laughter are pleasant,

1372a

whether people, or things said, or things done. The subject of the ludicrous, however, has been elsewhere discussed, in the treatise *On the Art of Poetry.*[1]

Of things pleasant, then, let this account suffice; from their opposites we see [the number and nature of] things painful. [The next chapter begins by suggesting that

[1] The causes of laughter are not systematically discussed in the extant *Poetics;* but the reference is intelligible if we admit that the so-called *Tractatus Coislinianus* contains an Aristotelian treatment of comedy, and is somehow related to the *Poetics* (see Cooper, *An Aristotelian Theory of Comedy*, New York, 1922).

men do wrong for the sake of pleasure or for the avoidance of pain; that is, the opening sentence seems to refer directly to the present chapter; but the reference properly includes the expedient and inexpedient, too; and among the causes of voluntary wrong-doing we must note habit and passion, though the immediate relation of habit and anger, as well as desire, to 'things pleasant' is marked in the present chapter. See above, 1.11, p. 60; 1.10, p. 59; 1.6, pp. 30–4; below, 2.2, pp. 93–9; 2.11–17, pp. 129–41.]

1. 12. [CHARACTER AND CIRCUMSTANCES OF WRONG-DOERS, AND OF THE VICTIMS OF WRONG.] These, then, are the incentives of wrong-doers; let us now consider the states of mind [conditions] in which they do wrong, and the persons whom they [tend to] wrong.

For the motives of wrong-doing, see above

Wrongs are done when the doers think the thing is possible, and possible for them; next, if they think they can escape detection, or think that, if detected, they will not pay the penalty; or that, given the penalty, it will be less than the gain to themselves, or less than the gain to persons they care for.

Conditions of wrong-doing

What sort of things seem possible, and what impossible, will be taken up later, for the subject belongs in common to all [three] kinds of speaking. [For the 'common topic' of the 'possible and impossible,' see 2. 19, p. 143.] The people who think that they, personally, can do wrong with the greatest impunity are able speakers, men of action and of much experience in legal contests; also those who have many friends, and the rich. The expectation is strongest with those who are themselves in the circumstances just mentioned, or who, lacking these advantages personally, have friends, supporters, or associates who possess them; for thus they can proceed, and can escape detection or avoid the penalty. Similarly men think wrong-doing possible if they are friends of the victims or of the judges; for our friends are not on their guard against

Classes of persons who think they can escape penalties

injury from us, and, besides, will come to terms before prosecuting us; while judges show favor to their friends, and either acquit them altogether, or make the penalties light.

Kinds of persons likely to escape detection

Wrong-doers likely to escape detection are those who [in character or situation] are the very opposite to that which the complaints will indicate; as when a feeble man is accused of assault and battery, or the ugly pauper is charged with adultery. [These were stock cases of improbability in the rhetorical treatises before Aristotle, and doubtless in those of his time; see 2.24, p. 177.] Men are likely to escape if their crimes are committed very openly, in full view; for against such acts no precautions are taken, since no one would imagine they could be committed. Similarly if the crimes are of such magnitude, or of such a nature, that you would think nobody ever could commit them; as with maladies, so with crimes, it is only the usual ones against which all men are on their guard. No one is on his guard against a disease from which nobody ever suffered. Again, wrong-doers think they can go unpunished if they have no enemy, or if they have a great number of enemies. Those who have none think to escape detection because they are not being watched; those who have many actually escape it because no one would think them likely to assail vigilant foes, and because, if accused, they have the defence that they were not likely to do it. Then there are those who have means of covering their tracks—some device, or advantage of locality, or easy way of arranging matters.

Other types and possibilities

And a certain number will do wrong when, though they cannot escape detection, it is possible to evade the trial, or to postpone it, or to corrupt the judges. Then there are those who expect that a penalty may be imposed, but think it possible to evade the payment or to delay it for a long time. Also those who are in such straits that they have nothing to lose. Also those for whom the gains are manifest, or great, or immediate, and the penalities small, or uncertain, or remote. Also those for whom there can be no punishment commensurate with the advantage [to be gained if the wrong-doing is successful]—as men suppose [when they aim at] despotic power [over the State]. And a certain number will do wrong when the gains are to be solid, and the penalty is but disgrace; conversely, there are those who will do wrong if the penalty means a fine, or exile, or the like, while the crimes will bring a measure of applause. For example, in committing a crime one might at the same time be avenging one's father or mother, as did Zeno. [This may be Zeno of Elea, or some other person now unknown.] Men will do wrong on both of the aforesaid grounds, and in both states of mind; not the same men, however, for the two types of character are direct opposites. Further, there are men who will do wrong if they have often escaped detection or escaped punishment. So also those who have often failed in their attempts [and have been punished]; for in crime, as in war, some are always ready to renew the struggle. And some will do wrong when the pleasure is immediate and the pain to come later, or when the gain is immediate and the loss to come later; such are the intemperate [unrestrained, incontinent], and intemperance [lack of restraint] is shown with respect to all the objects of human appetites. Conversely, there are men who will do wrong if the pain or loss is for the moment, and the pleasure and advantage are subsequent and more lasting—such being the objects sought by the temperate [continent] and the relatively prudent. Then there are those who do wrong when their deeds can appear to be the result of accident, or of necessity, or nature, or habit —in short, to be errors rather than crimes. [The incongruity between the classification in 1.10, pp. 56–7, and the list just given can be explained by the fact that *there* we are dealing with the causes of human actions, some of

1372b

them voluntary, others involuntary, while *here* we are viewing the excuses men make for wrong-doing. For actions arising from habit men are indeed responsible; but *here* the wrong-doer is thought of as prepared to excuse himself on the ground that a confirmed habit is beyond one's control.] Again, there are those who expect leniency [a merciful construction to be accorded their acts by the judges]. Then there are the needy; and these may be divided into two classes: some will do wrong on the ground that they lack a necessity of life—as the poor; and some on the ground that they lack a luxury—as the rich. Again, wrong is done by the highly respectable, because they will not be credited with it; and by the very disreputable, because they will incur no greater suspicion than before. [If anything, these latter think they stand to better their reputation.]

Persons likely to be wronged

Such, then, are the dispositions and circumstances of men who set out to do wrong. As for the dispositions and circumstances of persons likely to be wronged, and the kinds of injury done them, they are as follows. A man will wrong those who have things that he himself lacks, be it in the way of necessities, or of excess property, or of amusement. He will wrong persons far distant, and persons near at hand; when they are near by, the acquisition is speedy; and when they are far distant, the retribution is slow—as when Greeks plunder Carthaginians. Persons are likely to be wronged who are not cautious or vigilant, but confiding, for it is always easy to elude them. So also the easy-going, for a man must be ready to take trouble if he intends to prosecute. Likewise the retiring, since they are not keen about fighting for gain. Further, those who heretofore have been wronged by many without seeking justice—such people being, in the proverbial phrase, 'Mysian plunder.' [Compare our colloquial description of helpless prospective victims as 'easy meat.' The Mysians, with a reputation for meanness and cowardice, may at some juncture have been peculiarly defenceless.] They, too, are open to injury from us whom we never before have wronged, or whom we often have wronged; both classes are likely to be off their guard, the former from a notion that they are never to be injured, and the latter because they fancy themselves now at length exempt. Likewise people who have been subject to calumny, or may easily become so. Such people will not prosecute for fear that the judges will be against them, or, if they do prosecute, they cannot win the judges over; to this class belong the objects of popular dislike and envy. They also are likely to be wronged against whom the wrong- *1373a* doer has any pretext in an injury, or a threat of injury, by their ancestors, themselves, or their friends, to him or his ancestors or those for whom he cares; for, as the proverb has it, 'Villainy wants only a pretext.' Again, people will wrong their friends, and will wrong their enemies; friends will be wronged because it is easy, and enemies because it is pleasant. Also those who are without friends will be wronged. So also those who lack ability in speaking or action; for such people either make no effort to prosecute, or, if they start to prosecute, readily come to terms or in the end accomplish nothing. Also those who cannot afford to wait for a trial, or for damages—as foreigners and husbandmen; such persons tend to settle with the wrong-doer on easy terms, and will readily drop the prosecution. Again, they are likely to be wronged who themselves have committed many crimes, or crimes of the sort in which they now become victims; for it seems next to no injustice at all when a man has some such wrong done to him as he has been wont to inflict upon others—I mean, for example, when one man assaults another who has habitually been given to violence. And they are likely to be wronged [in requital] who have done or intended, or who intend or certainly will do, mischief to others; for the requital [anticipatory or subsequent] not only is pleasant, but satisfies a sense of honor, and seems next to no injustice. Further, they are likely to be wronged whose injury will gratify the friends of the wrong-doer, or those whom he admires or loves, or his masters—or in general those with respect to whom he governs his life. And they are likely to be wronged whose adversary may expect lenient consideration [from the judges]. Those, too, against whom some one has a grievance, and with whom he has already split—as Callippus did in the affair of Dion; for such deeds have the look of no injustice at all. [As ordinarily interpreted, the example of Dion, who was murdered at the instigation of Callippus, is not altogether clear. The Athenian Callippus, having joined Dion in the latter's expedition against Sicily, corrupted Dion's mercenaries; they slew Dion, and Callippus became master of Syracuse. The plot was known in advance to Dion, but he made no effort to protect himself. Aristotle seems to indicate that Callippus defended his act on the ground that Dion was aware of the 'grievance,' or difference in their interests, and that he, Callippus, had Dion killed by way of precaution, since otherwise Dion would have killed *him.*] Further, they are likely to be wronged by us, who will be wronged by others if we wait; here the wrong-doer thinks there is no time for deliberation. Thus when Gelon enslaved a certain town, Aenesidemus, as the story goes, sent him the cottabus-prize [eggs, cakes, and sweetmeats, the prize in this game of swiftness and dexterity] because Gelon got the start of him in a deed Aenesidemus also had in mind. Again, they are likely to be wronged through whose injury the wrong-doer can bring about many effects of justice, while he goes on the supposition that he can easily heal the wrongs. Thus Jason the Thessalian [—tyrant of Pherae] said that one should do some unjust things when it would give one power to do much justice.

Again, men are wronged in those things with respect

to which all or many of mankind are wont to do wrong, since here the wrong-doers expect to obtain forgiveness. And wrongs are done when concealment is easy. Thus men steal such things as are readily consumed—eatables, for instance. Similarly with things that may be quickly altered in shape, or color, or combination; or things that can be easily made to disappear in divers ways—such as portable things and objects that can be hid in holes and corners. And things [are stolen and injured] when the wrong-doer already has things that are indistinguishable from them, or has many like them. Wrongs are done, too, when they are of such sort that the victim will be ashamed to divulge them—such as outrages on the women of his household, or on himself, or on his sons. And wrongs will be done when the victim will be thought litigious if he prosecutes—petty offences and such as are commonly excused.

Circumstances tending to wrong-doing

The foregoing is an adequate account of the dispositions and circumstances in which men do wrong, and of the kinds of wrong they do, the kinds of people they wrong, and the reasons why wrongs are committed.

1. 13. [ACTIONS JUST AND UNJUST, IN RELATION TO LAW AND EQUITY.] Let us now differentiate the several kinds of wrong and right acts, starting out from the following consideration. Justice and injustice admit of a twofold distinction with reference both to the laws [two kinds of law] and to the persons affected. I mean that law is either particular or universal; by 'particular' law I mean that which an individual community lays down for itself (a law partly unwritten, partly written); and by 'universal' law I mean the law of nature. For there is a natural and universal notion of right and wrong, one that all men instinctively apprehend, even when they have no mutual intercourse nor any compact. This evidently is the law to which Sophocles' Antigone alludes when she

1373[b]

Classification of all unjust and just acts

Particular law

Universal law

says that, despite [Creon's] interdict, it is right to bury [her brother] Polyneices; the implication being that it is right according to nature [*Antigone* 456–7]:

> Not of to-day nor yesterday is this, but law eternal;
> None can say when first it came into being.

Similarly the utterance of Empedocles against killing any animate creature; it is not right in one land and wrong in another:

> But the law for living creatures all, one law,
> Extends through sovran sky and endless sunlight.

Similarly, again, the saying of Alcidamas in his *Messeniacus* [a declamation justifying the Messenians in their revolt from Sparta:

> God has left all men free; Nature made no man a slave.

—The quotation is supplied by the scholiast. Notice that Aristotle illustrates 'universal law' with passages that would be useful to the orator in persuasion.]

The community; the individual

As for the persons affected by justice or injustice, there is a twofold distinction; for what is obligatory or not allowable affects either the community or the individual in the community. Therefore acts that are wrong and acts that are right are rightly or wrongly done with this twofold distinction: either they are limited and affect an individual, or they affect the community. Thus the adulterer or beater wrongs a definite person; the man who avoids service in the army wrongs the State.

Recapitulation

Having thus classified all wrong acts, according as they affect either the State or one or more individuals, let us revert to our definition of wrong [1.10, pp. 55–60], and then proceed. To be wronged is to suffer injustice at the hands of a voluntary agent; for wrong-doing has already been defined as voluntary. And the person wronged must be harmed, and harmed against his will; while the nature of the various injuries is clear from what has gone before, a detailed list of goods and evils having been given above [1.6, pp. 29–34]. And by voluntary acts, as before [1.10, p. 55], are meant such as are done knowingly. It follows that all accusations must concern either the public interest or a private one, and, again, must concern acts that are done either unconsciously and involuntarily or voluntarily and knowingly, and the latter must be done either by deliberate choice or under the influence of emotion. The subject of passion will be discussed in our treatment of the emotions [2.2, pp. 93–9]; the subject of motives, with the dispositions and circumstances in which voluntary choices are made, has already been treated [1.11–12, pp. 60–73].

Now it often happens that the accused will admit the fact, but will deny the legal name the prosecutor gives it, or deny what is assumed under this name. For example, they will admit they have taken something, but will deny that they stole it; will admit having struck the first blow, but will deny having committed outrage; will admit intercourse, but will deny adultery; will admit theft, but will deny that the act was sacrilege (saying that the property stolen was not consecrated); will admit having encroached in cultivating land, but will deny that the land belonged to the State; or will admit having communicated with the enemy, but will deny that the communication was treasonable. Accordingly it would seem necessary to define these terms also—'theft,' 'outrage,' 'adultery'—in order that, whether we wish to prove the existence or the non-existence of the crime, we may put the case in a clear light. In all such cases the question is whether the accused is criminal and vicious, or the reverse; for the wickedness and injustice of an act lie in the purpose of the agent, and terms like outrage and theft connote, in addition to the acts themselves, this purpose. If a man has struck a blow, for example, it does not follow that he has committed wanton outrage; the blow must be struck with a certain

1374[a]

In distinguishing crimes, make clear the motive or its absence

motive such as insult to the victim or the gratification of the striker. Nor when a man has taken something privily does it follow that he has stolen; the act must be done to injure the victim and to benefit the taker. And similarly in all other cases of alleged crimes.

As we have seen, there are two sorts of right and wrong, corresponding to the written law and the unwritten. [Cf. 1.10, p. 55, and 1.13, p. 73. The various references to universal and particular law, and to unwritten and written law, do not fully agree, the reason doubtless being that the provinces of natural (universal) and particular (State) law overlap. In a given community there will be a body of written law having to do with specified rights and penalties, but there will also be prevailing, unwritten, concepts of justice and propriety which may or may not be 'universal' as belonging to mankind or nature, but for the moment are regarded as recognized in that community.] The acts regarding which the law is express have now been discussed. Of the unwritten, again, there are two kinds. First, there is the kind which concerns some unusual measure of virtue or vice [unwritten precepts suggesting higher considerations than mere 'obedience to law']; it refers to acts that bring disgrace or praise, degradations, honors, rewards—acts such as gratitude to a benefactor, return of generous treatment, service to friends in need, and all the like. The second kind of unwritten law supplies deficiencies of the particular, written, law; for equity [merciful consideration of circumstances] is regarded as a kind of justice, but is a justice that extends beyond the written law. This extension is made possible by the legislators, in some cases unintentionally, in others on purpose. It is unintentional when a point escapes their notice. It is intentional when they find themselves unable to make the law precise, and are forced to lay down a sweeping rule, but only one that is applicable to the majority of cases; also when the endless number of possible cases makes it hard

Equity distinguished from justice

Equity

to frame specific laws—hard, for example, in regard to 'wounding with an iron instrument,' to specify sizes and kinds. Life would be too short to enumerate them. If, then, the cases cannot be specified, and a law nevertheless must be laid down, it must be stated generally; so that if a man wearing a finger-ring lift his hand against another, or strike him, according to the letter of the law he is a criminal, but in reality he is not a criminal [not *1374b* liable to the penalty for striking with an iron instrument] —and there lies the province of equity. From this account we may see what sorts of actions fall within that province, and what without, and what sorts of persons are not equitable. To the province of equity belong all acts that should be excused; also it is equitable not to rate errors and wrongs as on a par, and, again, not to treat errors and mishaps as on a par. A mishap is something that cannot be foreseen, and is not the result of wickedness; an error something that could have been foreseen, but is not the result of wickedness; a wrong something that was not unforeseen, and does result from wickedness—for all such wrongs as come about through desire result from wickedness. It is equitable to excuse the common failings of mankind; to consider, not the law as it stands, down to the letter, but the legislator and his intention; not the action in itself, but the deliberate choice of the agent; not the part [as some detail of the crime], but the whole [including both the act and the moral purpose leading to it]; and not the momentary disposition of the agent, but his past character as invariably or usually displayed. It is equitable to remember benefits one has received more than injuries, and benefits one has received more than those one has conferred. It is equitable to be patient under wrong [not to retaliate]; to be willing that a difference shall be settled by discussion rather than by force; to agree to arbitration rather than go to court—for the umpire in an arbitration looks to equity, whereas the juryman sees only the law. Indeed, arbitration was devised to the end that equity might have full sway.

[For the purposes of rhetoric] let this suffice as a sketch of the nature and province of equity.

The topic of more and less in relation to wrongs

1. 14. [THE COMPARISON OF WRONGS.] The magnitude of a wrong depends on the degree of the injustice that prompts it; and hence the least of acts may be the greatest of wrongs. So with the crime of which Callistratus accused Melanopus—that he had cheated the temple-builders of an obol and a half [three half-pence] of sacred money. And conversely with regard to justice: [the degree of it is measured by the magnitude of the wrong to which one is tempted.] The reason is that the little act may potentially contain bigger ones; the man who would steal three sacred half-pence is capable of any wrong however enormous. Accordingly, the magnitude of the wrong is sometimes to be measured thus, and sometimes it is to be measured by the extent of the actual damage. In comparing wrongs, that is the greater for which no penalty exists that is commensurate with the offence—when any penalty [that exists or can be devised] falls short. Similarly where the injury is incurable; here any adequate penalty is hard, or even impossible, to devise. Or, again, a wrong for which the victim cannot obtain legal redress, for here also the wrong is incurable; [to victims] a verdict and a punishment [of the offender] are a healing. That, too, is the greater wrong which has led the victim, the person wronged, to inflict heavy chastisement upon himself; here the wrongdoer merits a heavier penalty [than the wrong by itself would merit]. So Sophocles, in pleading the cause of Euctemon, who had cut his own throat after suffering outrage, said he would lay on the aggressor no lesser penalty than the victim had laid on himself. And a wrong is the greater if the doer is the only person who ever did it,

1375a

or if he is the first to do it, or if he is one of a few who have done it. Again, it becomes a great offence if the same man goes wrong over and over in the same way. And that is a great offence which has caused people to seek and discover checks and penalties for such a crime; so at Argos a penalty is incurred by any one on whose account a law has been enacted, as also by those on whose account the prison was built. Again, a crime is greater in proportion as it is more brutal, or more premeditated; or as it arouses fear rather than pity in those who hear of it. Then there are the rhetorical means of magnifying the crime. Thus the speaker may say that the wrong-doer has subverted or transgressed many ties of justice—such as oaths, promises, pledges, marriage-vows; so you multiply the one wrong into many. Or you may say that the crime was committed in the very place where crimes are punished—that the man did what perjurers do; and you may ask: 'What place is there in which he would not do wrong, if he does it in the very hall of judgment?' [Similarly with theft in a temple, murder in a place of refuge, etc.] Yet further, wrongs are greater in proportion as they bring excessive disgrace upon the victims. And a wrong is the greater if it is done to a benefactor; here the wrong-doer is guilty in more than one way—he wrongs his man, and he fails to return the benefit. And an offence against the unwritten [universal] law [is greater than a violation of statute]; for it is the mark of the better character to be just without compulsion [and hence a mark of the worse character to disobey a law of justice that is not compulsory]. The written law is compulsory, the unwritten is not. [—But the speaker may argue the opposite.] In another way the wrong is greater if it is contrary to the written law: the man who does wrongs that will endanger him, and render him liable to punishment, will not shrink from wrong where he fears no penalty.

Rhetorical means of exaggerating a crime

So much on what will make a wrong greater or less.

1. 15. [NON-ARTISTIC OR NON-TECHNICAL MEANS OF PERSUASION.] Of the subjects thus far mentioned, we must next take a cursory view of the means of persuasion called 'non-artistic' [1.2, p. 8], as these belong especially to the forensic branch of Rhetoric. They are of five sorts: laws, witnesses, contracts, tortures, the oath. [The next sentence, in alluding to 'exhortation and dissuasion,' which suggests the deliberative branch, shows that the use of non-artistic proofs is not absolutely confined to forensic speaking.]

The five kinds of 'non-artistic' proofs

1. Laws

Let us begin by discussing the way in which the speaker should make use of laws in exhortation or dissuasion, and in accusation or defence. It is clear that, if the written law is adverse to our case, he must appeal to the universal law, and to the principles of equity as representing a higher order of justice. [He must say] that [the judge's obligation to decide] 'according to my best judgment' means that the judge will not be guided simply and solely by the letter of the statute. The speaker will contend, too, that equity is permanent and unchanging, and the universal law likewise—for it is the law of nature; whereas the written laws are subject to frequent change. Hence the speech in the *Antigone* [456, 458] of Sophocles; in defending herself Antigone pleads that she buried [her brother] contrary to the edict of Creon, but not contrary to the unwritten law:

1375b

> Not of to-day or yesterday is this, but law eternal . . .
> Whose precepts I was not [to violate] for any man.

Or the speaker may argue that justice is a genuine thing and beneficent, but the mere show of justice is not, and hence the written law is a sham, since it does not produce the effect of true law. Or he may contend that the judge is like an assayer of coin, whose function it is to distinguish spurious justice from the genuine metal; or that constant loyalty to the unwritten law is the mark of a better man, not continual obedience to the written statutes. The speaker may observe, too, that a given law [which tells against his case] conflicts with another, approved, law, or even contradicts itself; thus, perchance, one statute may prescribe that all contracts entered into shall be valid, while another prohibits the making of an unlawful contract. Again, he should note if a law is ambiguous, so that he may turn it [in either of two directions], and see which construction lends itself to justice, which to expediency [equity]; then he may employ the law with this construction, or with that, [according as he is pleading for justice or for equity]. Or, again, if the circumstances for which the law was made no longer exist, while the law remains in force, the speaker should try to make the situation clear, and in this way to combat the law.

On the other hand, if the written law favors his case, the speaker must say that [the judge's obligation to decide] 'according to my best judgment' is not intended to produce verdicts in opposition to the law, but to save the judge from perjury if he does not know what the law means. [And if his opponent argues for equity, as against strict justice according to the written law,] the speaker may contend that a man never chooses what is good in the abstract, but every one that which is good with reference to himself [and that the written law is impartial]. Or he may say that, if a law is not to be enforced, it might as well not have been enacted. Or he may say that in law, as in other arts—medicine, for example,—it does not pay to be wiser than the doctor, as the doctor's mistake will do less harm than getting into the habit of disobeying authority. Or [lastly] he may say that the effort to be wiser than the law is precisely what the most approved codes forbid.

On the [mode of appealing to] laws, let the foregoing analysis suffice.

2. Witnesses. Two kinds

As for witnesses, they fall into two classes (1) ancient [time-honored, venerable], and (2) recent [*viva voce*]; these latter, again, being divisible into those who share the danger [from the outcome of the trial], and those who are in no danger. By ancient witnesses are meant the poets and other men of note whose judgments are on record. Thus the Athenians cited the testimony of Homer in regard to Salamis; [Solon quoted, in support of the Athenian claim to Salamis, the lines (*Iliad* 2. 557–8):

Ancient witnesses

> And Ajax did twelve ships from Salamis bring;
> Did bring and set them where the Athenian phalanxes stood.

—The second line is said to have been interpolated by Solon for the purpose.] Likewise the people of Tenedos lately quoted Periander of Corinth [in their controversy] against the people of Sigeum. So also Cleophon quoted against Critias the verses of Solon, arguing that the family line must have been unruly of old, since otherwise Solon never would have written:

> Prithee bid Critias of the fiery locks obey his sire.

[Did Cleophon change Solon's epithet, 'of the *yellow* locks,' to suit *his* purpose?]

Persons like these, then, are witnesses in regard to things past. With regard to the future the soothsayers also are witnesses: thus Themistocles [counseled his fellow Athenians] to make ready to fight on their ships, citing [explaining that this was what the Delphic priestess meant (Herodotus 7. 141, 143) by] 'the wooden wall.' Proverbs, too, as has been said [perhaps in some other work on rhetoric], are a kind of testimony. Thus if the speaker is counseling [his audience] not to make friends with an old man [? an aging tyrant, say], the advice will find support in the proverb:

376ᵃ

> Ne'er do a good turn to a dotard.

Or if one counsels making away with the sons when one has slain their fathers, [one may cite the proverb:]

A fool is he who slays the sire, and leaves the children.

Recent witnesses

Recent witnesses are [first] any notable persons who have pronounced judgment on some matter; their judgments are useful to those who are contending about the same issues. Thus [the orator] Eubulus quoted in the law-court, against Chares, the saying of Plato [? the comic poet] with regard to Archibius—that the habit of admitting rascality had made strides at Athens. And [secondly] there are those who, if they are suspected of perjury, share [with the accused] the risk of the trial. All such witnesses are useful only for their evidence on such points as these: whether a thing has occurred, or not occurred; whether a thing is at present so, or not so. Their evidence is of no value on the quality of an act—as, for instance, whether an act is right or wrong [a question in forensic speaking], whether a policy is advantageous or the reverse [a question in deliberative speaking. These are questions to be decided by the judges in the case or by the assembly, not by witnesses concerned in the case.] On such points [for example, the quality of an act, which is related to the known character of the agent], the evidence of recent witnesses who are not concerned in the case [are remote from it, and in no danger] is very credible. Most credible of all are the ancient witnesses, since there is no possibility of corrupting them.

In dealing with testimony, the speaker may argue as follows. If he can call no witnesses, he may argue that the judges must decide on the basis of probabilities; that such is the meaning of [the judge's obligation to decide] 'according to my best judgment'; that you cannot bribe probabilities to deceive [the judges—as you can bribe witnesses]; and that probabilities are never convicted of false witness. If our speaker has witnesses that he can call, while the other side has none, he may argue that probabilities are not responsible beings [are not like persons, who can be tried and punished for false witness]; and that there would be no demand whatever for testimony, if all a case needed were argumentative speculation.

Now the testimony of witnesses will concern either our man or his adversary; and, again, it will bear either upon the [alleged] fact or upon the character [of an individual]. And hence it is clear that [the speaker] will never be wholly without resources in the way of serviceable testimony; for if you have no testimony regarding the fact from witnesses whose evidence will support your man or tell against his adversary, still you can always find witnesses in regard to character whose evidence will tend to establish the respectability of your man or the worthlessness of his adversary. As for other arguments [regarding testimony]—to show that a witness is friendly, hostile, or neither, and that he is estimable, disreputable, or betwixt and between, and to establish each and every such distinction in character—the speaker must draw upon the same topics as we use in deriving enthymemes [1. 9, pp. 46–55].

3. Contracts

Coming now to contracts [covenants, compacts, bonds, deeds, written agreements, recorded promises]: argument may be employed in a speech so far as to enhance or diminish their value, to establish or shake their credibility.

1376[b]

If there are contracts making for our side of the case, we must try to show that they are trustworthy and valid; if they make for the side of our opponent, we must do the reverse. The method of establishing or destroying the credit of contracts is precisely the same as the method of dealing with witnesses; for the credit of the document varies in accordance with the character of the persons who have endorsed it, or of those who have had it in their keeping. [The speaker must deal with their trustworthiness as he does with the trustworthiness of a witness.]

The genuineness of the contract being admitted, he must, if it tells for his side, magnify its importance; for the contract [one may urge] is a private and particular law, and while contracts do not give validity to the law, the laws impart validity to contracts that are legally made. And in general one may urge that the law itself is a species of contract, so that any one who violates or upsets a contract, upsets the laws. Add to this that, since most of the dealings between man and man, and in fact all voluntary transactions, are matters of contract, then to invalidate contracts is nothing less than subverting the customary intercourse of mankind. The other appropriate means [for magnifying the importance of contracts] are [so] obvious [that they need not here be dwelt on]. If, however, the documents are adverse to our case, and make for the other side, then, first, we shall find suitable the arguments one would use in contending against a law; we may urge that it would be strange indeed if we were forced to abide by [defective and mistaken] contracts, when we think we are not bound to abide by the ill-framed laws of mistaken legislators. Secondly, we may urge that it is the judge [not the contract] who is the arbiter of justice, and that he must regard, not the particular document, but the higher principle of what is right; and we may add that this principle, since it is the ordinance of nature, cannot be subverted by fraud or force, whereas contracts may be made by persons who are tricked or forced [into signing them]. Further, we should see whether the contract is in opposition to any written or any universal law—to any written law whether of our own land or foreign; and, next, whether it violates other contracts either subsequent or prior to it. [If it violates subsequent or prior contracts, then we may argue,] according as may suit our case, that the subsequent contracts are valid, and hence the earlier document in question is invalid, or that the earlier documents are sound, and the later document in question is fraudulent. Moreover we must have an eye for what may be advantageous to the judges, and see whether the contract may conflict with their interest; and so on, not neglecting other arguments of the same sort that are just as obvious. [The judges, like other citizens, have interests depending upon contracts; the speaker may show that it would be advantageous (or the reverse) to them if a given document were shown to be worthless.]

4. Tortures

Tortures [including tortures proper, tests, inquisitions, and the like] furnish a kind of testimony, and people regard this evidence as trustworthy because it is given under compulsion [is forced from a man against his will]. With respect to tortures it is again easy to indicate the available means of persuasion. If the evidence extorted is favorable to your side of the case, you may magnify its importance by arguing that tortures furnish the only sort of testimony that is genuine. If this evidence is against your side, and makes for that of your opponent, you may discredit it by saying what in general is perfectly true of evidence obtained by torture and the like—namely, that when you force men to testify, they are just as likely to utter what is false as what is true, and may persist in not telling the truth, or may readily utter false accusations so as to escape the sooner from the ordeal. The speaker should be prepared to illustrate his points with parallel cases that are known to the judges [cases of men who have steadily refused to tell the truth, or have lightly accused others in order to save themselves from the rack, and similar instances showing the worthlessness of such testimony].

1377a

5. Oaths: a fourfold distinction

Coming now to oaths: with respect to these we may make a fourfold distinction. A person (1) may both tender an oath and take one himself; or (2) he may do neither; or he may do one of these things and not the other—that is, (3) he may tender an oath and not take one, or (4) he may take an oath and not tender one. [The speaker may call upon the adversary to swear to the truth of his statements (that is, may tender an oath), or he may take an oath (accept it) when thus offered, and swear to the truth of his statements; out of this twofold distinction grows the fourfold distinction which Aristotle notes as useful to the speaker.] In addition to these [four possibilities (regarding oaths at the moment, oaths to be sought or avoided in the course of the speech)] we have to consider oaths [their utility] tendered or taken [or both] by either party [or both] in the past.

(1) If you do not [find it advisable to] tender the oath, [you may employ the following arguments. You may say] that men readily perjure themselves, and for the reason that they can take the oath, and so [by perjuring themselves] avoid making restitution, while you think that if your adversary is not called upon to swear, the judges will decide against him; and [you may say] that your chances are better when they rest with the judges, since you have confidence in them, but not in him.

(2) When you do not [find it advisable to] take the oath, [you may argue as follows. You may say] that the oath merely represents so much money, [and that you will not degrade it by taking it for pecuniary reasons]; and that if you had been a rascal, you would have taken it with a vengeance, since it is better to be a rascal for something than for nothing at all, and by taking the oath you get your money, whereas by not taking it you stand to lose. Thus you may argue that your refusal comes from a lofty motive, and not from a fear of perjury. And you may quote the maxim of Xenophanes [of Colophon]:

> Unequal is the challenge from a godless man to a pious.

[You may say] that such a challenge would be like the challenge of a strong man to a weakling to strike or be beaten.

(3) If you [find it advisable to] take the oath, [you may argue] that you have confidence in your side [can be trusted not to swear falsely], but distrust the adversary. And you may turn the maxim of Xenophanes the other way round, so as to argue that it is fair if the godless man tenders the oath and the pious man swears it, while you add that it would be monstrous in one not to be willing to swear to facts which you expect the judges to affirm under oath when they decide the case.

(4) If you [find it advisable to] tender the oath, [you may argue] that it is [the part of a] religious [man] to commit the issue to the gods, and that your opponent ought not to require others to judge for him, since you leave the decision in his hands. And [you may say] that it is absurd if he is unwilling to swear as to matters about which he expects others to swear.

As it is now clear how the speaker should proceed in dealing with the separate cases, we can see how he should proceed with them in combination—as, for example, (1) if you are willing to take the oath, but not to tender it; or (2) are willing to tender, but not to take it; or (3) are willing both to take and to tender it; or (4) are unwilling to do either. Such cases are necessarily combinations of those we have discussed, and hence the arguments to be used in dealing with them must be put together from the arguments in question.

1377b

Past oaths

If you have taken an oath before, and it contradicts this present oath, [you must argue] that there is no perjury; for [you will say] wrong-doing must be voluntary, and perjury is such, but things done under compulsion, and through being tricked, are involuntary; [you must therefore argue that either the former oath or the present one is the result of force or trickery, so that you cannot be held responsible for perjury.] And here you should use the argument, with regard to perjury in particular, that it is not the utterance, but the intention, that makes the crime.

On the other hand, if it is the adversary who has sworn [conflicting oaths], you must argue that the man who does not abide by his oath subverts the whole established order; that the laws themselves are enforced simply because the judges have sworn to enforce them. [If an oath is not sacred, then the laws have no sanction. And you may say to the judges:] 'We expect you when you judge the case to abide by the oath you have taken; are we not to abide by ours? And so the speaker [in dealing with the oath] may use all the other means of magnifying the importance of a thing.

So much for the non-artistic means of persuasion.

BOOK 2

[Book 1 has given us a general introduction on the nature of Rhetoric, with a definition, and has given us such analysis of Politics and Ethics as is adequate to a speaker; it has analyzed the three branches of Rhetoric—deliberative, forensic, and epideictic—and given a supplementary discussion of the non-artistic means of persuasion. In Book 1 Aristotle divides his subject into (1) the kinds of Rhetoric, and the artistic proofs or means of persuasion, namely, (2) logical means, (3) means having to do with characters, and (4) means having to do with emotions. Of the three kinds of artistic proofs or means of persuasion, that which Aristotle's division of them gives as the third, namely, the logical, has been analyzed in part. Without completing his discussion of this third kind, Aristotle now, in Book 2, passes to the other two, and for eighteen chapters deals with persuasion through character and emotion. In chapter 19 he considers the common topics (what is possible or impossible, etc.); and then, in chapter 20, he returns to the subject of logical proofs. Thus his arrangement is somewhat confusing. As might be expected, however, Book 2 begins with a recapitulation.]

Recapitulation

2. 1. [Means and Ends—Decisions.] So much for the premises from which the speaker must draw his arguments in exhorting or dissuading [Deliberative oratory], in praising or blaming [Epideictic oratory], and in accusing or defending [Forensic oratory], and for the popular beliefs and propositions that will serve toward effecting persuasion therein; for these [premises, no-

tions, and propositions] are the materials and sources of the enthymemes, when we take, as it were, each kind of speaking by itself.

Now Rhetoric finds its end in judgment—for the audience [of a deliberative speech] judges the counsels that are given, and [in forensic speaking] the decision [of the jury] is a judgment; and hence the speaker must not merely see to it that his speech [as an argument] shall be convincing and persuasive, but he must [in and by the speech] give the right impression of himself, and get his judge [audience] into the right state of mind. This is true above all in deliberative speaking, but it is true in forensic speaking also; for in conducing to persuasion it is highly important that the speaker should evince a certain character, and that the judges should conceive him to be disposed towards them in a certain way, and further, if possible, that the judges themselves should have a certain attitude towards him. Evincing the right character is more important in deliberative speeches, and producing the right attitude in the hearer is more important in forensic. The same thing does not appear the same to men when they are friendly and when they hate, nor when they are angry and when they are in gentle mood; in these different moods the same thing will appear either wholly different in kind, or different as to magnitude. To the friendly judge, the person about whom he is making a decision will seem either quite innocent or guilty of no great wrong; to the inimical judge, the same person will seem just the opposite. [The preceding instance has regard mainly to forensic speaking; the following to deliberative.] To the man [audience] that is eager and hopeful, the proposed object, if pleasant, seems a thing that will come to pass and will be good; to the man that is apathetic or disgruntled, the same object seems just the opposite.

Indirect means of persuasion

A certain character in the speaker

The attitude of the judges

1378a

As for the speakers themselves, the sources of our trust

The speaker must evince intelligence, character, and good will

in them are three, for apart from the arguments [in a speech] there are three things that gain our belief, namely, intelligence, character, and good will. Speakers are untrustworthy in what they say or advise from one or more of the following causes. Either through want of intelligence they form wrong opinions; or, while they form correct opinions, their rascality leads them to say what they do not think; or, while intelligent and honest enough, they are not well-disposed [to the hearer, audience], and so perchance will fail to advise the best course, though they see it. That is a complete list of the possibilities. It necessarily follows that the speaker who is thought to have all these qualities [intelligence, character, and good will] has the confidence of his hearers.

Intelligence and character: see analysis of the virtues

This being so, the means by which one may give the impression of intelligence and good character are to be found in our analysis of the virtues [1. 9, pp. 46-55]. The means are the same whether the speaker aims to establish this impression of himself or of another person.

For good will and friendliness, study the emotions

As for good will and a friendly disposition, these must be discussed [2. 4, pp. 102–7] under the head of the emotions. By these, the emotions, are meant those states which are attended by pain and pleasure, and which, as they change, make a difference in our judgments [of the same thing]; for example: anger, pity, fear, and all the like, and also their opposites. With respect to each emotion the points to be determined are three. Take, for instance, the emotion of anger. With respect to this we must note (1) what the mental state of angry persons is, (2) with whom they are wont to be angry, and (3) what are the things that commonly make them so; for a knowledge of one, or of two, of these points, without a knowledge of the third, will not enable the speaker to excite anger; and similarly with respect to the other emotions [the speaker must know all three points]. Accordingly, as in the former part of our treatise we outlined the

Three points to be noted for each emotion

available premises, so let us now analyze the emotions, using the [triple] division just indicated.

2. 2. [THE EMOTION OF ANGER.] Anger may be defined as an impulse attended by pain, to a revenge that shall be evident, and caused by an obvious, unjustified, slight with respect to the individual or his friends. If the definition is right, then it must be, when a man is angered, that he is always angry with some particular person—Cleon or the like—and not with 'man' in general, and is angry because that person has done or meant to do something against him or one of his friends; and it must be that anger is always attended by a certain pleasure arising from the expectation of revenge. [This last is so,] for it is pleasant to think that one will attain one's aim, and no one aims at what he thinks he cannot attain—and the angry man aims at things [a revenge] he can attain. And hence it has been well said of anger [*Iliad* 18. 109; cf. above, 1. 11, p. 62]:

Anger defined

1378b

> That sweeter far than dripping honey
> Waxeth [like smoke] in the breasts of men.

[Such is the case,] for a certain pleasure accompanies anger, both because of this [plan for revenge], and also because angry men keep imagining themselves in the act of vengeance; thus the image arising at the moment excites pleasure, like the imagery of dreams.

A slight is an active display of opinion about something one takes to be worthless. Positive evils, and positive goods, and anything conducing to either, we regard as worth serious attention; whatever has little or no tendency either way we consider unimportant.

Slights

There are three species of slight: contempt, spite, and insolence [outrage]. (1) Contempt is a form of slight; since men are contemptuous of what they deem worthless, and what they are contemptuous of they slight. (2) The spiteful person, too, shows contempt. Spite consists

Three species:
1. Contempt

2. Spite

in thwarting a man's wishes with a view, not to our own advantage, but to his loss. Accordingly, since the act is not done for one's own advantage, it is a slight; for clearly if you spite a man, you think that he can do you no harm worth mentioning (otherwise you would fear, not slight, him), and that he can do you no service worth mentioning (otherwise you would take care to be his friend).

3. *Hubris* or wanton insult

(3) Finally, *hubris* [wanton insult, outrage, insolence] is a form of slight. *Hubris* consists in doing or saying things that cause shame to the victim, not in order that anything may happen to you, nor because anything has happened to you, but merely for your own gratification. *Hubris* is not the requital of past injuries; this is revenge. As for the pleasure in *hubris*, its cause is this: men think that by ill-treating others they make their own superiority the greater.

And hence young men, and rich men, are given to *hubris*; they think that their insolence adds to their superiority. Again, under *hubris* falls disrespect, and to show disrespect [to fail in showing honor] is to slight; for if a thing is worthless it has no honor—is not esteemed either for good or evil. Thus Achilles, when angered, says [of Agamemnon (*Iliad* 1. 356)]:

> He hath dishonored me—hath [violently] seized, and keeps, my prize;

and again [*Iliad* 9. 648]:

> [Slighting me]
> . . . like some dishonored vagabond;

—indicating these [slights] as the cause of his anger. People think they have a natural right to consideration from their inferiors in birth, or power, or merit; to put it

1379a

generally, a man expects honor for anything in which he distinctly excels—as in regard to money the rich man excels the poor, and in oratory the eloquent man excels the man who cannot speak. So also the man who governs expects honor from him who is governed, and the man who thinks he deserves to govern expects it from the man whom he thinks he ought to be governing; and hence the sentiment [*Iliad* 2. 196]:

> Great is the anger of Zeus-fostered kings;

and again [*Iliad* 1. 80–2]:

> [More mighty a king, when vexed with a man inferior;
> Though he swallow his wrath for that day,]
> Yet thereafter he beareth a grudge.

[Both passages refer to the peril of ill-treatment from Agamemnon, 'that now avoweth him to be greatest by far of the Achaeans' (*Iliad* 1. 91).] It is the superiority [of the kings] that accounts for their vexation [when they are slighted]. Again, [a man is angered by a slight] from those to whom he looks for good treatment —persons, that is, who are indebted to him for benefits, past or present, which they have received from him, or through him, or who are similarly indebted to any of his friends, and persons whom he is trying, or has tried, to serve.

Conditions under which men become angry

From the foregoing it can now be plainly seen (1) in what mental state [or, under what conditions] men are when they become angry, and (2) with what persons, and (3) at what sort of things they become so. (1) Men are angered when they are annoyed [vexed, pained]; for the man in that state is always aiming at [eagerly desirous of] something. Accordingly, whether you cross such a man directly in anything—as, for example, if a thirsty man is crossed with respect to drinking—or cross him indirectly, to him your action appears the same. Whether you act against him, or fail to act with him, or bother him in any other way, when he is in this state of mind, he becomes alike angry. And hence people who are ailing, or needy, or in love, or thirsty—in a word, those who have any desire that is not being satisfied—are prone to anger, and are easily incensed, but above all at any one who shows indifference to [slights] their present aim. Thus a sick man is angered by indifference to his illness [by neglect or hindrance in respect to a cure], a poor man by indifference to his poverty, a man who is waging war by indifference to his war, one who is in love by indifference to his love; and so on in all similar cases, [the man who is aiming at something is angered by neglect or interference]. In each case the existing emotion predisposes the individual to his anger. Again, a man is angered by a result that runs counter to his expectations; for the pain is greater in proportion to the surprise—just as the pleasure is great in proportion to the surprise when [contrary to expectation] the thing turns out as he wished. And so from this analysis we can readily see the [application to] junctures and periods—[to] frames of mind and times of life—and [can perceive] which of these are easily moved to anger, in what places, and when, and [can observe] that the more a man is in these conditions, the easier it is to move him to anger. [For example, if a man is in love, and if the time of life is youth, if the place is in public, and the juncture brings the presence of his beloved, it is easy to anger him by a slight; or if he is needy, or engaged in fighting, or the like, the same is true. And the more he is in love, or needy, the easier it is to anger him; and as more of the conditions—frame of mind, age, place, and time—are fulfilled, the easier it is.]

Persons and things that make men grow angry

Such, then, are the conditions under which men grow angry. As for the persons with whom they grow angry, first come those who laugh at them, or sneer at them, or make scornful jests about them; for such persons insult them [commit *hubris*]. Next come those who do to them the kinds of injury that are marks of *hubris*; these injuries must be done neither by way of retaliation nor for the benefit of the doer; otherwise the intention will not seem to be that of *hubris* [2. 2, p. 94]. Then come those who disparage and despise a man in regard to the things which he has most at heart; thus any one will anger those who pride themselves on their devotion to philosophy if he disparages their favorite study, or those who pride themselves on their personal appearance if he disparages that, and so on. And he will anger them far more if they suspect that the advantages on which they pride themselves are things they really lack, or are not very strong in, or are not thought by others to possess; for once they 1379[b] are quite convinced that they do possess the advantages with [the lack of] which they are taunted, they are undisturbed [by the slur]. Again, [our anger is] more [readily excited] by our friends than by those who are not; for men think they are entitled to good treatment from their friends rather than bad. Again, people who have been wont to treat a man with honor or respect [will make him angry] if afterwards they treat him otherwise; for he will think they [have come to] look down on him; [were it not so, he thinks,] they would treat him as before. Again, people who do not requite good treatment with good treatment, or who return less good than they have received, [will make the benefactor angry]; and, similarly, people who act contrary to a man's interest, if they are his inferiors; for all such persons seem to look down on him, the latter sort treating *him* as inferior to *them*, and the former acting as if the benefits they have received came from an inferior. Further, those who are of no account, if they anger a man in any way, anger him the more [because of that]; for, on the assumption noted above [2. 2, p. 93], the anger aroused by a slight is directed against those who have no title to inflict one, and the natural duty of inferiors is not to slight [their superiors]. Again, friends arouse a man's anger if they fail to speak well of him, or to treat him well, and still more if they speak ill of him or treat him ill; or if they fail to perceive his need. So [in the *Meleager*] of [the tragic poet] Antiphon, Plexippus is angry with [his nephew] Meleager [? because the latter fails to recognize Plexippus' claim to the boar-skin]; for the failure to perceive is a sign [*semeion*] of slighting—when we really care for a man, his needs do not escape our notice. Again, people who rejoice in a man's misfortunes [anger him], and, in general, those who remain cheerful in them; for such conduct indicates [is a sign of] either an enemy or one who slights. Again, [anger is aroused] by people who are indifferent whether they give pain; that is why men are angry with messengers who bring bad news. Similarly, [it is aroused] by persons who hear [with indifference] the tale of a man's weaknesses, or [calmly] look on at [any display of] them. Such persons resemble either those who slight one, or one's enemies; for a man's friends share his pain, [your friend being your second, or other, self,] and every one is pained at the spectacle of his own weaknesses. Further, there are five classes of persons in whose presence a man is angered by a slight: (1) his rivals; (2) those whom he admires; (3) those by whom he wishes to be admired; (4) those of whom he stands in awe; (5) those who stand in awe of him. Any one who slights a man in the presence of [any of] these incenses him all the more. Again, people [arouse anger] who put a slight upon such objects as men are in honor bound to defend; for example, upon their parents, children, wives, or subjects. And they arouse anger who do not return a favor; here the slight is in violation of a natural claim. They, also, who are ironical with you when you are in earnest; for irony implies contempt. And they [arouse anger in a man] who treat others well, and fail to treat *him* so; this likewise argues contempt—not to rate him as high as you rate all the world. And forgetfulness also tends to produce anger—forgetting a man's name, say, trifling as the matter is; since forgetfulness is taken to indicate [be a *sign* of]

Things that make men angry

slighting. Forgetfulness arises from indifference, and indifference is a slight. [Aristotle has insensibly passed from the *persons* that cause anger to the *things* that do so; the dividing line is not easily drawn, since persons may unwittingly do things which the man thereby angered imagines to have been done on purpose.]

1380a

Thus the persons who arouse anger, the mental state [the condition] of the angry, and the things that give rise to anger, have all been discussed. [On occasion the speaker will apply this analysis in accordance with his end and aim.] Clearly, one must, by means of the speech, bring the judges into the state of those who are irascible [so that they shall be unfavorable to one's adversary], and must represent the adversary as obnoxious in those things which make men angry, and as the sort of person who arouses anger.

Application to speaking

2. 3. [MILDNESS.] Now the opposite of growing angry is growing mild [becoming calm, placated]—the opposite of anger, mildness [placability, calmness, patience]; and hence the speaker must ascertain (1) the mental state [condition] of those who are mild, (2) the persons towards whom they are mild, and (3) through what things they are rendered mild. The process of growing mild may be defined as a settling down and quieting of anger. Now we have seen that the persons who anger men are those who slight them, and that a slight is a voluntary action. If so, then obviously the persons towards whom men are mild will be those who do, or appear to do, nothing of the sort, or who do the thing, or appear to do it, unintentionally. Next, [a man is mild] towards persons who intended the reverse of what they actually did; and towards those who treat themselves in the same way as they treat him, the assumption being that people never put a slight upon themselves. And [a man is mild] towards those who acknowledge their fault and regret it; for he accepts

Mildness (calmness, placability)

Mildness defined

Persons towards whom men are mild

the pain they feel at their offence as an atonement, and ceases from his anger. The fact is well illustrated in our punishment of slaves: if they contradict us, and deny the fault, we chastise them more severely, but if they admit the justice of the punishment, our rage at them ceases. And the reason is that denial of the obvious is effrontery [absence of shame], while effrontery implies slighting and contempt; at all events, we feel no shame before those whom we hold in great contempt. Again, [a man is mild] towards those who humble themselves before him, and do not answer him back. They appear to admit his superiority; now a man's inferiors are afraid of him, and no one slights a man while afraid of him. That anger does subside towards those who humble themselves before us is manifest in the conduct of dogs: they do not bite you if you sit down [when they come at you]. Further, [a man is mild] towards those who take his serious interests seriously; their seriousness seems to exclude [the possibility of] their holding him in contempt. Again, [a man is mild] towards those who have done him greater favors [than he has done to them]. Also towards those who entreat him, and deprecate [his resentment]; for to that extent they are humble. And, again, [a man is mild] towards those who are not given to insulting [committing *hubris*], or to sneering, or to slighting—who do these things to no one at all, or to no virtuous persons, or to no persons like himself. (So in general we are to infer the means of rendering a man mild from their opposites [from the things that make one angry].) [A man is mild] towards those whom he fears or reverences; so long as he is in this state of mind he will not be angry; one cannot be afraid and angry at the same time. Further, with those who have acted through anger a man is either not angry at all or less angry, since they do not seem to have acted from a desire to slight; for no one who is angry slights—

1380ᵇ slighting implies the absence of pain, while anger is

attended by pain. [Persons who slight are indifferent to, contemptuous of, the person they are slighting.] And [a man is mild] towards those who respect him.

Conditions under which men are mild

And men are mild, obviously, under conditions that are opposed to anger; for example, when they are in sport or laughter, or at a feast, or in fine weather, or in success, or when they are well-fed—in a word, when they are free from pain and in pleasure that is not wanton [outrageous] and in a virtuous hope. Further, [they are mild (placable)] if time has elapsed and their anger is no longer fresh; for time makes anger to cease. Again, anger —even more violent anger—against one person will cease if vengeance is first taken on another. And hence Philocrates answered aright when some one said: 'The public is enraged at you; why do n't you defend yourself?' 'Not yet,' he replied. 'When will you, then?' 'As soon as I have seen some one else attacked.' The fact is, men become mild as soon as they have spent their anger on another person; and so it happened in the case of Ergophilus. The Athenians were more incensed at him than at Callisthenes, and yet they let him off because on the previous day they had sentenced Callisthenes to death. [People grow mild,] too, if they pity a man, and if he has suffered a greater ill than they in their anger would have inflicted upon him; for they think that, in a way, they have got their satisfaction. And [people are mild (placable)] if they think themselves to be in the wrong, and to be suffering justly; for anger is not aroused by justice. In this case they no longer think that they suffer beyond what is natural and fitting; but anger, we saw [2. 2, p. 93], involves this thought. Accordingly, we should administer reproof before [the actual penalty]; for then even slaves resent the punishment less. Further, [angry men are more placable] if they think [the man they desire to punish] will not perceive that his punishment is caused by them, and in return for what they have suffered; for anger is always directed against individuals, as is clear from our definition of it [2. 2, p. 93; cf. 2. 4, p. 106]. And hence the poetical representation is correct [when Homer makes Odysseus say to Polyphemus (*Odyssey* 9. 504):

> Cyclops, if any one of mortal men shall ask thee
> Concerning the hideous blinding of thine eye,]
> Say thou it was Odysseus, pillager of cities,
> [Who blinded it]

—as if [Odysseus'] vengeance were incomplete unless [the Cyclops] perceived both by whom and for what [he was punished]. And so men are no longer angry with those who cannot perceive it, nor angry any longer with the dead; the dead, they think, have paid the last penalty, and can feel nothing of that pain which the angry man aims at exciting. Accordingly, the poet has done well in the speech concerning Hector, when [Apollo] desires to make Achilles cease from his anger against the dead [*Iliad* 24. 54]:

> 'T is but senseless clay he is vexing in his fury.

Application to speaking

Obviously, then, when a speaker wishes to calm his hearers down [make them mild, placable], he must find his means in the foregoing topics; he must bring his hearers into such moods as have been described, and [according to circumstances] must represent those with whom they are angry as formidable, or as worthy of reverence, or as having conferred benefits, or as involuntary offenders, or as extremely distressed over what they have done.

Friendship and enmity

2. 4. [LOVE (OR FRIENDSHIP) AND HATRED.] Let us now discuss what persons men love, and what persons they hate, and the causes of these emotions; but first let us define love [friendship] and the act of being friendly.

Definition of loving (friendliness)

Let loving [liking, being friendly] be defined as wishing for a person those things which you consider to be good—

wishing them for his sake, not for your own—and tending so far as you can to effect them. And a friend is one who loves [likes], and is beloved [liked] in return; men deem themselves friends when they think that they stand in this mutual relation.

1381a

Definition of a friend

From these assumptions it follows that a friend is one who shares another's pleasure in good fortune, and his pain in what is painful, not for any ulterior motive, but simply for that other's sake. All men take pleasure in the realization of their own wishes, and are pained at the reverse; so it follows that our pains and pleasures are a sign of what we wish. [Your friend is your second self; the sign, proof, or test, of friendship—of identical wishes—is the identity of your pains and pleasures with his.] And they are friends who have come to regard the same things as good and the same things as evil, they who are friends of the same people, and they who are enemies of the same people; for between these there must needs be an identity of wishes [good, for example, to the common friend, harm to the common enemy]. And so one who wishes for another the very things he wishes for himself will, it appears, be that other person's friend. Further, men love [like] any one who has done good to them or to those for whom they are concerned—whether the service was great, or zealously done, or done at such and such a juncture—something done on purpose for the recipient; or [they love (like)] any one who, as they think, wishes to act in this way.

Persons whom men like (love)

A man will like [love] the friends of his friends, and people who like those whom he likes; will like those who are liked by those whom he likes; and will like those who have the same enemies as he has, who hate the people he hates, and who are hated by the people by whom he is hated; for all these consider the same things good as he does, and therefore wish such things as are good to him—and this, we saw, is the definition of a friend. [Cope remarks that 'these common hatreds, founded upon the principle of *idem velle atque idem nolle*, . . . are one of the strongest bonds of union by which religious and political parties, for example, are held together.'] Further, [men like (love)] those who are able and inclined to benefit them in a pecuniary way, or to promote their personal safety; for that reason they esteem the liberal and the brave, and the just; and they take to be such those persons who do not live at others' expense. Of this description are they who work for their living; chief among these, they whose livelihood comes from farming—and above all, they who work with their own hands. And [men like (love)] those who are temperate [who exercise self-control], because they are not unjust [refrain from wrong-doing]. And [they like] those who mind their own business—for the same reason. [We like] those with whom we wish to be friends, if they show the same inclination; such are the morally good, and those who are held in esteem either by all men, or by the best, or by those whom we admire, or by those who admire us. Further, [men like] those who are pleasant to live with, and to spend the day with; such are the good-tempered—people who are not given to catching up one's mistakes, and are not pertinacious or crossgrained. All such [fault-finders, the pertinacious, the crossgrained] are prone to contend with us, and those who are thus prone obviously wish the opposite of what we wish. And they are likable who are equally good at give and take in personal chaff; for here both parties are bent upon the same object—that is, mutual hilarity; each knows how to accept the chaffing, and returns it neatly. Further, we like those who praise our good qualities [such 'goods' as we possess], and especially if we are afraid we do not possess them.

1381[b] We like those who are clean and neat in person, in dress, in all their ways and habits. We like those who do not reproach any one with what he has failed to do for them, or with what they have done for him; either reproach shows a tendency to put people in the wrong. We like those who do not harbor grudges or nurse grievances, but are always ready for a reconciliation; for we think they would treat us as we believe they treat others. We like those who are not given to evil-speaking, and who will see, not the bad, but the good in us, as they do in their neighbors; for that is what the good man does. We like those who do not thwart men who are angry or in earnest; for such will not be likely to oppose us. We like those who take us seriously—who admire us, who show us respect, who take pleasure in our society; and especially if they are thus disposed regarding points in which we most desire to be admired or to show a deep interest or to seem pleasing. We like those who resemble us, and are engaged in the same pursuits [cf. 1. 11, p. 65], provided that they do not get in the way, nor draw their livelihood from the same source as we do; otherwise [if the interests clash] it will be the case of 'potter 'gainst potter' [Hesiod, *Works and Days* 25–6:

> And potter is grudging to potter, and builder to builder,
> And beggar is jealous of beggar, and minstrel of minstrel.]

We like those who desire the same things as we, if the case is such that we and they can share the things together; otherwise there is the same trouble here. We like those with whom our relations are such that, without any feeling of contempt, we have no feeling of shame in unconventional behavior before them; and those before whom we should be ashamed to do anything positively wrong. And those with whom we vie for distinction, or by whom we wish to be emulated—but not envied [envy being destructive of friendly feeling]—we either like these or wish to be liked by them. We like those with whom we join in efforts for their good, if the result does not promise undue ill for us. We are friendly to those who cherish their friends as much when the friends are absent as when they are present; and hence all of us are friendly to those who are faithful to the dead. And so in general we like those who are really faithful to their friends, and never desert them in time of trouble; among all the kinds of good men, they are especially liked who are good in the strength of their affections. And we like those who are straightforward with us; so this class includes those who mention their own failings [foibles]. As already noted [2. 4, p. 105], friends are not ashamed of unconventional behavior in the presence of friends; accordingly, if one who *is* ashamed is no friend, one who is not ashamed may be argued friendly. We like those who do not frighten us, and in dealing with whom we do not lose our aplomb —for no one likes a person of whom he is afraid.

Species of friendship

The several species of friendship [liking, love] are: companionship, intimacy, and ties arising from blood-relationship and the like.

Causes of friendship

Things that cause friendship [liking, love] are: favors [acts of kindness]; doing favors without being asked; and doing them without publishing the fact—for thus the recipient thinks they are done for his sake, and from no ulterior motive.

1382a

Enmity and hatred

Enmity and hatred obviously must be studied [by the speaker] from a consideration of their opposites [that is, love, liking, friendship]. Enmity is produced by anger, by spiting, and by calumny. Now whereas anger is excited by offences that concern the individual, enmity may arise without regard to the individual as such; for if we take a man to be of a certain sort, we hate him. Anger always has to do with particulars—with the individual Callias, or the individual Socrates; hatred is directed against the class as well. Thus every one hates a thief or an informer. And whereas anger may be cured by time, hatred is incurable. Again, the aim of anger is to give pain, while the aim of hatred is harm; the angry man wishes his victim to feel [and know], but to hatred this makes no difference. All painful things are felt; but of the greatest evils in a man—namely, wickedness and folly—he is least aware, since the presence of the vice gives him no pain. Again, anger is itself attended by pain, but hatred is not. The angry man is grieved; the hater is not grieved. Circumstances being altered, the angry man may come to pity the one who has angered him; hatred never pities. The angry man wishes the object of his anger to suffer in return; hatred wishes its object not to exist.

From the foregoing, then, it is clearly possible [for the speaker] to prove that men are enemies or friends; if they are not enemies or friends, to make them appear to be either; if their friendship or enmity is pretended, to refute them [to lay bare the pretense]; and if there be a dispute whether an act was done through anger or through hatred, to refer the act to either emotion as the speaker may choose. [That is, the preceding analysis of friendship and enmity, with their kinds and causes, will supply the speaker with the necessary arguments. The arguments regarding anger and hatred must be discovered through a study of the opposite emotions of love, friendship, liking; the persons whom we like, and our reasons for liking them, having been adequately analyzed for the purposes of Rhetoric.]

2. 5. [Fear and Confidence.] The sort of things men fear, the persons whom they fear, and the conditions under which they fear, may be learned from what follows. Fear may be defined as a pain or disturbance arising from a mental image of impending evil of a destructive or painful sort. [The evil must be of a destructive or painful sort;] for men do not fear all evils—as, for example, the prospect of becoming wicked or slothful—but only such as mean great pain or ruin, and these only when they

Fear

Definition of fear

appear to be, not remote, but close at hand, imminent. Of evils that are very remote men are not afraid; thus every one knows that he must die, but since people think they will not die soon, they do not care. From our definition, then, it must follow that fear is caused by whatever seems to have a great power of destroying us or of working injuries that are likely to bring us great pain. Accordingly, the very indications [signs] of such things cause fear, since they suggest that the thing is at hand; 'danger' means just this—the proximity of anything we dread. Such indications are the enmity and anger of those who have power to do us harm; for, since they clearly have the will to do it, the doing must be close at hand. So also injustice [wickedness, vice] joined with power; for it is the bad [unjust] man's will [choice] to do evil that marks him as bad [unjust]. Again, outraged virtue joined with power [is a cause of fear]; for, clearly, virtue when outraged always has the will [chooses to be avenged], and now has the power. Another cause of fear to us is the fear of us in those who have the power to hurt us; for such persons must always be in readiness to do it. And since the general run of men are worse rather than better—slaves to their own interest and cowards in time of danger—as a rule it is a cause of fear to be in the power [at the mercy] of another man; and hence one's accomplices in any tremendous crime will be feared as likely to turn informers [for gain or safety] or to leave one in the lurch. [They may run away, make off with the booty, or the like; compare Shakespeare, *Henry IV* 2. 2, and Chaucer, *The Pardoner's Tale*.] They who have the power to do wrong will be feared by those who are in a position [are peculiarly liable] to be wronged; for as a rule men will take advantage of each other when they can. And they are to be feared who are, or think themselves to be, wronged; for they are always watching their chance. And they who have already done

Causes of fear

1382[b]

some one a wrong are to be feared, if they have power, for they will be afraid of his retaliating [and are ready to forestall it by other wrongs]; we have already stated [2. 5, p. 108] that such a case [injustice joined with power] causes fear. And men fear those who compete with them for things which both parties cannot possess at the same time; with such competitors men are always at war. We fear those who are [by position, evident superiority] formidable to men more powerful than we are—if they could injure our betters, much more can they injure us; and, for the same reason, we fear those whom our betters actually fear [—less manifest enemies]. We fear those who have destroyed our betters. We fear those who have assailed persons inferior to us; either they were already formidable, or now they will be grown so. Of those whom we have wronged, and of our enemies or rivals, it is not the quick-tempered and outspoken that we fear, but the cool [composed], the dissembling, the unscrupulous; for since we never know whether they are upon us, we never feel that the danger from them is remote. All fearful things [situations] are more fearful if any mistake we might make regarding them cannot be remedied —if there will be no remedy whatever, or if the remedy lies, not with us, but with the adversary. And those things [situations] are more fearful in which no one can help us, or helping will not be easy. Speaking generally, we may say that those things make us fear which, when they befall, or threaten, others, make us pity.

Conditions under which men fear

Roughly speaking, then, of things that deserve fear, and of things that men do fear, those we have noted are the chief. Let us next take up the conditions under which men become frightened. If fear is accompanied by the anticipation of some destructive suffering, then, clearly, no one will be afraid who thinks that nothing is going to cause him suffering; he will not be afraid of things that he does not expect to suffer, nor of persons from whom he expects no injury, nor at times when he thinks himself safe. It follows, therefore, that fear is experienced by those who think themselves likely to suffer, and to suffer from particular persons particular things at particular

1383ª

times. People do not expect suffering when they are, or think they are, in states of great prosperity—conditions

Classes of people who are not likely to be afraid

that make them insolent [prone to outrage], contemptuous [prone to slighting], and bold [reckless]; such types of character as result from wealth, bodily strength, abundance of friends, power. Nor, on the other hand, do men expect suffering when they think they have already suffered the last extremity of horror, and are become callous to the future, like culprits who have been flogged until they are done for. If there is to be the anguish of uncertainty, there must be some lurking hope of deliverance; and that this is so would appear from the fact [a sign of this is] that fear sets men deliberating—but no one deliberates about things that are hopeless. Accordingly, when it is desirable that the audience should fear, the speaker must bring them into the right frame of

How the orator is to arouse fear

mind so that they shall take themselves to be the kind of people who are likely to suffer. He must argue that others greater than they have suffered; and must point out that others like them [in a like situation] are suffering, or have suffered, at the hands of people from whom they did not expect it, and things that they did not expect, and at times when they thought themselves safe.

Confidence [boldness]

From this explanation of fear and things to be feared, and the particular situations in which men are frightened, we can see what it is to be confident [bold, sanguine], and what sorts of things men are confident about, and under what conditions they are confident. Confidence [boldness] is the opposite of fear, and the thing that inspires confidence is the opposite of that which excites

Definition of confidence

fear. Therefore confidence is the hope [anticipation], accompanied by a mental image, of things conducive to safety as being near at hand, while causes of fear seem to be either non-existent or far away. Confidence is inspired both by the remoteness of calamities and by the proximity of sources of encouragement. And there is ground for confidence if there are means of rectifying mistakes and means of succor—either numerous means, or great ones, or both numerous and great. It makes for confidence if we have neither wronged others nor been wronged by them; if we have no rivals [competitors] at all, or if our rivals lack power; or if these rivals, having power, are our friends, and have treated us well or been well treated by us; or if those whose interests are at one with ours are more numerous than our rivals, or more powerful, or both more numerous and more powerful. [So much for *things* that inspire confidence.]

Causes of confidence

As for the conditions under which men feel confident: they do so if they think they have succeeded in much, and suffered little, or if they have often run into great danger, and have come off safely. There are, in fact, two things that render human beings indifferent to peril—inexperience and resourcefulness. Thus dangers at sea are faced boldly by those who never have met with a storm, and by those whom experience has taught how to meet one. We grow confident, too, when the danger we apprehend does not frighten our equals, nor yet our inferiors or those whom we take to be such. And such we take to be those whom we have conquered [surpassed], or whose superiors or equals we have conquered. We are confident if we think we possess in greater quantity or in a higher degree those superior qualities which would make our adversaries formidable; that is, if we think we are better off in respect to wealth, bodily strength, advantage in friends and territory, and, in the way of military preparations, either all or the most important. We are confident if we have injured no one, or few, or not such persons as men fear, and in general we are confident if we are sure of

Conditions under which men are confident

1383b

the favor of the gods, but above all when this is shown through signs [omens] and oracles; for anger brings confidence, and to suffer unjustly brings anger—and divine favor is supposed to aid those who are wronged. And we are confident when in any enterprise we think we are likely, or certain, to suffer no ill, or to attain success. So much for the causes of fear and confidence.

Shame [modesty] and its opposite

2. 6. [SHAME AND SHAMELESSNESS.] Let us take up shame and shamelessness. From what follows we shall see the kinds of things in regard to which men are ashamed, or unashamed, with reference to what people they have these feelings, and under what conditions they have them.

Definition of shame and shamelessness

Shame may be defined as a pain or disturbance regarding that class of evils, in the present, past, or future, which we think will tend to our discredit; and shamelessness as a certain contempt or indifference regarding the said evils.

Things that cause shame

Given this definition, it follows that shame will be aroused by such evils as are thought to bring disgrace to ourselves or those we care for.

Acts proceeding from each of the vices

These evils are, first, all acts that proceed from any of the vices; thus: throwing down one's shield, or running away—an act proceeding from cowardice. So also withholding a trust, or any similar wrong in money matters—an act proceeding from injustice. And having carnal intercourse with improper persons [or creatures], or in improper places, or at any improper time—an act proceeding from licentiousness. And taking profit from paltry sources, or base ones, or from the powerless, such as paupers and the dead—whence the proverb, 'He would take the sheet from a corpse'; for such acts proceed from low greed [avarice] and meanness. And not coming to the rescue when you have money, or helping less than you can; or getting assistance from those who are less able to give than you are; or borrowing when it will seem like begging, begging when it will look like asking for repayment of a favor, asking for repayment when it will look like begging, or praising a man in such fashion that you are seen to be begging—and hammering away at it when you have been refused; for all these acts indicate [are *signs* of] meanness. And praising a man to his face—a sign of flattery; praising his good points extravagantly and glossing over his bad, overdoing your sympathy when he is present and in distress; and all other acts of the same sort; for such acts indicate flattery. And refusing to bear hardships that are borne by older or more *1384ª* delicate people, or by persons of higher rank, or in general by those who are less fit and able to bear them than we are; for all this indicates effeminacy. And accepting favors, accepting many of them, and then abusing our benefactor for what he has done to us; for all this indicates littleness of soul and a groveling mind. And constantly talking about oneself, making large promises, and attributing to oneself the merits of others; for this appertains to boastfulness. And so with each of the remaining vices of character: the acts proceeding from each, the indications [signs] of each, and everything resembling them, are base, and cause shame.

Other causes of shame

In addition to the foregoing, it is a cause of shame not to have any part in the honorable things in which all men, or all or most persons like ourselves, participate. By 'persons like ourselves' I mean those of the same race, or city, or age, or kin, or, in general terms, those who are on our own level. Once we are on a given level, it makes us ashamed not to be as well educated, say, as the rest are; and similarly with respect to all else. And the shame is the greater if the fault appears to lie with the individual himself, for then the deficiency will have proceeded rather from inward badness [vice], if the man is responsible for his present, past, or future condition. And it causes shame if one is undergoing, has undergone, or is about to undergo such treatment as tends to bring one into dishonor and reproach; that is, subservience of the body or submitting to base acts—under which head comes submission to wanton outrage. Yielding oneself to another's licentiousness [lust] causes shame, whether willingly or unwillingly—and when the unwilling person is forced to yield. The submission, and the failure in self-defence, appear to come from a want of manliness or from cowardice.

These, then, and the like, are the things that make men ashamed. Now since shame is a mental image of discredit [ignominy]—a discredit considered in and for itself, and not with regard to further consequences; and since we care for the opinion that is formed of us only because of the people who form it; it follows that the persons before whom [with respect to whom] a man feels shame are those of whom he takes account. A man takes account of those who admire [look up to] him; those whom he admires; those by whom he would like to be admired; those whom he is ambitious of rivaling; and those whose opinion he does not despise. Those by whom we wish to be admired, and whom we admire, are they who possess any good that is in high esteem, or they from whom we vehemently desire to obtain something that they have power to bestow—as lovers, for example, [vehemently desire favors from the beloved]. Those whom we are ambitious of rivaling are such persons as are like us. Those whom we respect as uttering veracious opinions are our elders, well-educated people, and the like. And more shame is felt for things that are done before men's eyes, and things done conspicuously; whence the proverb, 'Shame sits in the eyes.' [That is, she turns away from disgraceful conduct.] Accordingly, we are more ashamed of things done in the presence of those who will always be with us, or of those who pay attention to us; for in both cases the things are done before [critical] eyes. We feel shame before those who are not liable to the same imputations [for shameful acts] as we are; since it is plain that here their attitude must be the direct opposite of

Persons with respect to whom men feel shame

1384[b]

ours. And we feel it before those who are severe in judging people who seem to err; for if a man does a thing himself, he is commonly supposed not to resent it in another who does the same, so that, conversely, if he does not do that sort of thing himself, he obviously will resent it in another. And we feel shame with respect to those who tell tales [gossip]; having no tales told is as good as not being considered in the wrong. Tale-bearers are of two classes: those who have been injured, and are watching their chances to retort, and habitual evil-speakers; for, if the latter speak ill of the innocent, how much more will they talk of the erring! We feel shame with respect to those whose chief occupation is with the failings of their fellow men; satirists, for example, and comic poets—for these are, in effect, evil-speakers and tale-bearers. We feel shame with respect to those who never have known us to fail, since hitherto they have been in a position to admire us. And hence we are ashamed to deny those who make a first request of us—our sentiment being that we never before have given them a bad opinion of us. And these are either such as have but recently conceived the wish to be friendly with us, having hitherto seen only our best side (and hence the merit of Euripides' reply to the Syracusans [?—'If for no other reason, men of Syracuse, you ought to respect our humble admiration because this is the first request we Athenians ever have made to you']); or else they are such of our old acquaintances as know nothing to our discredit. And we are ashamed not only of the shameful facts as aforesaid, but of the indications of them [the 'signs'—anything that commonly betrays such facts]; as in the case of sexual intercourse, not merely of the facts, but of anything that would indicate them; and not only of disgraceful things, but of disgraceful talk as well. Similarly we are ashamed not only before the persons above-mentioned, but also before those who will reveal our doings to them, such as servants and their friends. In general, however, we are not ashamed before those for the validity of whose opinion we have a great contempt; thus no one feels shame before small children or before animals. Nor, again, are we ashamed of the same things before our intimate friends as before strangers; with respect to intimate friends we are ashamed of things that are considered essentially disgraceful, while with respect to outsiders the standard is that of convention [—law or custom].

Conditions under which men feel shame

As to the conditions under which men may be ashamed, they are these. First, if there are people standing in such relations to them as we have said [p. 114] cause shame. These, as we saw, are those whom we admire, or who admire us, or by whom we should like to be admired, or from whom we desire some advantage which we shall not obtain if they do not think well of us. Such persons may be actually looking on—as Cydias represented them in his speech on the assignment of lands in Samos, when he asked the Athenians to imagine all the Greeks to be standing in a circle about them, eye-witnesses of the voting, not simply men who were going to hear afterwards about the result. Or they may be persons near at hand, or persons who are sure to learn of what befalls us. And hence in time of misfortune we do not wish to be seen by our former rivals—rivals being in the class of admirers. And we are in a situation to feel shame when there are deeds and achievements to our credit which we may tarnish; these may be our own, or our progenitors', or may appertain to various other persons with whom we are closely connected. To speak generally, we feel shame before those persons whose own disgrace would affect *us*. These are they who have been mentioned [relatives, ancestors, persons with whom we are connected by various ties], and they who defer to us as their standards—they to whom we have stood in the relation of guides and advisers, or any others, if such there be, persons of our own

1385a

level whom we regard as rivals for distinction. Many, in fact, are the things we do and refrain from doing on account of such persons through a sense of shame. And when we are likely to be seen by those who know of our disgrace, and to mix with them in public, the greater is the tendency to feel ashamed. That was the point in the remark of the poet Antiphon as he was about to be flogged to death by Dionysius [tyrant of Syracuse]; when he saw his fellows (doomed to die with him) covering their faces as they all went through the city-gates, he said: 'Why hide your faces? Do you fancy any of these [bystanders] will see you to-morrow?'

So much for shame. As for shamelessness, obviously we shall be well supplied with arguments from a study of the opposite cases. [That is, the speaker must turn the foregoing study of shame around, whereupon he will see from what causes, with respect to what persons, and under what circumstances, men are not ashamed. Thus, for example, he will know with what arguments to allay, as well as to arouse, a sense of shame in his audience; see the illustrations from Euripides, Cydias, and Antiphon.]

2. 7. [Benevolence. The term represents the emotion toward disinterested kindness in doing or returning good to another or to all others; the same term represents the kind action as an action, or the kind thing done considered as a result.] The persons toward whom men show kindness, and the reasons for it, or the conditions under which men have the feeling, will be clear when we have defined the term. Let us take benevolence [favor, kindness] to be this: the feeling in accordance with which one who has it is said to do a favor to one who stands in need, not in return for anything, nor for any advantage to the doer, but for the advantage of the recipient. The favor [benevolence] is great if shown to one who is in urgent need, or in need of things that are great and are hard to

Benevolence [or favor—including gratitude]

Benevolence defined. Its relation to needs

Persons in need

effect, or of things that must be effected in important or difficult crises, or if the benefit is the only one, or the first, of its kind, or if the doer has helped more than any one else. Our natural impulses [wants, cravings] represent needs, and, above all, the impulses [cravings] which when unsatisfied are attended with pain; such are the desires—sexual desire, for instance. Then there are the desires connected with the ills of the body and attendant on dangers—for a man who is in danger desires, and so does a man in pain. And hence those who stand by us in poverty or in exile [flight], even if the things they do for us be but small, gain our favor because our need is great and the assistance timely—as the man [won favor] who gave the mat in the Lyceum. [The circumstances of this example are unknown. The reference may be to an actual occurrence in the Lyceum; or it may be to an episode in some play or story. But the point is clear: giving the mat was perhaps a trifle to the doer, but of great importance to the recipient, who measured the service by his own extreme need—he may have been in poverty or in exile (flight), or both.] Therefore the service must preferably tend to satisfy these needs [urgent bodily wants, or the desires attendant on peril], or if not, then to satisfy equal or greater needs [of some other kind]. Accordingly it is plain who are the persons toward whom kindly feeling is shown, what are the reasons for it, and under what conditions it is shown; and obviously the speaker must draw his arguments from these sources. [He must argue from these basic concepts if, for example, he aims to arouse kindly feeling (favor, benevolence) for his client in his hearers.] He must show that *these* persons [the objects of the feeling] are, or have been, in such need and pain as we have mentioned, and that *those* [the benevolent ones] gave, or are giving, them assistance of the sort described, in such circumstances of distress. It is equally plain from what sources the speaker can draw arguments

Application to the ends of the speaker

to rob a deed and its doers of benevolence. He may argue either that the alleged doers are rendering, or did render, the service for their own advantage (and by definition this is not benevolence), or that the service was accidental—a coincidence—or done under constraint, or that it was in the nature of repayment, and not a free gift—whether the doers were aware of this or not; for, whether they were or not, there was a *quid pro quo*, and accordingly [by definition] no benevolence. And [in testing alleged motives of benevolence] we must examine [a given act] under all the Categories; for an act is benevolent either in being a particular thing [the Category of Substance], or in having a particular Magnitude, or in having a particular Quality, or in occurring at a particular Time, or in a particular Place. [Aristotle evidently thinks that these five Categories are here of special interest to the orator (Rhetoric is a less scientific discipline than Dialectic). Strictly considered, 'all' should mean ten (cf. *Categories* 4), namely: (1) Substance (=Essence), (2) Magnitude (=Quantity), (3) Quality, (4) Relation, (5) Place (=Where), (6) Time (=When), (7) Position (e.g., sitting or standing), (8) Possession (=Having), (9) Activity (=Doing), (10) Passivity (=Suffering, Undergoing).] Thus it is a sign [of the absence of benevolent feeling] if a man has failed [refused] to do us a smaller service [than the alleged one], or if he has done the same service [as the alleged one], or an equal service, or a greater, to our enemies; for then it is clear that the alleged service was not done for our sake [was not disinterested]. Or the speaker may indicate [the absence of benevolent feeling (it is a 'sign' of this)], if the doer knew that the alleged service to us was worthless; for no one will admit that worthless things are *needed*.

1385b

2. 8. [Pity.] Having now discussed benevolence and the lack of it, let us turn to the emotion of pity. Let us

Pity

consider what sort of things are piteous, what persons men pity, and under what conditions the feeling is aroused. Pity we may define as a sense of pain at what we take to be [what vividly strikes us as] an evil of a destructive or painful kind, which befalls one who does not deserve it, which we think we ourselves or some one allied to us might likewise suffer, and when this possibility seems near at hand. In order to feel pity, one obviously must be the sort of man who will think that some evil may befall either himself or some one allied to him—an evil such as we have mentioned in the definition, either resembling it or equally momentous. And hence pity will not be felt by those who are utterly lost and ruined, since they think they can suffer nothing more—they have done their suffering; nor again will it be felt by those who conceive themselves to be eminently prosperous—rather will these be given to insolence. Supposing themselves to be in the possession of all good things that are, they obviously think that no evil can possibly befall them—this impossibility being itself included in 'all good things.'

Definition of pity

Conditions in which pity is not felt

Conditions in which it is felt

Persons who tend to think that evil may befall them [and hence to feel pity] are such as the following. Those who have already experienced disaster and survived it. Men advanced in years, both because they are reflective and because of their experience. Men who are physically weak. Men who are somewhat over-timid. Educated people, since they reckon duly with possibilities. Men who have parents living, or children, or wives; for these are a part of the man himself, and are liable to suffer the evils in question. [They may die, suffer pain, and the like.] Those who are neither in a state of courageous emotion like anger or boldness (for such emotional states take no thought about what may be coming), nor in a mental frame of insolent presumption (for the insolent also give no thought to the possibility of their suffering evil), nor, on the other hand, in a condition of excessive fear (for the panic-striken do not feel pity—they are absorbed in their own emotion). Pity is felt by men in a state between these extremes. Men will feel pity, too, if they think that some people are good; the man who believes no one to be good will think that every one deserves to suffer ill. Finally, as a general rule, [we may say that a man will feel pity] when he is in a position to remember that similar ills have befallen him or his friends, or to anticipate such ills for him or his friends.

1386[a]

Things that arouse pity

So much for the conditions in which men pity. The things that arouse pity are readily seen from our definition [p. 120]. Whatever brings pain and anguish, and is in its nature destructive, is piteous—and whatever brings utter ruin; likewise all ills of a sufficient magnitude that result from chance. Under the head of things painful and destructive come all forms of death, bodily injuries and afflictions, old age, sickness, lack of food. Under evils that result from chance come the total or relative lack of friends (and hence to be torn away from friends and companions is pitiable); deformity, constitutional weakness, mutilation; an ill result coming from a source from which good was to be expected; the frequent occurrence of the like; and the arrival of good when disaster has already occurred—as in the case of Diopeithes, who was lying dead when the gifts came in for him from the Persian King. And it is pitiable never to have attained any good thing at all, or, when good things have been attained, to miss the enjoyment of them

Persons whom we pity

The things that cause pity are the foregoing and the like. The people whom we pity are as follows. Those whom we know well, so long as they are not too closely allied to us. In the latter case [if they are near and dear], we have the same feeling [of alarm, not pity] as if we ourselves were threatened. That is why Amasis [rather Psammenitus] did not weep when, as the story goes, his son was led by to execution, but did weep when he saw his friend of old now begging; this latter sight was piteous, the former terrible. The terrible is different from the piteous; it tends to drive out pity, and often serves to arouse the opposite emotion. [The speaker will find terror useful in arousing fear.—'Amasis' takes us to the story of Psammenitus in Herodotus 3. 14: 'Psammenitus, thy lord Cambyses asketh thee why, when thou sawest . . . thy son on his way to death, thou didst neither utter cry nor shed tear, while to a beggar, who is, he hears, in no wise related to thee, thou gavest those marks of honor.' 'O son of Cyrus, my own misfortunes were too great for tears; but the suffering of my friend and follower deserved them. When a man falls from splendor and plenty into beggary at the threshold of old age, one may well weep for him.'] Further, we pity men when the terrible thing comes close to us. We pity those who are like us in age, or character, or habits of mind, or social standing, or birth and blood; for [when something terrible happens to one who is like us] in any of these points, we have the deeper impression that it may likewise happen to us. Here again one must assume a general rule: whatever men fear for themselves will arouse their pity when it happens to others. Now, as we have observed, it is when suffering seems near to them that men pity; as for disasters that are ten thousand years off in the past or the future, men cannot remember or anticipate them, and either feel no pity at all for them, or at all events feel it in no comparable measure. Accordingly, the speaker will be more successful in arousing pity if he heightens the effect of his description with fitting attitudes, tones, and dress—in a word, with dramatic action; for he thus makes the evil seem close at hand—puts it before our eyes as a thing that is on the point of occurring or has just occurred. Events of the recent past or the near future are more piteous [than remote ones], for the same reason. Piteous, too, are the signs [of woe], and the acts of the victims,

You vivify the impression by making the case seem near

1386[b]

their garments and all similar tokens, their words, or whatever they said or did in the midst of their suffering—for example, at the moment of death. [Compare Antony's use of a 'sign' when he speaks to the citizens in *Julius Caesar* 2. 3. 169 ff.: 'If you have tears, prepare to shed them now. You all do know this mantle. . . . Look! in this place ran Cassius' dagger through.' See also Caesar's piteous last words, *ibid.* 3. 1. 77: '*Et tu Brute!* Then fall Caesar!'] Most affecting of all is it when in these critical moments the victims maintain a noble bearing. All these circumstances increase our pity, because they make the evil seem near to us, and the suffering undeserved, and set the picture of it before our very eyes.

2. 9. [Indignation.] The nearest antithesis to pity is the feeling they call indignation; for pain at the sight of undeserved good fortune corresponds in a way to pain at the sight of undeserved ill fortune, and proceeds from the same sort of character. Both emotions are characteristic of good men, who are bound to feel sympathy and pity for undeserved ill fortune, and indignation at undeserved prosperity; since whatever comes to a man against his deserts violates the principle of justice. Accordingly, we ascribe indignation to the gods themselves. It might indeed be thought, on the same grounds, that the opposite of pity should be envy, on the supposition that envy is very close to indignation, even identical with it. But envy is something different. True, it also is a disturbing pain, and is directed at good fortune. But here the good fortune is not undeserved; it is the good fortune of an equal, a person like the one who envies him. Envy and indignation have this in common: if we are to have either emotion, there must be an absence of the belief that anything untoward will happen to us; our emotion must arise on our neighbor's account only. If the pain and perturbation are caused by the thought that our neighbor's good fortune

Indignation

The opposite of pity

Envy

will result in some disadvantage to us, the emotion will no longer be either indignation or envy; it will be fear. And it is obvious that hand in hand with these emotions will go their counterparts. Thus the man who is pained at a case of undeserved misfortune will feel pleasure, or at least no pain, at a case of deserved misfortune. No good man, for example, will be grieved when punishment overtakes parricides and murderers. He is bound to rejoice at such things, as he is bound to rejoice when good fortune comes to those who deserve it. Both rewards are just, and both will make the fair-minded man rejoice. He is sure to hope that what has happened to a man like himself will happen also to him. All these feelings belong to one and the same type of character. And the opposite feelings belong to the opposite type: thus one and the same kind of person will rejoice at another's mischance and be envious of his good fortune; for if a man is pained when something is acquired and possessed, he must necessarily be glad at the want or destruction of it. Accordingly, all these emotions [indignation, envy, and malicious joy] tend to check the emotion of pity, while they are caused, as we saw, in different ways; and hence all of them will serve alike in representing situations as not pitiable. [The speaker, by arousing any of them, may prevent pity in his audience.]

1387a

How the speaker may check pity

Reserving the other emotions for subsequent treatment, let us first discuss indignation. With respect to what persons do we have this feeling, what are the reasons for it, and under what conditions is it aroused? These points are clear from what has been said above. If being indignant is being pained at what we take to be unmerited good fortune, then, first, it is obvious that we do not have this feeling with respect to all 'goods' [cf. 1. 5–6, pp. 24–34]. Thus no one will be indignant at another for being just or brave, or for acquiring any virtue; just as no one will pity another for the opposite reason [—for being unjust or cowardly, or failing to acquire a virtue]. It is wealth, power, and the like that cause indignation—in a word, such things as are deserved by good men and by those who possess the goods of nature, as noble birth, beauty of person, and all the like. Further, the 'old' [the possession long since acquired] seems akin to the 'natural' [the possession as a natural gift]; and hence, of those who possess a given good, they who have recently acquired it, and fare well on this account, will arouse the more indignation. Thus the newly rich give more pain than the people of long-established and hereditary wealth. The same principle applies to those who govern, or have influence, or an abundance of friends, or fine children, or any other of the 'goods' in this class. And similarly we feel indignation if through [possessing some of] these advantages the men come into some other; thus here again the newly rich who come into office because of their wealth give more pain than do those that are wealthy from of old. And so in the other cases: [for example, when a man who has recently acquired one external advantage (as power) thereby acquires another (as wealth) he gives more pain than does a man who has long had power and thereby has come into wealth—and so throughout the list.] The reason is that the possessor from of old is considered to have what is his own, and the new possessor what is not; for what has all along appeared to be as we now see it is regarded as real—and hence the new men seem to have what is not theirs. Further, each several good is not the desert of every chance possessor; rather, there is a certain correspondence and fitness [as between the good and its possessor]. Thus splendid weapons befit, not the just man, but the brave, and distinguished marriages suit, not the newly rich, but the well-born. Accordingly, a man may be good enough, and yet, if he gains an advantage that does not befit him, it is a case for indignation. And people have this feeling against

Causes of indignation

Persons who arouse indignation

a worse man who enters into rivalry with a better—above all, when they are worse and better in the same pursuit; [as when an upstart poet or painter sets himself up as a rival to Dante or Leonardo.] And hence the lines [cf. *Iliad* 11. 542–3]:

> But he [Cebriones] avoided encounter with Ajax, Telamon's son;
> For Zeus would have had indignation if he fought with the mightier man.

1387[b] But even when they are not better and worse in the same respect, we are indignant with one who is inferior in any way, when he sets himself up against his superior; for example, with the musician if he contends with the just man—since justice is better than music.

What persons arouse indignation can be seen from the foregoing; and also what are the grounds for it. Now for the conditions under which indignation is felt. Men tend to have this emotion if they deserve to possess the greatest goods, and do possess them; it is unjust [unfair] that people unlike them should have been thought worthy of the like rewards. Secondly, they tend to have it if they are in fact good and upright, for then they make sound judgments, and hate anything that is unfair. And they tend to have it if they are ambitious, and eager to gain particular ends, and especially if they aim at things [honors, for example] that others get without deserving them. In general, those persons tend to feel indignation who are worthy of things of which others are unworthy; they tend to have it towards those others, and with respect to those things. Accordingly, the servile, the worthless, the unambitious, are not given to indignation, for there is nothing that they think they deserve.

Conditions under which men feel indignation

Summary, with reference to the aims of the speaker

From all this one can see the cases of misfortune and disaster, or of failure to succeed, at which men will rejoice, or anyhow will not be pained; for from what we have said the opposite cases become obvious. And so, if the speech puts the judges into the appropriate frame of mind; and if it shows that the persons who ask for pity, and the special grounds on which they ask for it, deserve, not pity, but the reverse; then it will be impossible for the judges [those who listen and decide] to feel pity.

Envy

2. 10. [Envy.] The persons whom men envy, the grounds for the emotion, and the conditions under which men have it, are likewise clear from the definition. We define it as a pain at what strikes one as being good fortune, with respect to the advantages we have mentioned [cf. 1. 5–6, pp. 24–34; 2. 9, p. 125], coming to persons like oneself, the pain being felt, not because one desires something, but because the other persons have it. Envy is felt by those who have, or think they have, equals; and by 'equals' [persons like the one who envies] are meant persons of like race, like family connections, like age, like disposition, like reputation, like possessions. It is felt by those who barely fall short of having everything; and hence by those who do great things, and by men who succeed—they think that every one else is getting what belongs to *them*. It is felt by those who are pre-eminent in their reputation for a given thing—above all, if they are thus noted for wisdom or good fortune. And the ambitious are more envious than the unambitious. Pretenders to wisdom are given to envy, since they are ambitious to be thought learned. So all, generally, who aim at a reputation for anything are envious in regard to that particular thing. The little-minded [small-souled] are envious, for to them everything seems great, [and hence they envy any one who gains anything].

Persons who tend to be envious

Grounds of envy

1388a

The things that excite envy are the 'goods' already mentioned. The objects of the desire for reputation and honor, whether deeds or possessions; whatever men strive for with a view to fame; and the various gifts of fortune—with virtually all these things envy is concerned; but especially with the things that the individual longs for, or thinks he himself should have, or the things in the possession of which he is a little above, or a little below, the average.

Persons whom men envy

It is clear, too, who are the objects of envy—that is included in what we have said. The persons men envy are persons near them in time, in place, in age, in reputation. And hence the line:

> Ay, kinsfolk can envy their kin.

And men will envy those with whom they compete—who are included in the previous list; for we do not compete with folk who lived ten thousand years ago, nor with men yet to come or now dead, nor with those who dwell at the Pillars of Hercules [at the world's end], nor with those whom, in our own judgment or that of our fellows, we take to be far below or far above us. And as we are disposed toward these persons, so are we disposed toward the corresponding things. [That is, competition (rivalry) and envy are not concerned with things far off in time or space, or out of reach above us, or far beneath our consideration.—A variant reading would give: 'So, too, we compete with those who pursue ends that are similar to ours.'] We compete with our rivals in some contest, with our rivals in love—in a word, with those who seek the things that we seek; so that these persons above all must be the ones whom men envy. And hence the saying [of Hesiod—see 2. 4, p. 105]:

> And potter 'gainst potter.

We envy those whose acquisitions and successful efforts are a reproach to us (these also will be persons near at hand and like us); for it is evidently our own fault that we have missed the 'good' in question, and the consequent pain makes for envy. We envy those who have what by rights would be ours, or have got what once belonged to us. Thus old men envy their juniors. And those who have spent much for a thing envy those who get it at slight expense.

It is evident, too, what things and persons give pleasure to the envious, and under what conditions the pleasure is felt. If in a given situation an envious man is pained, the opposite situation will give him pleasure. Consequently, if by your speech you bring the masters of a situation into a state of envy; and if the others who ask for pity, or who lay claim to some good [a favorable award, for instance] shall appear in the said light [if you cause them to be envied]; then these others obviously will not win pity from those masters.

Application to the ends of the speaker

2. 11. [EMULATION.] The conditions under which men are emulous, the objects of their emulation, and the persons who excite this feeling in men, will be clear from what follows. Let emulation be defined as a pain at what we take to be the presence, in the case of persons who are by nature like us, of goods that are desirable and are possible for us to attain—a pain felt, not because the other person has these goods, but because we do not have them as well. Accordingly, emulation is a good emotion, and characteristic of good men; whereas envy is a bad emotion, characteristic of bad men. Through emulation a man prepares himself to win what is good; through envy he proceeds to keep his neighbor from having it. It follows that they are emulous who think themselves worthy of good things which they do not possess [—attainable things, of course]; for no one aspires to what he believes impossible of attainment. Accordingly, the young [2. 12, p. 132] and the high-minded [the magnanimous, the great-souled] are emulous. So also they who possess such goods as befit men that are held in honor—namely, wealth, abundance of friends, public office, and all the like; because they have what a good man deserves, they

Emulation

Emulation defined

1388b

People who are emulous

assume that they themselves ought to be good, and hence they are emulous for this sort of advantages. Emulous, again, are they whom the world thinks deserving. [If people praise a man, he will strive to win further praise.] And if a man's ancestors, or kinsmen, or friends, or nation, or city, have been honored for particular things, he will tend to be emulous for the same distinction; he will look on those things as proper to him, and himself as deserving them.

Things that excite emulation

Since all goods that are held in honor excite emulation, the moral virtues must do so, and whatever is useful and beneficial to our fellows, for men honor the virtuous and the beneficent. And emulation is excited by those goods which bring enjoyment to one's neighbors—as, for example, wealth, and personal beauty rather than health.

Persons who excite emulation

We can see, too, what persons are the objects of emulation. They are the ones who possess these and similar goods—the goods we have mentioned, such as courage, wisdom, public office; for men in office can render service to many, and so can generals, orators, and all who have the like power and influence. Emulation is excited, too, by those who have many imitators; or whose acquaintance or friendship many desire; or whom many admire, or whom we ourselves admire. And it is excited by those whom poets or panegyrists celebrate in praises and encomiums.

Contempt

Toward the opposite sorts of persons men feel contempt; this emotion is the antithesis of emulation, and the corresponding activities are mutually opposed. Consequently, men who are in a condition to emulate or to be emulated must tend to feel contempt for those who are subject to any evils [defects and disadvantages] that are opposite to the goods arousing emulation, and to feel it with respect to these evils. Hence there is often contempt for the lucky, when fortune favors men who lack the goods that are held in honor.

So much for the means by which the several emotions are produced or are dissipated, the sources from which we derive the persuasive arguments that concern these emotions.

The emotions, concluded

[The foregoing treatment of anger and mildness, friendship and hatred, fear and boldness, shame and shamelessness, kindness and unkindness, pity, indignation, and envy, emulation and contempt, will furnish the speaker with means of persuasion subsidiary to logical arguments. The study of these emotions enables him to color his speech with his own character in a desirable way, and to give the color he desires to the persons and their acts that are dealt with in his speech. This study also throws light on the nature of audiences, their emotions, the ways of utilizing those emotions as they are, or of arousing or allaying them.

The next six chapters treat of character in another aspect, but still for the purpose of discovering means of persuasion that are subsidiary to logical arguments. They perhaps mainly concern the nature of audiences, and the kind of argument that will appeal to a given audience, or a given part of an audience. Thus the analysis of the character of the young will enable the speaker to find the right appeal, and to avoid the wrong, for an audience made up wholly or in part of young men; but this analysis would also help an orator or a poet to devise a speech suitable for utterance by a young man. Again, it would be useful in explaining acts and motives if a case involved the deeds and impulses of the young. And so with the characteristics of the old, of the intermediate age, and of persons in the various states of fortune, the rich or the poor: what will be the emotions of a man who is young and rich, old and rich, old and poor, and the like, and what argument will be suited to each?]

2. 12. [TYPES OF CHARACTER.] Let us now discuss the various types of human character in relation to the emo-

Character

Summary: emotions, moral states, times of life, fortune

tions and moral states, to the several periods of life and the varieties of fortune. By emotions are meant anger, desire, and the like—which we have already discussed [2. 2–11]. By moral states are meant virtues and vices; and these, too, have already been treated [1. 9, pp. 46–55], along with the characteristic choices, and characteristic acts, of the men who are subject to them [cf. 1. 5–6, pp. 24–34]. By periods of life are meant youth, the prime of life, and old age; by varieties of fortune [states or conditions of life] are meant health, wealth, power [in its several kinds], and their opposites—in a word, good fortune and bad.

1389a

Times of life

Characteristics of the young

We shall begin with the characteristics of youth. Young men have strong desires, and whatever they desire they are prone to do. Of the bodily desires the one they let govern them most is the sexual; here they lack self-control. They are shifting and unsteady in their desires, which are vehement for a time, but soon relinquished; for the longings of youth are keen rather than deep—are like sick people's fits of hunger and thirst. The young are passionate, quick to anger, and apt to give way to it. And their angry passions get the better of them; for, since they wish to be honored, young men cannot put up with a slight; they are resentful if they only imagine that they are unfairly treated. Fond of honor, they are even fonder of victory, for youth likes to be superior, and winning evinces superiority. They love both honor and victory more than they love money. Indeed, they care next to nothing about money, for they have not yet learned what the want of it means; the point is brought out in the saying of Pittacus about Amphiaraus. [The apophthegm of Pittacus is unknown. In order to illustrate the point, a speaker might refer to the parable of the Prodigal Son; the young man squandered his money, and later 'began to be in want.' Aristotle's character-sketch is general, as befits the study of Rhetoric. In arguing with a group of young men, the speaker assumes that the majority will not be avaricious. The brother of the prodigal son is exceptional—though it is to be noted that he is the 'elder.'] The young think no evil [are not cynical], but believe in human goodness, for as yet they have not seen many examples of vice. They are trustful, for as yet they have not been often deceived. And they are sanguine; for young men glow with a natural heat as drinkers are heated with wine, while as yet their failures have not been many. They live their lives for the most part in hope [anticipation], as hope is of the future and memory of the past; and for young men the future is long, the past but short; on the first day of life there is nothing to remember, everything to expect. They are easily deceived, and for the same reason, since they are quick to hope. Being passionate as well as hopeful, they are relatively brave; the passion excludes fear, and the hope inspires confidence—no one is afraid when he is angry, and an anticipation of good makes one confident. And they are shy; for as yet they have no independent standard of good conduct, but only the conventional standards in which they were reared. They are high-minded [have lofty aspirations]; first, because they have not yet been humbled by life, nor come to know the force of circumstances; and secondly, because high-mindedness means thinking oneself fitted for great things, and this again is characteristic of the hopeful. In their actions they prefer honor to expediency; for their lives are rather lives of good impulse [moral instinct or feeling] than of calculation [reason]; and calculation aims at the expedient, virtue at the honorable. They are fond of their friends, intimates, and associates—more so than are men in the other two periods of life; this comes from their love of company, and from the fact that as yet they judge nothing, and hence do not judge their friends, by the standard of expediency. All their mistakes are on the side of intensity and excess, running

1389b

counter to the maxim of Chilon ['Moderation in all things']. They carry everything too far: they love to excess, they hate to excess—and so in all else. They think they know everything, and are positive about everything; indeed, this is why they always carry their doings too far. When they wrong other people, the injuries are wanton [insolent], not malicious. The young are prone to pity, because they think every one good, or at all events better than people really are. That is, they judge their fellow man by their own guilelessness, and hence assume that his sufferings are undeserved [cf. 2. 8, p. 120]. They are fond of laughter, and therefore facetious, facetiousness being a subdued insolence.

Characteristics of the elderly

2. 13. [ELDERLY MEN.] Such, then, is the character of the young. As for elderly men—men who are past their prime—we may say that their characteristics for the most part are the opposite of these. The old have lived long, have been often deceived, have made many mistakes of their own; they see that more often than not the affairs of men turn out badly. And so they are positive about nothing; in all things they err by an extreme moderation. They 'think'—they never 'know'; and in discussing any matter they always subjoin 'perhaps'—'possibly.' Everything they say is put thus doubtfully—nothing with firmness. They think evil [are cynical]; that is, they are disposed to put the worse construction on everything. Further, they are suspicious because they are distrustful, and distrustful from sad experience. As a result, they have no strong likings or hates; rather, illustrating the precept of Bias, they love as men ready some day to hate, and hate as ready to love. They are mean-souled [small-minded], because they have been humbled by life. Thus they aspire to nothing great or exalted, but crave the mere necessities and comforts of existence. And they are not generous. Property, as they know, is one of the neces-

sities, and they have learned by experience how hard it is to acquire, how easy to lose. They are cowards, apprehensive about everything—in temperament just the opposite of youth; for they are grown cold, as youth is hot, so that advancing age has paved the way to cowardice, since fear in itself is a species of chill. They cling to life, and all the more as the latter end of it comes nearer; for, as the object of all desire is the absent, so the thing they most lack will be the thing they most desire. They are unduly selfish [their self-love exceeds the right measure]—another trait of the mean-souled. And through selfishness they live their lives with too much regard for the expedient, too little for honor; by expediency we mean what is *1390c* good for oneself, by honor what is good absolutely. They are not shy, but tend to be shameless; because they have less regard for honor than for expediency, they do not care what people think of them. They are slow to hope; partly from experience—since things generally go wrong, or at all events seldom turn out well; and partly, too, from cowardice. They live in memory rather than anticipation; for the part of life remaining to them is but small, while the part that is past is large—and hope is of the future, memory of the past. Here, again, is the reason for their garrulity; they are for ever talking of bygone events, which they thus enjoy in recollection. Their fits of passion, though quick, are feeble; as for their desires of sense, these have either wholly failed, or are weakened. Accordingly, the old are not characterized by passion, and their actions are governed, not by impulse, but by the love of gain. And hence men in this period of life are thought to be temperate [appear to have the virtue of self-control]; the truth is that their desires have slackened, and they themselves are mastered by the love of gain. Their lives are rather lives of calculation than of moral bias; for calculation aims at expediency, whereas the object of morality is virtue. When they wrong others, the injuries are done out of malice, and not from insolence. Old men, too, as well as young men, tend to feel pity, but not for the same reason. Young men feel pity out of human kindness, old men out of their infirmity. Because they are weak, they take all possible sufferings to be near them; and this, as we saw [2. 8, p. 120], is the state of mind in which pity is felt. And hence they are querulous, not given to jesting or laughter; for the querulous disposition is just the opposite of the mirthful.

Application to the ends of the speaker

Such, then, are the characteristics of young men and of the elderly. Now the hearer is always receptive when a speech is adapted to his own character and reflects it. Thus we can readily see the proper means of adapting both speech and speaker to a given audience. [In addressing young men, for example, the speaker should assimilate his character to theirs. Or, again, in pleading for a gift to the poor and ailing, one would appeal to the kindness and generosity of the young, but to the fears and doubts of the old.]

Character of men in their prime

2. 14. [The Prime of Life.] As for men in the prime of life, their character evidently will be intermediate between these two, exempt from the excess of either young or old. They will be neither excessively confident—which means confident to the point of rashness—nor yet too timid; they will be both confident and cautious. They will neither trust every one nor distrust every one; rather they will judge each case by the facts. Their rule of life will be neither honor alone, nor expediency alone; they will duly observe both standards. And so with regard to parsimony and prodigality: their economy will be fit and proper. So, too, with regard to passion and desire: they will combine self-control with valor, and valor with self-control. In the young and the old these qualities are not combined; young men are brave, but lack self-control, and old men, while temperate, are cowardly. To put it

1390b

generally: all the valuable qualities which youth and age divide between them are joined in the prime of life; and between the respective excesses and defects of youth and age, in every case it strikes the fitting mean. The body is in its prime from thirty years of age to five-and-thirty, and the soul about forty-nine. [Thirty-five and forty-nine are multiples of seven, like the Biblical three score and ten, which is twice thirty-five. Aristotle's figures are not essentially mystical, however, but are based rather upon his observation of men. Apart from these figures, he does not precisely mark the limits of youth and age; he doubtless realized that some men are mature before the age of thirty, and that the mind or soul, the intellectual and moral faculties, may continue in full vigor long after the age of fifty. In the *Republic* 7. 539–40, Plato suggests that the study of philosophy should be carried on between the ages of thirty and thirty-five, and that rulers should hold office between thirty-five and fifty, after which they are to lead the contemplative life, with an occasional return to politics. In dealing with a mixed audience of old and young, and men of middle age, Aristotle's speaker, while not neglecting the old and the young, should doubtless adapt his speech, and his own character as therein evinced, mainly to the intermediate type of hearer; for in persuading this type, which unites the best qualities of the two extremes, he will tend to win the entire audience.]

2. 15. [Character as Modified by Fortune.] So much for youth, old age, and the prime of life, with the characteristics that distinguish each of them. Let us turn to those gifts of fortune which also modify human character. And let us first take the character of the well-born. Good birth has the effect on its possessor of making him more ambitious; for if a man has something to start with, he will tend, as men commonly do, to add to the pile; and

Gifts of fortune

Character of the well-born

good birth means an inherited distinction. [It is something to start with.] The well-born will tend to look down even on people who are as good as his ancestors, since the distinction from afar carries more weight, and is easier to boast of, than the same distinction near at hand. [His ancestors gained a certain honor, and hence the man is 'well-born'; he can look down on people who have only now gained the same honor, social standing, or the like. Or, again, the honor has come to him from a foreign city; it is easier to boast of, and the recipient can look down upon one who gains the same honor from their native city. 'Distance,' in time as well as in space, 'lends enchantment to the view.'] The term 'well-born' applies merely to descent from a good stock. It must not be confused with 'generous' ['noble'], which means that the character still runs true to the ancestral nature. For the most part that character does not run true in the 'well-born'; such persons usually are insignificant enough. Indeed, in the generations of men, as in successive crops of grain, the yield will vary; now and again, where the stock is good, there will come a succession of exceptional men, and then there will be a falling off. The clever stocks, when they degenerate, tend towards the type of insanity, as witness the descendants of Alcibiades and those of Dionysius the elder [tyrant of Syracuse]. And the sedate stocks degenerate into stupidity and dulness, as in the descendants of Cimon, Pericles, and Socrates.

Character of the wealthy

1391a

2. 16. [The Influence of Wealth.] The effect of wealth upon character lies on the surface for all to see. The rich are insolent and superior. The possession of wealth so upsets them that they feel as if they owned every kind of 'good' there is. Since money is taken as a standard of value for other things, wealth fancies there is nothing that cannot be bought. Rich men are given to luxury and ostentation. They are luxurious because of

the ease and style [display of prosperity] in which they live. They are ostentatious and vulgar, because, like the rest of mankind, they give their time and thought to what they love and admire, and because they think that every one else is keen for the same things as they are. [And hence they flaunt their wealth, and display their ill-breeding.—Their vulgarity is shown in various ways, as, for example, in faulty speech. They do not give time and thought to propriety.] Nor is it unnatural that they should be thus affected [—there is much to encourage their insolence, ostentation, and ill-breeding]; for many are the suitors to those who can give. And hence the saying of [the poet] Simonides about the wise and the wealthy, when he was asked by the wife of Hiero [tyrant of Syracuse], 'Is it best to be wealthy, or wise?' 'To be wealthy,' said he; 'for the wise, I observe, mark time at the rich men's doors.' It is characteristic of the rich to believe themselves fit for public office; for they think they already possess that which gives title to authority. To sum up, the character resulting from wealth is that of a prosperous fool. But there is this difference within the type: as between the newly rich and those who have long had wealth, the newly rich have all the characteristic vices in an accentuated and baser form. And the reason is that to be newly rich means, so to speak, to lack training in wealth. The wrongs committed by the rich are not malicious, but are wrongs either of insolence [outrage, *hubris*] or of licentiousness [self-indulgence], as, for example, either assault or adultery.

2. 17. [THE INFLUENCE OF POWER.] As for power: here again the resulting type of character would seem to be in most points obvious enough; some of the traits are common to power and wealth. The rest are better. As compared with men of wealth, men in power are characterized by a higher ambition and greater manliness, because they

Character of men in power

aspire to such notable deeds as their power gives them the opportunity of effecting. They are more energetic because of their responsibilities; they have to be on the alert for all that concerns their power. They are dignified rather than overbearing; for their rank heightens their impressiveness, and so they tone their self-importance down—dignity being a tempered and becoming sense of importance. The wrongs, if any, that are done by men in power are not petty misdemeanors, but crimes on a larger scale.

Effect of good fortune on character

As to good fortune: this shares in its effects upon character with the conditions [of good birth, wealth, and power] which we have just treated; for the kinds of fortune that are considered highest tend toward these [three conditions]. In addition, good fortune brings advantages in the way of domestic happiness and bodily excellence of various sorts [cf. 1. 5, p. 24]. In general, it makes men more arrogant and less judicious; yet it is attended by one very excellent trait: the prosperous are god-fearing. They maintain an attitude of reverence, trusting in the divine power because of goods that come from luck.

1391 b

Here we may close the discussion of the types of character that belong to the different times of life [2. 12–14, pp. 131–7] and the several kinds of fortune [2. 15–17, pp. 137–40]. As to the kinds of fortune opposite to those described—for example, the character of the poor or the unlucky, or the character of the powerless—one will ascertain the types by substituting the opposite traits. [Thus, if the wealthy are insolent and superior, the poor will be just the reverse, and so in other details; similarly with the opposites of good fortune and power. It is perhaps noteworthy that Aristotle does not mention the opposite of good birth; this may fall under the general head of ill luck or misfortune, which includes the other two opposites that he does mention.—In the next chapter he takes a fresh start in his subject, recapitulating as it were the substance of Books 1 and 2 up to this point, and looking forward to the remainder of Book 2.]

2. 18. [GENERAL RECAPITULATION.] The function of all persuasive utterance is realized in some decision—for when we know a thing, and have reached a decision about it, there is no need of further argument. Such is the function of speaking, even to a single listener, when you urge him on, or try to turn him—as you do if you tax an individual about his conduct or seek to alter his views. The individual man is as truly a judge or decider as an entire audience; so, in the wider sense, whoever it is you have to persuade is 'judge.' Nor does it make any real difference whether you are addressing an actual opponent or merely arguing against an impersonal thesis. However impersonal the case, what you say must function like a speech; you have to upset the opposite hypothesis, and you frame your discourse against that as if it were your opponent. [That is, any kind of persuasive discourse must observe the method of rhetoric; of written discourse—of ordinary prose—the reader is the 'judge.' You aim to make the reader 'decide' in your favor.] And the same thing holds good of epideictic speaking [—of panegyrics, declamations, and the like]; you compose your speech for an audience, and the audience is the 'judge.' As a rule, however, the term 'judge' means simply and solely one of the persons who decide the issue in the disputes of civil life, where, as in law-suits, there is a question of fact to be settled, or, as in deliberations of State, a question of policy. [In the narrower and usual sense, a 'judge' is one whom either the forensic or the deliberative speaker seeks to persuade, with a view to obtaining a decision.] The typical forms ['characters'] of government have previously been discussed [1. 8, pp. 44–6] in our section on deliberative speaking. [And character

The function of speaking

Retrospect

in relation to the individual has likewise been discussed (2. 1–17, pp. 90–141). This is perhaps of especial interest to the forensic speaker; though we must bear in mind that the interests of the epideictic, the forensic, and the deliberative speaker are not mutually exclusive; what is specially useful to any one of them is generally useful to the other two.] Accordingly the manner and means of investing a speech with the necessary character have now, it would seem, been adequately determined.

As we have seen [1. 3, p. 18], each of the three kinds of speaking has its own distinct purpose. And, again, for all three, we have ascertained the popular notions and accepted premises [2. 1, p. 90] from which speakers may draw their means of persuasion in deliberative, epideictic, and forensic oratory [1. 4–8, pp. 20–46; 1. 9, pp. 46–55; 1. 10–14, pp. 55–79]. Still further, we have determined the means by which a speech may be invested with the requisite ethical quality. But we have yet to discuss the forms of argument that are common to all speeches. The topic of the Possible and Impossible, for instance, is an appliance that every one is bound to use in speaking; some [as forensic speakers] must use it in trying to prove that a thing has happened, others [as deliberative speakers] in trying to show that a thing will happen. So also the topic of Size is common to all speeches; every one will use the device of magnifying and minifying things—whether in speaking on the public weal, or in praising or blaming, or in prosecuting or defending. When we have analyzed the common topics of Possibility and Size [2. 19, pp. 143–7], we must try to say what we can of Enthymemes and their general use, and of Examples [2. 20–26, pp. 147–8]; in order that, by adding what [? then] remains of our subject, we may complete what we set out to do at the beginning of the treatise. [Cf. 1. 1, p. 7. 'What remains' may refer to the substance of Book 3, which is superadded to the discussion outlined in

Universal appliances

1392[a]

Outline of the rest of this treatise

the present chapter for the rest of Book 2, and does fill out the general plan of the *Rhetoric* as announced at the end of the first chapter of Book 1.] Of the topics common to all three kinds of speaking, that of magnifying (as we have said [1. 9, p. 54]) is most closely associated with the epideictic kind; that of the past with the forensic (since here the decisions concern past facts); and those of the possible and the future with the deliberative.

The topic of the Possible and Impossible

2. 19. [FOUR COMMON TOPICS.] Let us take first the argument concerning the Possible and Impossible. [Here the speaker will use the following assumptions.] If it is possible for one of a pair of contraries to exist or come to pass, then you may assume that it is possible for the other. For instance, if a man can get well, then a man also can fall sick; any two contraries are equally possible if considered only in relation to each other. Further, if two things are alike, and one is possible, then so is the other. And if the harder of two things is possible, then so is the easier. Similarly, if a thing can come to pass in an excellent and beautiful form, it can come to pass in general: to be a fine house is harder than to be just a house. Again, whatever can have a beginning can also have an end; for no impossibility comes, or begins to come, into existence. Thus the diagonal of a square cannot begin, and never could begin, to be commensurate with the side. [If a thing cannot have a beginning, it cannot have an end; Aristotle's illustration of equal impossibilities is the familiar one of attempting to 'square the circle.'] Similarly, whatever can have an end can also have a beginning; for everything that occurs has a beginning. Again, if one thing (B) follows another (A) in essence or in the order of development, and if that subsequent thing (B) can come into being, so can the antecedent thing (A): thus, if a man (B) can come into existence, so can a child (A)—childhood being antecedent. And conversely; for example,

if a child can come into existence, so can a man—on the principle, too, that if a thing can have a beginning, it can also have an end. Further, the natural objects of love or desire are possible: as a rule, nature will not lead any one to be enamoured or desirous of impossible objects. Again, when any science or art exists, its proper object can exist or come to pass. And if the conditions governing the first step in any process lie within our control—if we can compel the first step by force or persuasion, through our superior strength or authority, or through friends—then the thing thus conditioned is possible. And if the parts of a thing are severally possible, then the whole is possible. Conversely, if the whole is possible, so, as a rule, is each several part. Thus if the several parts of a shoe—sole, cap, and foot-covering—can be had, then a shoe can be had; and if a shoe can be had, then sole, cap, and foot-covering can be had. Similarly if a given genus can be pro-

1392[b] duced as a whole, then a given species under that genus is possible; and if the species can come into existence, then the genus is possible. Thus, if vessels can be built, then a war-vessel can be; and if a war-vessel can be built, then a vessel is possible. Again, if two things are by nature dependent on each other for their possibility, and one is possible, then so is the other. Thus, if 'double' can exist, so can 'half'; and *vice versa*. Again, if a thing can be produced without art or preparation, much more can it be produced with the help of art and care. And hence the lines of [the poet] Agathon:

> Without art there are things that no bard can attain;
> Some things by main force or sheer luck he may gain.

And if a thing is possible for inferior, weaker, less intelligent people, it is more so for persons with the opposite qualities. Thus Isocrates said it would be passing strange if he could not discover a thing that a man like Euthynus had learnt. [Cf. Isocrates, *Or*. 18. 15.]

As for the Impossible, the speaker obviously will have his stock of arguments in the opposites of the foregoing.

Past Fact

In dealing with the past—with the question whether a thing has or has not occurred—he will look to the following principles. First, if the less probable of two things has occurred, the more probable should have occurred as well. If one thing (B) that naturally follows another (A) has occurred, then the antecedent (A) has occurred; for instance, if a man has forgotten something, then at some time he must have learnt it. Again, if a man had the power to do a thing, and also the wish, then he has done it; on the principle that every one has his way when he can, since then there is nothing to stop him. Further, you may argue that a man has done a thing, if he wished to do it, and if there was no external hindrance; or if he could have done it, and was in a state of anger; or if he was in a position to do it, and was spurred on by desire. The general rule is that men will gratify their longings when they have the chance—bad people through lack of self-control, and good people because they have a steady desire for good ends. And you may argue that whatever was about to happen did actually occur; the general probability being that a man who intends to do a thing will do it. And you may argue that if the natural [usual] antecedents, or the necessary steps showing intention, occurred, the thing itself must have followed. Thus: 'If there was lightning, thunder followed'—if he made the attempt, he accomplished the act. Conversely, if all the natural [usual] results, or the results that must follow intention, occurred, you may argue that the [usual or necessary] antecedent occurred. Thus: 'If there was thunder, it was preceded by lightning'—if the act was committed, then he made the attempt. [For example, in a case of alleged seduction or rape, granted the occurrence of the act, you argue that it was preceded by the natural (usual) tentatives, or by the necessary force or deceit or other means to its accomplishment.] In all these sequences you distinguish between necessity [cause and effect] and probability [what happens as a rule].

Arguments against the occurrence of things in the past can obviously be found in the opposites of the foregoing.

1393a

Future Fact, probable or inevitable

On questions touching the future, it is clear that you must argue from the same considerations. You may argue that a thing will come to pass when the power and the wish to have it so are joined; as likewise when such power is coupled with desire, or with anger, or with calculation [considered purpose]. And you may argue that a thing so prompted will occur, if the persons concerned have started to do it, or if they intend to do it shortly; on the principle that what people intend to do is more likely to be done than the reverse. And, again, you may argue that the consequences will occur, if their natural antecedents have occurred: 'If the clouds are gathering, it is likely to rain.' Or, again, that the intended result is likely to come, if the means to it have been effected: 'If the foundation is laid, there will be a house.'

The topic of Size, and the process of magnifying or minifying

As to arguments respecting the Greatness or Smallness of things—the relative greatness or smallness of one thing in comparison with another, or their greatness or smallness generally considered—the method to be followed is clear from what we have previously said. In dealing with deliberative speaking we took up the importance of various goods, and, quite simply, the comparison of greater and lesser values [1. 7, pp. 34–44]. Now in each of the three kinds of speaking [1. 3, pp. 16–20] the object under discussion is some sort of good—either something expedient, or something honorable, or something just; and hence all speakers, when they come to magnify [or minify], will employ the means we have there analyzed. Our analysis need go no further. To consider greatness or superiority in the abstract would be a waste of time; for practical purposes the concrete instance is more effective than any general speculation.

So much for arguments about (1) the possibility and impossibility of things; for questions respecting (2) the occurrence or non-occurrence of things in the past, or (3) of things in the future; and for the treatment (4) of the relative greatness and smallness of things.

2. 20. [MEANS OF PERSUASION COMMON TO ALL BRANCHES OF SPEAKING.] We have now discussed the [four] special means of persuasion [belonging to the three kinds of speaking (epideictic, forensic, and deliberative)]; it remains to discuss the means that are common to all [three]. These common [universal] means are generically two [—that is, under one genus there are two species, namely,] Example and Enthymeme. As for the Maxim [which some take to be a third species], it is to be included under the Enthymeme. Accordingly, let us first speak of (1) the Example; for [in Rhetoric] the Example corresponds to the process of induction [in Dialectic], and induction is the basis [of all reasoning].

The two universal means of persuasion are Example and Enthymeme

The Maxim belongs under the Enthymeme

There are two kinds of argument by example. One consists in the use of a parallel from the facts of history; the other in the use of an invented parallel. This last may take the form of a comparison [parable, invented by the speaker], or one may employ fables such as Aesop's or the African beast-tale. The use of the parallel from history would go as follows. The speaker, say, is urging us to arm against the King of Persia, and not let him conquer Egypt; then the argument from parallels would be: 'Darius in his day did not cross [the Aegean] until he had seized Egypt; but once he had seized it, he crossed [the sea against us]. And Xerxes, again, did not invade us until he had seized Egypt; but once he had seized it, he likewise crossed [against us]. And so this man, if he seizes Egypt, will cross, too. We must therefore prevent him.'

(1) The Example; two species: (*a*) historical, (*b*) invented

Examples from history

1393[b]

Instances of the invented comparison are those employed by Socrates. Let us suppose the speaker to be urg-

Examples by invented comparison

ing that public officials should not be chosen by lot. He may argue thus: 'It is like choosing athletes for a contest by lot, instead of picking those who can play the game; or it is as if the choice of a helmsman from a crew had to go by the toss of a coin, and not to the man who knows how to steer.'

Examples from fables

Instances of the fable are the example used by Stesichorus in regard to Phalaris, and that used by Aesop in defence of the demagogue. When the people of Himera had made Phalaris their military leader, and were about to give him a body-guard, Stesichorus closed his discussion of the plan with this story. There was a horse that had a meadow all to himself, until a stag came and began to spoil his pasturage. Thirsting for revenge, the horse went to the man, and asked: 'Could you help me to punish the stag?' 'Yes,' said the man, 'if you will let me bridle you, and mount upon your back with javelins in my hand.' The horse agreed, and was mounted; but, instead of getting his revenge, he became the slave of the man. 'See to it,' said Stesichorus, 'that in your desire for vengeance on your enemies you do not fare like the horse. With the military master you have chosen, you already have taken the bridle. If you give him a body-guard, and so let him mount you, from that moment you will be slaves to Phalaris.'

So Aesop, at Samos, in defending a demagogue who was on trial for his life, told the following story. A fox, while crossing a river, was swept into a cleft in the bank; unable to get out, she was for a long time in sorry plight, and many dog-ticks fastened upon her. Then a hedgehog that was wandering about spied the fox, took pity on her, and asked if he might not pull the ticks out of her. But she would not let him; and being asked 'Why not?' replied: 'These already have taken their fill of me, and no longer draw much blood. If you take these away, others will come, ravenous, and will drain all the blood I have left.' 'And to you, too, men of Samos,' said Aesop, 'my client will do no further harm, for he already has got his wealth. If you put him to death, others will come in their poverty, and by theft will utterly consume your public funds.' *1394ᵃ*

Fables are suited to speeches in a popular assembly; and they have an advantage in that it is hard to find parallels in history, but easy to find them in tales. In fact, the speaker must contrive with the fable as he contrives a comparison; all he needs is the power to see [in some fable] the analogy [to the case in hand]—and facility in this comes from literary training. But if it is easier to find parallels in tales, nevertheless for deliberative speaking the parallels from history are more effective, since in the long run things will turn out in future as they actually have turned out in the past.

In the absence of Enthymemes, the speaker must make Examples serve the ends of logical proofs, since it is proofs that carry conviction in the audience. If, however, he has Enthymemes, he must use Examples for the ends of confirmation, subsequent and complementary to the Enthymemes. The Examples should not precede, for then the argument will seem like an induction; but [anything like a scientific] induction is not appropriate in Rhetoric, save in rare cases only. When they follow the Enthymemes, Examples function like witnesses—and there is always a tendency to believe a witness. Accordingly, when the speaker puts the Examples before, he must use a good many of them; if he puts them after, one may suffice—on the principle that a single witness, if you have a good one, will serve the purpose.

So much for Examples and their several kinds, and how and when they should be employed.

2. 21. [Maxims; the Kinds and Their Use.—Maxims, as we have seen (2. 20, p. 147), come under the head of the **Maxims.**

Enthymeme; so that we enter the subject of the Enthymeme by a discussion of the Maxim, which is a general sentiment (sententious generalization, 'sentence,' *sententia*) respecting human life and action.] For the use of Maxims, the best procedure is to define the thing; and then we shall see what are the proper objects, times, and persons for the application of it in our speeches. A Maxim is a statement [declaration]; not about a particular fact, such as the character of Iphicrates, but of a general nature; yet not a general statement concerning any and every sort of thing—thus 'Straight is the opposite of curved' is not a Maxim; but a statement about those things which concern human action, about what is to be chosen or avoided in human conduct. Now Enthymemes are a kind of syllogism which almost entirely deals with such matters; take away the syllogistic form, then, and a premise or a conclusion of an Enthymeme is a Maxim. Thus [Euripides, *Medea* 295–6]:

The Maxim defined

> No man of native sense should ever
> Have his children taught to be too clever.

There you have a Maxim. Now add the cause or reason [*ibid.* 297–8]—

> It makes them useless, and they gain
> Jealous dislike throughout the town—

1394b

and you have an entire Enthymeme. Again [Euripides, frag. 661, N²]:

> There is no man in all ways happy.

Or [Euripides, *Hecuba* 864]:

> There is none of mankind that is free.

Taken so, it is a Maxim. You have an Enthymeme when you add the next line [*ibid.* 865]:

> For each is a slave to money or chance.

In view of what has been said, there must be four kinds of Maxims. The Maxim either will or will not have a reason subjoined. Such demonstration is needed when the statement is paradoxical or open to dispute; maxims that state nothing paradoxical need no supplement. Of the latter sort, (1) some need none because the truth in them is already known. Thus [the line from (?) Epicharmus]:

Four kinds of Maxims

> Methinks there is no such wealth as excellent health.

It is the view entertained by most people. (2) Others need no added reason because they are plain [and acceptable] at first glance. Thus [Euripides, *Troades* 1051]:

> No lover true but loves for ever.

Of the maxims that do have a reason added, (3) some are part of an enthymeme, like [the one first given]:

> No man of sense, etc.

(4) Others have the nature of an enthymeme, but are not part of one; and these are considered the best; here the added reason is only suggested. Thus the line [unidentified]:

> Mortal as thou art, nurse not wrath immortal.

The statement, 'A man should not nurse his wrath for ever,' is a maxim; the conjoined phrase, 'Mortal as thou art,' suggests the reason. Similarly [in the line from (?) Epicharmus]:

> The mortal should have mortal thoughts, not thoughts immortal.

From what has been said we can see how many kinds of Maxims there are, and to what subjects each several kind is adapted. When the statement is open to dispute, or is paradoxical [startling], you must not omit the supplementary reason. [In such cases you have the following choice.] You may put the reason first, and make

How to frame Maxims

a maxim of the conclusion. Thus [reverting to the first example (p. 150)] the speaker might say: 'For my part, since one should not incur envy or be idle [useless as citizens], I deny that it is better to be [finely] educated.' Or you may put the maxim first, and then put the former clause after. When a statement, though not paradoxical [startling], is not convincing, the reason should be added as tersely as possible. In such cases Laconic and enigmatic sayings are alike suitable; thus one might say what Stesichorus told the Locrians: 'It is better not to be insolent, lest the cicalas chirp on the ground.' [They would chirp there if a ravaging enemy felled the trees.]

1395[a]
Laconic and enigmatic Maxims

How and when to use Maxims

The use of maxims is suited to speakers of mature years, and to arguments on matters in which one is experienced. In a young man, uttering maxims is—like telling stories—unbecoming; and to use them in a realm where one lacks experience is stupid and boorish. An adequate sign of this is that rustics are specially given to coining maxims, and always ready to vent them.

Illicit generalization [the use of maxims that state as a universal truth what is not always true] is best-suited to the arousing of distress and indignation, whether by way of preface or after you have shown your case. Even well-worn and familiar maxims should be used if they fit the situation. Precisely because they are familiar, and thought to be universally admitted, they will be accepted as true. Thus a leader who calls on his men to risk battle in the absence of favoring omens may use [the saying (*Iliad* 12. 243) of Hector to Polydamas, who has threatened him with an adverse omen]:

> The best of omens is to fight for our land.

Similarly, [if one asks men to run the risk] against superior forces, [one may use the saying of Hector (*Iliad* 18. 309) when he is ready to fight Achilles]:

> The War-god gives an even chance.

So [if one urges] the slaughter of an enemy's children, though they have done us no harm [one may use the saying in the *Cypria* of Stasinus (see 1. 15, p. 83)]:

> A fool is he who slays the sire, and leaves the children [alive to avenge him].

Some proverbs are also maxims; for example, 'An Attic neighbor.' [The complete statement would be: 'An Attic neighbor is a restless neighbor.'] And [on occasion] you must utter maxims that run counter to sayings which have become public property; I mean, to saws like [Solon's] 'Know thyself,' and [Chilon's] 'Do nothing in excess.' [You may contradict them] when it will raise your character [or that of your client] in the eyes of the audience, or produce the effect of strong emotion. This emotional effect would be gained, for example, if an indignant speaker said: ' "It is well to know thyself" is a lie. If my client had known himself, he never would have presumed to be general.' [Yet observe his military success!] And it would raise our character in the eyes of the audience to declare: 'We ought not to treat our friends, as men say [see the precept of Bias (2. 13, p. 134)], like potential enemies; rather we should treat enemies like potential friends.' The wording should convey a clear impression of the speaker's ethical choice [his moral excellence]. If not, the reason [for his dissent from the maxim] should be subjoined; thus, having said, 'One must not treat friends as the proverb advises, but as if they were to be our friends for ever,' the speaker should add: 'The other sort of love is designing.' Or you may put it thus: 'That proverb does not content me; for the genuine friend should love as expecting to love for ever.' So you may say: 'The proverb, "Nothing in excess," does not content me; for we are bound to hate bad men to excess.'

One great advantage of maxims to a speaker arises from *1395b* the uncultivated mentality of an audience. People are

The services of the Maxim

delighted when he succeeds in expressing as a general truth the opinions they entertain about special cases. What I mean will be clear as I proceed to show how one is to hunt down the maxims required. A maxim, as was said above [p. 150], is a general statement; and people like to hear stated in general terms what they already believe in some particular connection. Thus any one who is afflicted with bad neighbors, or bad children, will gladly listen to a speaker who says: 'There is no greater trial than a pack of neighbors'; or, 'Nothing so foolish as the begetting of children.' The speaker, therefore, must feel his way to the subjects on which his audience has prepossessions, and guess how these came about, and then must express the same views, on the same subjects, as general truths. The foregoing is one advantage of using maxims. Another advantage, and a greater, is that it invests a speech with moral character. This quality is present in every speech that clearly evinces a moral purpose. Now maxims always produce the moral effect, because the speaker in uttering them makes a general declaration of ethical principles [preferences]; so that, if the maxims are sound, they give us the impression of a sound moral character in him who speaks.

How to hunt for Maxims

So much for the Maxim—its nature, its kinds, its proper use, and its services.

2. 22. [ENTHYMEMES.] We now come to Enthymemes [proper]. Let us first discuss in general terms the method by which the speaker should look for them, and then take up the question (a distinct one) of their topics. [A topic is a 'head,' under which are grouped arguments, or lines of arguments; in a *topos* ('place,' *locus*, 'region') the speaker has a stock of arguments to which he may turn for a particular need. If he knows the *topoi* (regions, places, lines of argument)—and a skilled speaker will know them—he will know where to find what he wants

The two universal means of persuasion: (2) the Enthymeme proper for a special case. The general topics, or *common*places, are regions containing arguments that are common to all branches of knowledge; these are the topics of *more and less*, of *magnifying and minifying*, of *past and future*, and of *possible and impossible*—the four *commonplaces* in the strict sense. But there are also special topics (regions, places, *loci*) in which one looks for arguments appertaining to particular branches of knowledge, special sciences, such as ethics and politics. In these *special* regions the orator hunts for arguments as a hunter pursues game. Knowing where a particular kind of game (or argument) is to be found, he will hunt for it there, and not in some other place or places. But if he is to know these places, he must have a thorough and detailed knowledge of the special sciences which mainly concern the art of Rhetoric—that is, ethics and politics, above all, since they have to do with the conduct of men as individuals, and with men in groups. Of course he must have an adequate knowledge of other special sciences, too; no knowledge comes amiss to the speaker. His head must be filled with knowledge, and the knowledge must be well-ordered so that he may know *where* to look for a particular kind of argument. The topics or places, then, may be indifferently thought of as in the science that is concerned, or in the mind of the speaker. The two questions which are said at the opening of this chapter to be distinct ones are: *how* to look for enthymemes, and *where* to hunt for the arguments the speaker is to embody in them. The chapter begins by recapitulating the nature of the enthymeme.]

General nature of the Enthymeme

We have already stated [1. 2, p. 10–12] that the Enthymeme is a syllogism, and in what sense it is so. And we have noted [1. 2, p. 12] how enthymemes differ from the syllogisms of Dialectic: [when you wish to persuade,] you must not begin the chain of reasoning too far back, or its length will render the argument obscure; and you must not put in every single link, or the statement of what is obvious will render it prolix. These are the reasons why uneducated men are more effective than the educated in speaking to the masses—as the poets say [cf. Euripides, *Hippolytus* 989] that the unlearned 'have a finer charm . . . for the ear of the mob.' Educated men lay down abstract principles and draw general conclusions; the uneducated argue from their everyday knowledge, and base their conclusions upon immediate facts. Our speaker, accordingly, must start out, not from any and every premise that may be regarded as true, but from opinions of a definite sort—the [actual] opinions of the judges [audience], or else the opinions of persons whose authority they accept. And the speaker must make sure that his premises do appear in this light to most, if not all, of his audience. And he must argue not only from necessary truths, but from probable truths as well.

1396[a]

The speaker must have real knowledge

Now, first of all, let this be understood: Whatever the subject on which we have to speak or reason—whether the argument concerns public affairs or anything else—we must have some knowledge, if not a complete one, of the facts. Without it, you would have no materials from which to construct an argument. How, let me ask, could we advise the Athenians whether they should go to war or not, if we did not know their forces, whether these were military or naval or both, the size of these forces, what were the public revenues, and who were the friends and foes of the State, what wars it had waged, and with what success—and so on? Or how could we eulogize them, if we knew nothing of the sea-fight at Salamis, or the battle of Marathon, or all they did for the Heracleidae, or anything else of a like import? The eulogist necessarily draws his materials from the noble deeds, actual or reputed, of the man he is praising. And similarly with speeches of censure. The materials are drawn from facts of the opposite kind, and the speaker looks for the base deeds, actual or reputed, that stand to the discredit of the man he attacks;

for example, that [the Athenians] brought Greece into servile subjection, enslaved their gallant allies—Aegina, Potidaea, and so on—who had fought at their side against the Persians, and any other like offences that may stand against them. So, too, in forensic speaking; prosecution and defence alike must be based upon a study of the facts. It makes no difference whether the subject is the Athenians or the Lacedaemonians, a man or a god; the same thing has to be done. Suppose it is Achilles whom we are to advise, or to praise or blame, or to accuse or defend; we must acquaint ourselves with the facts, actual or accepted for such, about him. From these we must take our materials for praising or blaming any noble or base deed of his, for accusing or defending him in respect to his acts of injustice or justice, and for advising him about his interest or hurt. The same thing applies to any subject whatever. Thus, in arguing whether justice is or is not a good, we must start from the [ascertainable] facts about justice and goodness. So we see that this is the only way in which people ever make their point about anything, whether they argue [syllogize] more rigorously *1396*[b] or less; because they do not start out from any and every fact, but from the characteristic facts belonging to their particular subject.

And, manifestly, in speaking you cannot make your point in any other way. Consequently, as may be seen in our treatise *On Topics*, the speaker must, first of all, be provided with a selection of premises [facts] from which to argue on the possible and most timely subjects he may have to discuss; and in emergencies he must seek his premises in the same way, by referring, not to vague generalities, but to the facts of the subject on which he is speaking, including just as many of the most pertinent ones as he can. The more facts he has at his command, the more easily will he make his point; and the more closely they touch the case, the more germane will they be to his purpose, and the less like sheer commonplace. By 'commonplace' I mean, for instance, praising Achilles for being a man and a hero and joining the expedition against Troy; these things are true of many besides him, so that such a speaker praises Diomede as much as he does Achilles. By 'special' facts I mean things that are true of Achilles alone—that he slew the great Hector, bravest among the Trojans, and Cycnus the invulnerable, who prevented the entire Greek army from landing; that he was the youngest of those who joined the expedition, and was not bound by oath to join it; and so forth.

Here, then, we have one principle, and the first, for selecting enthymemes; and it refers to the choice of materials for them. Let us now pass on to their elementary forms; and by 'elementary form' I mean the same thing as the class [*topos*] to which an enthymeme belongs.

Two primary species of Enthymemes: (1) Demonstrative; (2) Refutative

Let us begin where one must begin. There are two primary species of enthymemes, namely: (1) Demonstrative Enthymemes, which prove that a thing is, or is not, so and so; and (2) Refutative Enthymemes, [which controvert the Demonstrative]. The difference between the two kinds is the same as that between syllogistic proof and disproof in dialectic. By the demonstrative enthymeme we draw a conclusion from consistent propositions; by the refutative we draw a conclusion from inconsistent propositions.

We may now be said to have in hand the special topics [heads] for arguments on those various matters which a speaker will find it useful or necessary to treat. We have selected the propositions [premises] suitable in various cases—have, in fact, already ascertained the topics from which enthymemes are to be drawn [the lines of argument which enthymemes are to follow] about good and evil, the noble and the shameful, justice and injustice [1. 4–14, pp. 20–79], and likewise about types of character, emotions, and moral qualities [2. 1–18, pp. 90–143].

Let us now approach the subject in a different way, and get universal topics for enthymemes on all matters. We will indicate the refutative and the demonstrative topics side by side [2. 23, pp. 159–72]; and also the topics for apparent enthymemes—that is, spurious enthymemes which correspond to spurious syllogisms [2. 24, pp. 172–7]. And when these points are clear, we will determine the several modes of destroying or attacking enthymemes [2. 25, pp. 177–80].

1397a

Plan for the rest of Book 2

2. 23. [A List of Topics.] (1) One *topos* of demonstrative enthymemes is from opposites. [If there are two things, one of which (B) is said to be true of the other (A), then] we must observe whether the opposite of A is true of the opposite of B. If it is not, you upset the original proposition [that B is true of A]; if it is, you establish the original proposition. For example: 'Self-control (A) is beneficial (B); for licentiousness is harmful.' Or as in the Messenian oration [of Alcidamas (see 1. 13, p. 74)]: 'If war is the cause of our present evils, it is peace that we need to correct them.' Or [an example from (?) Agathon]:

A list of 28 *Topoi* ('places' or 'lines' of argument) from which to draw Enthymemes

1. Opposites

> If, now, it is not fair to grow enraged
> When evil-doers injure us unwittingly,
> Then neither do we owe a grain of thanks
> To him who does us good when forced to do it.

Or [an example from Euripides (*Thyestes*, frag. 396, N.[2])]:

> But if falsehood is persuasive in this world,
> Be sure now that the opposite holds good:
> In the world there 's many a true word ne'er believed.

(2) Another *topos* is from inflections of the same stem. What can or cannot be said of one inflected form [of a word] can or cannot be said of another. Take, for example, the word 'just.' You may argue that 'just' does not always mean 'beneficial,' otherwise 'justly' would al-

2. Inflections

ways mean 'beneficially'; but it is not, in fact, desirable to be justly put to death.

3. Correlative terms

(3) Another *topos* is from correlative terms. If it is the fact that A gave honorable or just treatment to B, you may argue that B received such treatment from A; or if A had the right to command, that B was right in obeying. So Diomedon the tax-collector argued about the farming of taxes: 'If there is no disgrace in your selling the privilege of collecting them, there is no disgrace in our buying it.' And if 'well' or 'justly' is true of the person to whom a thing is done, you may argue that it is true of the doer. But here the argument may be fallacious; for, granting that the man deserved what he got, it does not follow that he deserved it from you. Accordingly, we must keep the two questions distinct—must see (1) whether A deserved what he suffered, and (2) whether B was right in so treating him; and then we can apply our results in whichever way fits the case. There actually are cases of this discrepancy, where the justice of the punishment does not hinder the act of the man who inflicts it from being wrong. So it is in the *Alcmaeon* of Theodectes. [Here Alcmaeon is asked whether no one thought the death of his mother Eriphyle (whom he slew for her deadly betrayal of his father) to be her just reward]:

1397[b]

Did none abhor thy mother for her crime?

The son replies:

Why, the question must be taken in two parts.

And when Alphesiboea asks, 'How?' he rejoins:

Her they deemed fit to die; me, not to slay her.

Or, again, take the trial of Demosthenes [? the general] and the men who killed Nicanor; since they were held justified in killing him, he was thought to have deserved his death. Or take the case of the man [Euphron, tyrant of Sicyon] who was killed [by Sicyonians] at Thebes; here the spokesman [of the defendants] asked the judges to decide whether the man deserved to die, arguing that it could not be wrong to kill one who deserved it.

4. More and less

(4) Another *topos* is that *a fortiori* [from degrees of more and less]. Thus you may argue that if not even the gods are omniscient, much less are men; on the principle that, if a thing cannot be found where it is more likely to exist, of course you will not find it where it is less likely. Again, you may argue that a man who strikes his father will also strike his neighbors; on the principle that, if the less frequent thing occurs, then the more frequent thing occurs—for people strike their fathers less frequently than they strike their neighbors. So the argument may run; or it may run as follows. [You may argue that,] if a thing does not exist where it is more frequent, it does not exist where it is less frequent; or that, if it exists where it is less frequent, it exists where it is more frequent—according as you may need to prove that it does not exist [in a given instance], or that it does. And you may also employ this line of argument in a case of parity; so it is used in the lines [from the *Meleager* of (?) Antiphon, where (?)Oeneus says (?)to his wife Althaea whose brothers had been slain by Meleager, and who caused the death of Meleager]:

> Thou pitiest thy sire who lost his children;
> No pity, then, for Oeneus who has lost his gallant son?

Similarly you may argue that if Theseus did no wrong [? in abducting Helen], neither did Paris; or that if the sons of Tyndareus [Helen's brothers, Castor and Polydeuces] did no wrong [? in abducting her], neither did Paris; or that if Hector did well to slay Patroclus, so did Paris to slay Achilles [see below, No. 7, p. 163]. Or, again: 'If other followers of an art are not bad men, neither are philosophers.' Or: 'If their frequent condemnation to death does not show generals to be bad men, neither does the like show sophists to be bad men.' So, too: 'If it behoves each citizen among you to care for the reputation of your city, it behoves you all as a city to care for the glory of Greece.'

5. Time

(5) Another *topos* is from considerations of time when. Thus Iphicrates, in the case against Harmodius, said: 'If before doing the deed I had demanded that, if I did it, I should have a statue, you would have given me one. Now that the deed is done, will you refuse me the statue? You readily make promises when you look for a benefit; do not withdraw them when you have reaped it.' Again, to induce the Thebans to let Philip pass through their land

1398[a]

into Attica, [his ambassadors argued]: If he had pressed for this [as a condition] before he helped them against Phocis, they would have promised to do it. How monstrous to refuse him a passage now, merely because he let the matter go, and trusted them.

6. Opponent's utterance turned against him

(6) Another *topos* is from utterances made by your opponent against you and turned against him. The turn is singularly effective, as may be seen in the *Teucer* [of Sophocles (cf. 3. 15, p. 227)]. It was employed by Iphicrates in his reply to Aristophon. 'Would you,' asked Iphicrates, 'betray the fleet for money?' 'Never!' said Aristophon. 'Very good,' was the reply. 'You, who are Aristophon, would not betray it—then would I, who am Iphicrates?' Our adversary, of course, must strike the audience as the more likely of the two to commit such a crime, or our speaker will make himself ridiculous—it would be ludicrous to retort in such fashion to an accuser like Aristides ['the just']. The function of the retort is to discredit the accuser, who as a rule poses for a better man than the defendant, a pretension which it is desirable to upset. But in general the device is absurd if a man upbraids others for doing what he does or would do himself,

or urges them to do what he himself neither does nor ever would do.

(7) Another *topos* is from definition. Thus [Socrates in Plato's *Apology* 27 C–E defines his term]: 'What is "the divine"? It must be either a god or the work of a god. Well, then, any one who believes in the existence of a work of a god must needs believe in the existence of gods.' So Iphicrates [in meeting the charge of lowly birth defines and argues]: '"True nobility" is *goodness*. There was nothing noble about Harmodius and Aristogeiton until they had done a noble deed.' And he argues further that he himself is more akin [to those heroes than his adversary (a contemporary Harmodius) is]: 'At any rate, my deeds are more akin to those of Harmodius and Aristogeiton than yours are.' Another example is found in the [*Apology for*] *Paris* [(?) by Polycrates (see above, No. 4, p. 161)]: 'We shall all admit that by "incontinent" people we mean those who are not content with the enjoyment of one love.' [And Paris was content with Helen.] Or take the reason Socrates gave for not visiting the court of Archelaus: '"Ignominy" consists as much in not being able to repay a benefit as in not being able to requite an evil.' Each of the persons mentioned defines his term, gets at its essential meaning, and then proceeds to reason from it on the point at issue.

7. Definition

(8) Another *topos* is from the various senses of a word. See our treatise *On Topics* [1. 15; 2. 3] for the correct use of [ambiguous] terms. [Or perhaps: 'An example, "rightly," is found in the *Topics*.' (Consider the various senses of 'rightly'; establish the sense which fits your case —'rightly' in the sense of 'technically right,' or in the sense of 'with justice'; and then argue from that sense.— But this example is not found in the extant *Topics*.)]

8. Ambiguous terms

(9) Another *topos* is from [logical] division. Thus you may argue: 'All men do wrong from one of three motives, A, B, C. In my case, the first two of these motives are out

9. Division

of the question; and as for the third, C, the prosecution itself does not allege this.'

10. Induction

1398b

(10) Another *topos* is from induction. Thus, beginning with [?Antiphanes'] *Woman of Peparethus*, you might argue that the women everywhere can settle questions touching the legitimacy of the children. This happened, you may add, at Athens, in the case between the orator Mantias and his son, where the mother established the legitimacy of the son; and happened, again, at Thebes, in the case between Ismenias and Stilbon, where Dodonis proved that Ismenias was the father of her child Thettaliscus, and the latter in consequence was declared to be the son of Ismenias. Another instance of induction may be taken from the *Law* of Theodectes: 'If we do not entrust our horses to men who have mishandled other people's horses, nor our ships to those who have capsized the ships of others, and if this is our way with everything else, then beware of employing for the safety of our State men [mercenaries] who have ill protected the safety of others.' Or take the argument of Alcidamas that all men honor the wise: 'Thus the Parians honored Archilochus, though he had a bitter tongue; the Chians Homer, though he did not reside among them; the Mityleneans Sappho, though she was a woman; the Lacedaemonians even made Chilon a member of their senate, though they are the least literary of peoples; the Italian Greeks did the like to Pythagoras; and the people of Lampsacus gave Anaxagoras, though an alien, a public burial, and honor him to this very day.' . . . [Or take the argument that states are sure to prosper when they get their laws from philosophers:] 'For Athens grew prosperous under the laws of Solon, and the Lacedaemonians under those of Lycurgus, while at Thebes no sooner did philosophers [Epaminondas and Pelopidas] become the leading men than the State began to prosper.'

(11) Another *topos* is from an existing decision. The

decision may be on the point at issue, or on a point like it, or on the opposite point—preferably a decision that has been accepted by all men at all times; but if not that, then a decision accepted by the majority of mankind; or by wise or good men, all or most of them; or by the actual judges of our question; or by men whose authority these judges accept, or by masters of the situation whom they cannot gainsay, or by persons whom it is not fitting to gainsay, such as the gods, or a father, or our teachers. Thus Autocles said, in attacking Mixidemides: 'How! were the Dread Goddesses [the Eumenides] content to submit to the judgment of the Areopagus, and Mixidemides is not?' Or as Sappho said: 'Death is an evil; the gods have so judged it, or they would die.' Or take the reply of Aristippus to Plato, who, as Aristippus thought, had said something rather dogmatically: 'Well, our friend,' meaning Socrates, 'never talked that way.' So Agesipolis, having first consulted the oracle [of Zeus] at Olympia, inquired of Apollo at Delphi 'whether he took the same view as his father,' implying that it would be a shame to contradict his father. And so Isocrates [*Helen* 18–38] argued that Helen was a worthy woman, since Theseus decided that she was; and Paris a worthy man [*ibid.* 41–8], since the [three] goddesses preferred him to all others; and Evagoras, again, says Isocrates [*Evagoras* 51–2], was a worthy man, since Conon, after he 'met with his misfortune' [at Aegospotami], 'went straight to Evagoras,' trying nobody else on the way.

11. Existing decisions

1399a

(12) Another *topos* is from the parts of a subject, taken separately. [The whole is the genus, and its parts are the species. What is true, or untrue, of the whole must be true, or untrue, of part 1, part 2, etc.; and you argue from part by part to the whole.] As in our treatise *On Topics* [2. 4; 4. 1]: 'What kind of motion is the soul? It must be *this* kind, or *this* kind.' The *Socrates* of Theodectes will

12. From the parts to the whole

supply an illustration: 'What temple has he profaned? To which of the gods recognized by the State has he failed to pay honor?'

13. Simple consequences good and bad

(13) Another *topos* is from consequences. Since it commonly happens that a given thing has consequences both good and bad, you may argue from these [to their antecedents] in urging or dissuading, in prosecuting or defending, in praising or blaming. For example: education results in unpopularity, a bad consequence, and in wisdom, a good consequence [cf. 2. 21, p. 150]. And so you may argue: It is not well to be educated, since it is not well to be unpopular. Or: It is well to be educated, since it is well to be wise. The *Art of Rhetoric* of Callippus is simply this *topos*, with that of Possibility and the other [two common *topoi*] which we have discussed above [2. 19, pp. 143–7] superadded.

14. Criss-cross consequences

(14) There is another *topos* when we have to urge or dissuade with reference to contrary alternatives, and have to apply the method just stated to both. The difference between this *topos* and the foregoing is that there any two things are contrasted, while here the things contrasted are opposites. For instance, the priestess urged her son not to engage in public speaking: 'For,' said she, 'if you speak honestly, men will hate you; if you speak dishonestly, the gods will hate you.' [But one may deal with the contrary alternatives thus:] 'Now you *ought* to engage in public speaking; for if you speak honestly, the gods will love you; if you speak dishonestly, men will love you.' There we have in effect the proverbial 'buying the marsh along with the salt' [—the unwholesome marsh with the valuable salt]. And for this form of argument we have the term 'criss-cross' [*blaisosis* = 'knock-knees'—with legs diverging like the extended hind-legs of a frog], when each of two opposites has both a good and a bad consequence opposite respectively to each other.

(15) Another *topos* comes from the fact that men approve one thing openly, and another in their secret thoughts. In public they make a great show of praising what is just and noble; but inwardly they prefer what is to their own advantage. From the premises of your opponent you must try to draw the inference which he does not. [If he assumes a moral tone, you appeal to the inward self-interest of the audience; if he assumes that men act from self-interest alone, you appeal to the motives of justice and nobility which they openly profess.] No other *topos* of paradox is so effective as this.

15. Inward thoughts and outward show

(16) Another *topos* is from the proportion between this and that result. For example, when they would compel the son of Iphicrates, a youth under the legal age, to discharge a public duty because he was tall, Iphicrates said: 'If you make big boys count as men, you will have to enact little men into boys.' So Theodectes says in his *Law*: 'You enfranchise mercenaries like Strabax and Charidemus for meritorious service; will you not exile those among the mercenaries who have wrought irreparable harm?'

16. Proportional results

1399[b]

(17) Another *topos* is the argument from identity of results to the identity of their antecedents. Thus Xenophanes said that to affirm the birth of the gods was as impious as to say that they die; either way, it results that there is a time when they do not exist. [You argue from this identical result (which contradicts the notion, 'the gods are eternal') that the two antecedents are equally untenable.] This type of argument assumes for a general rule that the result of any given thing is absolutely constant. For example: 'You are about to decide upon the value, not of Isocrates [? Socrates], but of philosophical pursuits in general. Or again, 'to give earth and water' means slavery [to Persia]; or 'to share in the Common Peace' means obeying [? Philip's] orders. [Of the alternative arguments, positive and negative,] the speaker must take the one that suits his purpose.

17. Identical results: identical antecedents

18. Altered choices

(18) Another *topos* depends on the fact that men do not always make the same choice on a later as on an earlier occasion, but reverse it. For example, take the following enthymeme [from Lysias (*Orations* 34. 11)]: 'When we were exiles, we fought to return; now that we have returned, it would be monstrous to choose exile rather than fight.' In the one case, that is, they chose to preserve their homes at the cost of fighting, in the other to avoid fighting at the cost of deserting their homes.

19. Attributed motives

(19) Another *topos* is the treatment of some conceivable motive as the actual motive for an event or state of affairs; for example, the argument that A has given something to B with the motive of paining B by withdrawing it. This is the motive in the lines:

> Heaven to many men gives great prosperity,
> Not out of favor, but that later they
> May come to grief the more conspicuously.

Similarly in the passage from the *Meleager* of Antiphon:

> Not for to slay the boar [the heroes came],
> But for to witness unto Greece the valor
> Of doughty Meleager.

And similarly the argument [of Ajax against Odysseus] in the *Ajax* of Theodectes, that Diomede chose Odysseus [for his companion (cf. *Iliad* 10. 218–54)], not to do him honor, but in order that his companion might be an inferior man to himself. That is a possible motive for the act. [This *topos* belongs rather to forensic speaking.]

20. Incentives and deterrents

(20) Another *topos* is common to forensic and deliberative speaking. Here you consider the incentives and deterrents as the motives people have for doing or avoiding the acts in question. These are the conditions which, according as they are for or against us, make us act or refrain from action. We are moved to act if the thing is possible, easy, and advantageous to us or our friends, or hurtful to our enemies; this is true even if the act is damaging to us,

so long as our loss is outweighed by a solid gain. From these considerations a deliberative speaker will urge a course of action; and from the opposite considerations he will argue against it. And from the same considerations a forensic speaker will argue in accusation or defence—arguing from the deterrent motives for the defence, and from the incentives for the prosecution. This *topos* represents the whole *Art of Rhetoric* of Pamphilus as well as that of Callippus. [But see, on Callippus, No. 13, above, p. 166.]

1400a

(21) Another *topos* is from things that are thought to occur though they seem incredible. You may argue that no one would have believed in such an occurrence if the thing had not actually, or almost, happened; even that it is more likely to be true because it is incredible. [That the incredible thing is believed is a proof that it happened;] for the things men believe are either facts or probabilities, and hence, if the thing in question is neither credible nor probable, it must be true, since the reason why it is believed is surely not its credibility or plausibility. An example is the reply made by Androcles of Pitthus when he was arraigning the [existing state of the] law. The assembly was in uproar when he said: 'Our laws need a law to correct them.' [This the audience found incredible; so he added:] 'Why, so do fish need salt [to preserve them], however unlikely and incredible it is that, bred as they are in the brine, they should need salt; and olive-cakes need olive-oil, however incredible it is that the source of olive-oil should need it.'

21. Incredible occurrences

(22) Another *topos*, useful in refuting an opponent, is this: See what inconsistencies you can find in all the facts—conflicting dates, acts, and statements. And do this under three separate heads. First, with respect to your opponent; for example: 'He says he loves you—yet he conspired with the Thirty.' Secondly, with respect to yourself; for example: 'He says I am litigious—yet he

22. Conflicting facts

cannot prove that I ever engaged in a single lawsuit.' Thirdly, with respect to you and your opponent together; for example: 'He never has lent one of you a penny, but I ransomed a goodly number of you.'

23. How to meet slander

(23) Another *topos* is useful for persons or causes that have fallen under odium or slanderous suspicion. Here you state the reason why the facts appear in a wrong light; for then there is something that accounts for the false impression. Thus a mother who had palmed off her son on another woman was thought to be his mistress because she embraced him; but when the cause was explained, the calumny was quashed. Thus, too, in the *Ajax* of Theodectes Odysseus tells Ajax the reason why he is not thought braver than Ajax, though he really is so.

24. From cause to effect

(24) Another *topos* consists in arguing from the presence or absence of the cause to the existence or non-existence of the effect. If you prove the cause, you at once prove the effect; and conversely nothing can exist without its cause. Thus Thrasybulus accused Leodamas of having had his name recorded as a criminal on the Acropolis, and of erasing it in the days of the Thirty Tyrants; and Leodamas replied: 'Impossible! The Thirty would have trusted me all the more if my hostility to the populace were there on record.'

25. Course of action

(25) Another *topos* for the deliberative and the forensic speaker is this: See if it is or was possible to devise a better course than the speaker is recommending, or than is or was taken. If this better course was not taken, the accused obviously has not done the deed; for no one willingly and wittingly chooses a bad method.—This argument, however, is fallacious; for it often becomes clear after the event how an affair could have been better managed, though before the event this was not clear.

1400[b]

26. Actions compared

(26) There is another *topos* when an intended action runs counter to one's previous actions. Bring them together and compare them. [And, in deliberative speak-

ing, advise accordingly.] Thus, when the people of Elea asked Xenophanes whether they should or should not sacrifice to Leucothea [who as a mortal was Ino,] and mourn for her, his advice was: 'If you think her a goddess, do not sing the dirge; if you think her a human being, do not sacrifice to her.'

27. Previous mistakes

(27) Another *topos* is from previous mistakes, which you make the basis of accusation or defence. Thus, in the *Medea* of Carcinus the accusers allege that Medea has slain her children: 'At any rate,' it is urged, 'they have disappeared'—Medea having made the mistake of sending the children away. She defends herself by arguing that it is not her children, but Jason, whom she would have slain; for, supposing her to be capable of the other murder, it would have been a blunder for her not to do this [not to kill him]. This *topos* and species of enthymeme constitute the whole Art of Rhetoric before the treatise of Theodorus.

28. Meaning of names

(28) Another *topos* is from the meaning of names. Thus Sophocles plays on the name [Sidero (*sideros* = hardened iron), in his *Tyro*—the reference being to the cruelty to Tyro of her step-mother]:

> Steel, truly, like the name thou bearest.

This type of inference is common in panegyrics of the gods. Thus, too, Conon called Thrasybulus *rash counselor*. And Herodicus said of [the orator] Thrasymachus, 'You are ever *rash in combat*'; of Polus, 'You are ever a *colt*'; and of the legislator Draco that his laws were 'not the laws of a human being, but of a *dragon*'—so cruel were they. So the Hecuba of Euripides [*Troades* 990] says of Aphrodite:

> And rightly the name of the goddess begins as
> does folly [*aphrosyne*].

And so Chaeremon [? in his *Dionysus*]:

> Pentheus, prophetic name of grief [*penthos*] to come.

Refutative Enthymemes are better liked than the Demonstrative, because the refutative kind brings out, in small compass, two opposing arguments, and the two things, side by side, are plainer to the audience. But of all syllogisms, whether refutative or demonstrative, those are most applauded of which we foresee the conclusion from the outset—so long as it is not too obvious, for part of our pleasure is at our own sagacity—or those that we just keep up with as they are stated.

A list of 9 *Topoi* of Sham Enthymemes

2. 24. [A List of Sham Enthymemes. Besides genuine arguments (the foregoing) which the honest speaker may use, there are spurious arguments which he must be prepared to meet.] Since the enthymeme is a kind of syllogism; and since there can be syllogisms that look genuine, but are not; it follows that, besides genuine enthymemes, there must be enthymemes that look genuine, but are spurious.

1401[a]

1. Diction

(1) Among the *topoi* of these Spurious Enthymemes the first is from the Diction; and under this head there are two sub-heads.

a. Structure of the diction

(*a*) In Dialectic a final statement can be made to pass for the conclusion of a logical process, when no such process has been performed: 'So it is not thus or thus'; 'So, too, it must be thus or thus.' Similarly, then, in Rhetoric a compact and antithetical sentence will pass for an enthymeme. This sort of language is the very habitat of the enthymeme, and it seems that the fallacy resides in the structure of the sentence. In giving their language the air of a logical process, speakers find it useful to summarize the results of a number of their previous arguments; thus [Isocrates (*Evagoras* 65–9)]: 'Some he saved'; 'others he avenged'; 'he liberated Greece.' Each of these points has been proved from something else; when they are brought together, it seems as if we had some novel conclusion.

(*b*) The second head is that of homonyms [equivocal terms, the same or similar names for different things]. Thus [Polycrates] says that the *mouse* is a noble creature, since it gives its name to the most august of all rites—the *Mys*teries—for such they are. Or you may put into the eulogy of a dog an allusion to the dog-star of heaven; or to Pan, on whom you may quote Pindar:

b. Homonyms

> Blest one, whom the gods of Olympus
> Call the manifold dog of Cybele;

or you may argue: 'Since it is a great shame to have no dog [*kuna*] in the house, plainly it is honorable to be a dog [i.e., a *Cynic*]. Another example is the statement that 'Hermes is the readiest of the gods to go shares [in communicating], for about no other god is there a phrase like "Go shares in Hermes' luck" ' [addressed to a lucky finder]. Another, that 'Speech [*logos*] is the best of things, since good men are not "worth money," but "worth esteem" ' [*logos*]; the phrase *logou axion* having more than one sense.

(2) Another *topos* consists in asserting of the whole what is true of the parts, or asserting of the parts what is true of the whole. A whole and a combination of its parts seem to be identical, but very often that is not the case. The procedure is to combine, or to disjoin, as may the better serve the purpose. This is the method of Euthydemus, when, for example, he argues: 'You know there is a trireme in the Peiraeus.' The man knows the details separately. [(?) You know there is a trireme; you know this in the Peiraeus.] Similar is the argument that one who knows the letters knows the whole verse, since the verse is the same thing as the letters which compose it; or again that, if a double dose of a thing is harmful, a single dose cannot be called wholesome, since it is absurd that two good things should make a bad one. Put thus, the enthymeme is refutative; put as follows, demonstrative:

2. Fallacious combination and separation

For one good thing cannot be made up of two bad things. The whole *topos* is fallacious. Take, again, the praise of Thrasybulus by Polycrates, that he 'put down thirty tyrants'; here the speaker adds up the parts. [—An illicit combination; Polycrates argued that Thrasybulus deserved thirty rewards, one for each tyrant.] Or take the argument in the *Orestes* of Theodectes; here you go from the part to the whole [—an illicit division]:

'T is right that whoso slays her spouse should die.

1401 b

'And it is right that a son should avenge his father. Well, then, these two things are what [Orestes] has done.' [But this is fallacious;] for perhaps the two put together do not form one right act. The fallacy might also be described as one of omission, since the speaker does not say by whose hand she [the mother who slays her husband] should die.

3. Indignation

(3) Another *topos* consists in the use of indignation, whether to support a case or to upset it. Such means are used when the speaker, without having proved his case, elaborates on the nature of the deed. If the defence thus amplifies, it produces the impression that the accused is innocent; if the prosecutor goes into a passion, it produces an impression that the accused is guilty. There is no genuine enthymeme; the listener falsely infers guilt or innocence; the fact has not been proved.

4. A 'sign'

(4) Another *topos* is from a 'sign' [a single instance, used as a logical proof]. Here, too, we have no logical argument. For example, suppose some one says: 'Lovers are useful to their countries; for the love of Harmodius and Aristogeiton caused the downfall of the tyrant Hipparchus.' [The single case does not prove the rule.] Or suppose that one calls Dionysius a thief 'because he is a rascal.' Here, too, we have no logical argument; not every rascal is a thief, though every thief is a rascal.

(5) Another *topos* is from the accidental, [treated as if it were essential]. Thus Polycrates says in his eulogy of mice that 'they came to the rescue' by gnawing through the [enemy's] bowstrings. Or one might urge that an invitation to dine is a very great honor, for [in Sophocles' *Assembly of the Greeks*] it was the lack of an invitation [from Agamemnon] that enraged Achilles against the Greeks at Tenedos. What really enraged him, however, was the slight; it was quite accidental that this took the shape of his not being invited to dinner.

5. The accidental

(6) Another *topos* is the fallacious argument from consequence. Thus in the *Apology for Paris* [of Polycrates] it is argued that Paris was high-minded, since he disdained the society of the crowd, and dwelt by himself on Mount Ida. Because men of lofty souls act thus, therefore we are to believe that Paris, too, was high-minded. Or, again, if a man goes smartly dressed, and roams about at night, he must be a rake, for such are the ways of rakes. A like argument is [the one on the happiness of beggars and exiles]: Beggars sing and dance in the temples; and exiles can live wherever they please; such liberties are enjoyed by those we account happy; and hence all who enjoy them may be regarded as happy. But there is a difference: How [under what circumstances do men enjoy them]? Accordingly, this *topos* also falls under the head of fallacies of omission.

6. Consequence

(7) Another *topos* consists in treating as a cause what is not a cause; for example, in taking what happened along with or before a thing as the cause of it. People assume *post hoc* to be *propter hoc*; and this is especially true of men in public life. Thus Demades said that the policy of Demosthenes was the cause of all the mischief; 'for after it came the war.'

7. *Post hoc* for *propter hoc*

(8) Another *topos* consists in omitting any reference to time and manner [the time when, and the circumstances under which, a thing was done]. Thus, [Polycrates

8. Time and manner

argues] that Paris had a right to take Helen, since her father left her free to choose [a husband]. [Here the element of time is neglected;] for she doubtless was not to be perpetually free—the permission concerned only her first choice, beyond which her father's authority did not extend. Or one might argue that to strike a free citizen is an act of wanton outrage; this is not true, however, in all circumstances—it is true only when the act is unprovoked.

1402a

9. Substituting the absolute for the particular

(9) Further, [in public speaking] as in 'eristical' combats, a spurious syllogism [enthymeme] may arise from a substitution of the absolute for what is not absolute but particular. Thus in Dialectic it may be argued that the non-existent *is*, since the non-existent *is* non-existent, and that the unknowable can be known, since we can know that it is unknown. [Here the universal statement, 'the unknowable can be known,' is substituted for the particular statement, 'the only thing we can know about the unknowable is that it cannot be known.'] Similarly, then, in Rhetoric a spurious enthymeme may arise from the confusion of particular probability with probability absolute; but the probability of a thing is not something universal. As Agathon holds:

> And some perchance will say 't is probable
> That many improbable things will happen to men.

Since what is against probability does occur, it follows that something improbable is likely to occur. If that is so, the improbable will be probable. [Here the fallacy lies in the fact that] probability is not something absolute. [The probability or improbability of an occurrence is not with regard to things in general, but with regard to specific antecedents.] As, in Eristic, it is the failure to add a limitation of relationship, of reference, or of manner, that does the trick, so here: the probability is not general, but specific. It is out of this *topos* [of the likely and unlikely] that the *Art of Rhetoric* of Corax is composed. For example, if the defendant is not open to the charge—if, say, a weakling is accused [by a strong man] of assault and battery—the defence will be: 'It is not probable.' But if the defendant—a strong man, say—is open to the charge, still the defence will be: 'It is not probable, for it was sure to be thought so.' [The strong man could be sure that people would think him likely to use violence.] And similarly with any other charge. [Whatever it be,] the defendant must either be open or not open to it; in either case, then, there is an apparent probability. In the first case, however, there *is* an actual probability; but in the second the probability is not absolute—it is, as we have said, particular. This [fallacious procedure of substituting the absolute] is what is meant by 'making the worse appear the better cause.' And therein lies the reason why people, rightly, could not abide the training advertised by Protagoras. The thing is a [logical] fraud; the probability concerned is not genuine but spurious, and has no place in any art except [mere] rhetoric and quibbling.

2. 25. [METHODS OF REFUTATION.] Having now described enthymemes, genuine and apparent, we have next to speak of their Refutation.

Refutation of Enthymemes

An argument may be refuted either by a counter-syllogism or by bringing an objection. As for the counter-syllogism, obviously it can be constructed from the same *topoi* as the original argument; for the sources are the ordinary opinions of men, and such opinions often contradict one another. Objections as we see in our treatise *On Topics* [cf. *Topics* 8. 10; *Prior Analytics* 2. 26], may be brought in four different ways: (1) you may attack your opponent's own premise; (2) you may adduce another premise like it; (3) you may adduce a premise contrary to it; (4) you may adduce previous decisions.

Counter-arguments

Objections

(1) By 'attacking a premise of your opponent' is

meant such a procedure as follows. Suppose his enthy- 1402b meme to argue that 'All love is good.' Then your objection can be brought in two ways; you may either make the general statement that 'All want is an evil,' or the particular statement that 'If there were not evil loves as well as good, there would be no such proverb as "Caunian love"' [the incestuous passion of Byblis for her brother Caunus].

(2 [=3]) As an instance of an objection from a contrary premise, suppose the enthymeme to have been: 'The good man does good to all his friends.' You object: 'No, the bad man does not do evil to all his friends.'

(3 [=2]) As an instance of adducing another premise like your opponent's, suppose his enthymeme to have been: 'Victims always hate those who have ill-used them.' You object: 'No, men who have been well-treated do not always like their benefactors.'

(4) The decisions available for objections are those of well-known men. Suppose your opponent's enthymeme to have been: 'Some allowance must be made for drunken offenders, since they did not know what they were doing.' You object: 'Then [the wise] Pittacus is no authority, or he would not have prescribed heavier penalities for crimes committed when the offenders were drunk.'

Enthymemes are derived from four sources; these are: (1) Probabilities, (2) Examples, (3) Infallible Signs, (4) Ordinary [fallible] Signs.

(1) Enthymemes taken from Probabilities are those which argue from what as a rule is or is thought to be true. (2) Enthymemes taken from Examples are those which proceed by induction from one or more parallel cases until the speaker abstracts a general rule, from which he then argues to the case in point. (3) Enthymemes taken from Infallible Signs are those which proceed from what is necessarily and invariably true. (4) Enthymemes taken from Fallible Signs are those

which proceed from what is generally or partly true—possibly so, possibly not.

Probabilities

(1) Now since the Probable is that which happens as a rule but not always, it is clear that enthymemes taken from Probabilities are always open to refutation; that is, you may raise an objection to them, though the objection is not always valid, but may be spurious; for the objector can refute a conclusion by showing, not that it is not probable, but that it is not inevitable. Thus it is always possible to gain an unfair advantage by the use of this fallacy. Yet the advantage lies rather with the defence than with the accusation; for the accuser uses probabilities to prove his case, and refuting a conclusion as not probable is a different matter from refuting it as not inevitable. Any conclusion from what happens as a rule is open to objection—otherwise the thing would not be a probability but an invariable and necessary truth. But if the refutation is made thus [if the conclusion is shown to be not necessary], the judges think either that the accuser's case is not probable, or that they are not warranted in deciding that it *is* probable—reasoning falsely, as we have said. The truth is, they must decide, not from necessary conclusions alone, but on grounds of probability as well. This, in fact, is what is meant by 'a verdict in accordance with their best judgment' [1. 15, p. 80]. Therefore it is not enough if the defendant shows that the charge is not necessarily true; he must refute it by showing that it is not likely to be true. Now this can be done if his objection states something more generally true [than is the point in the accusation]. And the objection may be more generally true in two ways: either with respect to time, or with respect to details. [Cope, *Introduction*, p. 274, explains: 'If you can make out that there is more analogy in the ordinary course of events for your account of the case in respect of the time and circumstances of it, your account of it is more probable than that of the accuser.']

The objection will be most effective if it satisfies both [these conditions of time and details]; for if a majority of instances are in our favor, the balance of probability will be on our side.

1403a

Fallible Signs

(2) Fallible Signs, and the enthymemes which employ them, can be refuted, even if the facts are correct, as was said at the outset [1. 2, p. 14]; for we have shown in the [*Prior*] *Analytics* [2. 27] that no Fallible Sign can enter into a strictly logical proof.

Examples

(3) Enthymemes depending upon Examples may be refuted in the same way as those depending upon Probabilities. A single negative instance on our side will disprove the conclusion of our opponent, so far as concerns its necessity, even though a majority of instances or the usual course of things is against us. If these are both against us, we must contend that the present case is unlike the rest in its nature or conditions, or at least presents some point or other of difference.

Infallible Signs

(4) Infallible Signs, and enthymemes taken from them, cannot be refuted on the ground that they are logically inconclusive; this, too, we have shown in the [*Prior*] *Analytics* [2. 27]. Our only resource is to prove that the fact alleged does not exist. If there is no doubt about the fact, and no doubt that it is an Infallible Sign, refutation is no longer possible; for this amounts to a complete and manifest demonstration.

2. 26. [Supplementary Remarks.] Magnifying and Minifying do not constitute merely an elementary form of enthymeme—and by this is meant the same thing as a *topos*. ('Elementary form' and *topos* signify a class into which many particular enthymemes fall.) Magnifying and minifying are a kind of enthymeme—the kind which tends to show that a thing is great or small. So there are enthymemes to show that a thing is good or bad, just or unjust, or the like; all these things are the subject-matter

Two possible errors

of syllogisms and enthymemes; none of them is the *topos* of an enthymeme. Accordingly, neither do magnifying and minifying constitute a *topos*.

Nor are Destructive Enthymemes a different species from Constructive; for it is clear that refutation consists either in offering positive proof or in raising an objection. In the first case you prove the opposite [of your adversary's statements]. Thus, if he shows that a thing has happened, you show that it has not, and *vice versa*. The distinction, then, if there were one, could not lie here. The same means are employed on both sides; enthymemes are advanced to show that the facts are, or are not, such and such. An objection, on the other hand, is not an enthymeme at all; rather, as we have said in our treatise *On Topics* [cf. *Topics* 8. 10], it consists in stating some accepted opinion, from which it shall appear that our opponent has not reasoned correctly, or has made a false assumption.

The provinces of study which concern the making of a speech are three. Of these we have now adequately treated the first, having discussed (1) Examples, Maxims, and Enthymemes, and the element of thought in general —the way to invent and refute arguments. We have yet to consider (2) Style and (3) Arrangement. *1403b*

BOOK 3

3. 1. [STYLE.] The provinces of study which concern the making of a speech are three: (1) the means of effecting persuasion; (2) the style [language, diction]; (3) the right ordering of the several divisions of the whole. We have already dealt with the sources of persuasion, and have shown that they are three in number [1. 2, pp. 8–11]. We have explained their nature, and have shown why there are but these three; for we have seen that persuasion can be effected only (1) by working on the emotions of the audience [judges], or (2) by giving the audience the right impression of the speaker's character, or (3) by convincing them all with proof.

Enthymemes have also been discussed, with the sources from which they must be derived, these sources being either the special or the common *topoi* for enthymemes.

[Books 1 and 2 deal with the first of the three provinces of study. We come, then, to the second—that is, *lexis*, the way in which the thoughts of the speaker are expressed; by *lexis* is meant everything that has to do with expression—choice of words, syntax, and delivery.]

Style (= *Lexis*, Diction)

We have next to treat of Diction [i.e., Style, and the like]; since it is not enough to know *what* to say—one must also know *how* to say it. The right way of doing this contributes much to the right impression of a speech. It was natural that we should first investigate the subject which comes first in the natural order—the facts themselves as a source of persuasion. But next comes the question, how to state [set out] these facts in language. A third question would touch the art of correct delivery; for success in delivery is of the utmost importance to the

Delivery

effect of a speech. [In Rhetoric,] however, the subject hitherto has been neglected; [nor is this surprising,] for not until late did the art of delivery make its way into the arts of tragedy and epic recitation, since at first the poets themselves delivered their own tragedies. [And the epic poets recited their own poems; so that the technique of professional actors and rhapsodists necessarily was a later development.] Now, plainly, for the art of rhetoric delivery is of as much concern as it is for the art of poetry, in connection with which it has been treated by various persons, including Glaucon of Teos. The art of delivery has to do with the voice: with the right management of it to express each several emotion—as when to use a loud voice, when a soft, and when the intermediate; with the mode of using pitch—high, low, and intermediate; and with the rhythms to be used in each particular case. These are, in fact, the three things that receive attention: volume, modulation of pitch, and rhythm. And it is contestants who look after these points that commonly win the prizes in the poetical competitions; further, just as there the performers now count for more than the authors, so is it with the delivery of speeches in the contests of public life—because of our corrupt institutions. [That is, here delivery exerts more influence than the substance of the speech.] Yet so far we have no systematic treatise on delivery in public speaking; and the reason is that the whole subject of style [utterance, *lexis*] was late in coming to the front; moreover, in a fine perspective, delivery is regarded as something vulgar. Still, the whole affair of Rhetoric is the impression [to be made upon an audience]; and hence delivery must be cared for, not on grounds of justice, but as something we are bound to do. Strict justice, of course, would lead us, in speaking, to seek no more [of an emotional effect] than that we should avoid paining the hearer without alluring him; the case should, in justice, be fought on the

The voice in delivery

1404[a]

strength of the facts alone, so that all else besides demonstration of fact is superfluous. Nevertheless, as we have said, external matters do count for much, because of the sorry nature of an audience. Meanwhile attention to style necessarily has some real, if minor, importance in every kind of exposition; it does make a difference in the clearness of an exposition whether you put a thing in this way or that—and yet not so much difference as people think, since all these devices of style and the like are of the imagination, and meant for the ear. No one uses them in teaching mathematics!

Well, then, when rhetorical delivery comes to be studied, it will have the same effect as the art of acting has had on the drama; hitherto, only slight progress has been made, by some few, towards dealing with it, as by Thrasymachus in his *Rules of Pathos* [*Eleoi*]. The capacity for acting is, indeed, a natural gift, and hardly within the province of art, save in respect to the diction. To diction artistic principles may be applied; and hence, again, we find able writers who win prizes [that is, through artistic management of the diction], just as prizes are won by declaimers who excel in delivery; for the written compositions owe more of their effect to their diction than to their thought.

Prose and poetic diction

It was the poets, naturally, who gave the first impulse [toward the cultivation of style]; for words represent [imitate] things, and the poets had also the human voice, which of all our organs can best imitate. Thus the arts of epic recitation and acting were fashioned, and more besides. And since the poets were thought to have won their fame by their fine language, when their thoughts were not profound, so the language of prose at first took on a poetical cast—for example, that of Gorgias. Even now the uneducated mostly think such discourses very fine. But it is not so. On the contrary, the language of prose is distinct from that of poetry. We can see this from what has happened in tragedy, where the poets no longer follow the old method. As they passed from the use of tetrameters to an iambic measure, because this, of all metres, most resembles ordinary discourse, so they have discarded all those words, not in idiomatic use, which the early poets employed for ornament, and which even to-day are so employed by the writers of hexameter verse [in the epic style]. Accordingly, it is absurd to imitate the poets in a fashion which the poets themselves have dropped. And so it is obvious that we need not enter minutely into the whole subject of style; we have only to discuss so much of it as concerns our present interest [namely, Rhetoric]. The other kind of style is treated in the *Poetics* [20–22].

3. 2 [THE QUALITIES OF STYLE.] We may therefore assume the general observations of the *Poetics*, and regard it as settled that a good style is, first of all, clear. The proof is that language which does not convey a clear meaning fails to perform the very function of language. The style, again, should be neither mean nor above the dignity of the subject, but appropriate; the poetical style, say, is not mean, but it is unsuited to prose. Clearness is secured through the use of name-words [=nouns and adjectives] and, verbs, that are current terms; freedom from meanness, and actual embellishment, through the use of the other terms mentioned in the *Poetics* [21–22]. These deviations from ordinary usage make the style more impressive. Words are like men; as we feel a difference between people from afar and our fellow townsmen, so is it with our feeling for language. And hence it is well to give the ordinary idiom an air of remoteness; the hearers are struck by what is out of the way, and like what strikes them. In verse there are many things to produce this effect, and to verse they are fitting; for there the subject-matter—both things and persons—is more remote

1404[b]

The style should be clear

And appropriate

Current terms

Deviations from ordinary usage

from daily life. But in prose such devices are far less often to be used, since the subjects are humbler. Even in poetry, it is hardly appropriate if fine language is used by a slave or a very young man, or for very trivial matters; even in poetry, the language, if it is to be appropriate, must rise and fall with the subject. Thus we see the necessity of disguising the means we employ, so that we may seem to be speaking, not with artifice, but naturally. Naturalness is persuasive, artifice just the reverse. People grow suspicious of an artificial speaker, and think he has designs upon them—as if some one were mixing drinks for them. The difference is illustrated by the effect of Theodorus' voice as against the voices of all other actors; his seems to be the actual voice of the person he represents, and the other voices sound like voices assumed. In style, the illusion is successful if we take our individual words from the current stock, and put them together [with skill]. That is what Euripides does, and he led the way to this style.

Language is composed of name-words [=nouns and adjectives] and verbs. And name-words are of the various kinds we observed in the *Poetics* [21]; of these, the speaker should use rare words, compound words, and coined words, but sparingly and seldom. On what occasions they may be used we shall state by and by; why they should be sparingly used has already been explained —they diverge too far from custom toward the extreme of excess. In the language of spoken prose, only the current term, the distinctive name, and metaphors can be used to advantage; we so infer because these, and these alone, are what every one uses in ordinary conversation. Every one does use metaphors, as well as distinctive names and current terms. So it is plain that good composition will have an air of novelty [remoteness], while the art can escape notice and the style is clear. And this, as we saw [3. 2, p. 185], is the character of good oratorical prose. [Compare Lincoln's 'Fourscore and seven years ago our fathers brought forth': 'brought forth' is a metaphor; 'fathers' a distinctive name; the remaining words, individually, are current terms; the combination has an air of novelty or remoteness—but the art escapes notice; and the whole is clear.] Homonyms [equivocal terms] are useful specially to the sophist—with these he juggles and misleads; synonyms, to the poet. By synonyms that are in current use I mean such words as 'going' and 'walking,' which are at once accepted [=current] and synonymous terms.

1405ᵃ

Metaphor

In the *Poetics*, as we have said, these various kinds of words have been explained, and metaphors classified. And there it is stated that metaphor is of the utmost value in both poetry and prose [*Poetics*, end of chapter 22]. But in prose all the more attention must be devoted to metaphors because here the resources of the writer are less abundant than in verse. It is metaphor above all else that gives clearness, charm, and distinction to the style; and the use of it cannot be learned from without [—cf. *Poetics, ibid.*] The speaker must find epithets and metaphors alike that are fitting; their appropriateness will arise from the correspondence [proportion, between epithet or metaphor and the thing to which it is applied]. Otherwise the impropriety will be glaring; the disproportion between contrary terms is most evident when they are put side by side. Instead, we must search thus: a crimson cloak befits a young man; what dress befits an old one? The same clothing is not appropriate to both. And if you aim to adorn a thing, you must take your metaphor from something better in its class; if to disparage, then from something worse. For example: since opposites belong to the same class [genus], you may do what has just been mentioned if you say that the man who begs 'prays,' or that the man who prays 'begs'; for begging and praying are both forms of asking. So Iphicrates called

Proportional metaphor

Callias a 'mendicant priest' instead of a 'torch-bearer'; and Callias replied that Iphicrates must be uninitiated, or he would not call him a 'mendicant priest,' but a 'torch-bearer.' Both titles have to do with religion, but the one is honorable, and the other base. Again, some one calls actors 'parasites of Bacchus'; they call themselves 'artists.' Each of these terms is a metaphor—the one abusive, the other ennobling. So pirates nowadays call themselves 'purveyors' [compare Pistol (*Merry Wives of Windsor* 1. 3. 30) on the word 'steal': ' "Convey" the wise it call']; and by the same rule one may describe crime as error, error as crime, and stealing as either 'taking' something or 'plundering' a victim. An expression such as Telephus uses in the play of Euripides—

> Lord of the oar, on the Mysian coast having landed—

Inappropriate metaphors

is inappropriate; the word 'lording' is too dignified for the subject—so that the art is unconcealed. A metaphor, again, may miss the mark by reason of its syllables, when the sound that is suggested is unpleasing; thus Dionysius 'the Brazen' in his elegies calls poetry 'Calliope's clamor.' True, poetry and clamor [screaming] both fall under the head of vocal sounds; but the metaphor is bad, because 'clamor' suggests unintelligible discord. Further, the metaphors by which we give names to nameless things must not be far-fetched; rather we must draw them from kindred and similar things; the kinship must be seen the moment the words are uttered—as in the popular riddle:

Riddles are metaphorical

1405[b]

> A man I saw gluing bronze on a man with fire.

The operation lacks a name; but both it and gluing are in the nature of an application, and that is why the riddler called the application of the cupping-instrument 'gluing.' Clever riddles do, in general, furnish one with happy metaphors; for metaphor is a kind of enigma, so that

Sources of metaphor

obviously a metaphor taken from a good enigma will be good. Again, a metaphor must be derived from something beautiful; and the beauty of a word, or its ugliness, as Licymnius [in his *Art of Rhetoric*] says, will lie either in the sound or in the sense. And there is yet a third consideration—one that upsets Bryson's sophistical argument that there is no such thing as foul language; he said it made no difference what words you employed so long as you meant one and the same thing. But that is false. One word may come closer than another to the thing described, may be more like it, and, being more akin to it, may set it more distinctly before our eyes. Further, two different words will not signify the same thing in the same light; so on this ground, too, one term must be regarded as fairer or fouler than another. Both words may denote something fair, or both may denote something foul; but not simply as it is fair or foul [—the associations of two words will hardly be the same], or, if so, not fair or foul to the same degree. Our metaphors must be drawn from the province of things that are beautiful in sound, or in effect, or to sight or some other of the senses. It makes a difference whether we say, for instance, 'rosy-fingered morn' [*Iliad* 1. 477, etc.], or 'purple-fingered,' or, still worse, 'red-fingered.'

Epithets

As for epithets, they, too, may be formed from the bad and ugly side of a thing—as 'Orestes the matricide'; or from the better aspect—as 'the avenger of his sire' [cf. Euripides, *Orestes* 1587–8]. Thus Simonides, when the victor in the mule-race offered him a small fee for an ode, declined to write one—'did not care to write poetry about *half-asses*'; but on receiving a proper fee, he wrote:

> All hail, ye daughters of storm-footed mares!

Diminutives

(Yet they *were* the daughters of asses, too!) The same effect is attained by the use of diminutives; the diminutive makes a bad thing less bad, a good thing less good.

See, for example, the banter of Aristophanes in the *Babylonians*, where he uses 'goldlet' for *gold*, 'cloaklet' for *cloak*, 'curselet' for *curse*, and 'poxlet.' But in the use of epithets and diminutives alike we must be on our guard, and never lose sight of the golden mean.

Faults of of taste (=frigidities)

3. 3. [Four Faults of Style. From excellences of style we pass to defects—(1) the misuse of compound words, (2) the use of strange words, (3) mistakes in the use of epithets, and (4) bad figures of speech (metaphors and similes).]

1. Compound words

Bad taste in style has four sources. (1) The first is the misuse of compound words. Thus Lycophron speaks of 'the *many-visaged* heaven' above 'the *giant-peaked* earth,' and of 'the *narrow-pathed* headland'; and Gorgias of

1406[a]

a '*beggar-poet-toady,*' and of 'men forsworn or *over-veracious.*' So also the phrases of Alcidamas: 'his soul with passion filling, his face with *flame-flush* kindling,' and 'he thought their zeal would prove *end-executing,*' and '*end-executing* he made his words' persuasiveness,' and '*steel-dark* is the floor of the sea.' All these phrases, from the way in which they are compounded, seem too poetical. This, then, is one source of bad taste.

2. Strange words

(2) Another is the employment of strange words [=archaic, obsolete, alien]. Thus, with Lycophron, Xerxes is a 'vasty' man, and Sciron a 'baleful' man; and Alcidamas speaks of 'a *gawd* [toy, bagatelle] for poetry,' and of 'the *witlessness* of his nature,' and says, '*whetted* with the *heady* anger of his thought.'

3. Epithets

(3) A third source lies in the use of long, or untimely, or crowded epithets. In poetry it is fitting enough to say 'white milk'; but in prose such epithets are less appropriate; and when used to excess they betray the artifice, and we see that the author grows poetical. There is, of course, some need of epithets; they diversify the usual idiom, and give our language an air of distinction. But

we must aim ever at the golden mean, for using too many epithets works more harm than does sheer carelessness about them; neglect does no good, but excess brings a positive evil. That is why the epithets of Alcidamas leave us so cold; he does not use them as sauce for the meat, but as the meat itself, so crowded and prolix and obtrusive are they. For instance, he does not say 'sweat,' but 'the *moist* sweat'; not 'to the Isthmian games,' but 'to *the general assembly* of the Isthmian games'; nor yet 'laws,' but 'laws *the rulers of states*'; not 'with a rush,' but 'with *a rushing impulse from within*, taking captive,' not 'a haunt of the Muses,' but '*Great Nature's* haunt of the Muses.' Again he says: 'the thought of his soul *sullen-visaged*'; 'the *demiurge*,' not 'of gratification,' but 'of *universal* gratification,' the '*general steward* of pleasure to his audience'; 'he [? Odysseus] hid,' not 'with boughs,' but 'with boughs *of the forest*,' and '*veiled*,' not 'his body,' but '*his body's nakedness*.' And again: '*counter-mimic* is the heart's desire' (the word is at once a compound and an epithet, so that here we get poetry); and '*so outflying* is the excess of his villainy.' We thus see how this poetical diction by its inappropriateness injects absurdity and bad taste into speeches, while it makes them obscure, too, through its wordiness; for when a matter is plain, piling up words only dissolves the clearness and beclouds the sense.

Compound words

The ordinary use of compound words is this: when there is no word for a thing, and the combination is readily made, people form a compound—as *chrono-tribein* ['pass-time' = *pastime*]. but if the practice is abused, the effect is entirely poetical. Accordingly, the language of compounds is especially useful to writers of dithyrambs, who love mouth-filling phrases; while rare words are most useful to epic poets, for their works are lofty and austere; and metaphor is most useful in iambic verse, which, as we noted above [3. 1, p. 185], is now employed for tragedy.

1406[b]

4. Metaphor

(4) The fourth and last cause of bad taste lies in metaphor; for metaphors, too, may be inappropriate. Some are so because they are ridiculous—for comic poets use metaphors to this end. Others are too grand, too much in the vein of tragedy, and, if far-fetched, are obscure. Thus Gorgias speaks of 'events that are fresh and full of blood,' and says: 'In shame you sowed, in misery reaped'—which is too poetical. And so Alcidamas calls philosophy 'a bulwark of the laws,' and the *Odyssey* 'a mirror fair of human life,' and talks of 'offering no such gawd [toy, bauble] to poetry.' All these expressions are unconvincing, for the reasons we have just given. As for Gorgias' address to the swallow flying overhead, when she let her droppings fall on him—'For shame, O Philomela!'—it is in the best tragic manner. If done by a bird, the act would not be shameful; it would be shameful in a maiden; and so it was a good joke to abuse her, not as she is, but as she once was.

Similes

3. 4. [Similes; their Use and Formation.] The simile also is a metaphor; the difference is but slight. When Homer says of Achilles [cf. *Iliad* 20. 164],

He sprang at the foe as a lion,

that is a simile. When he says of him, 'The lion sprang at them,' it is a metaphor; here, since both are courageous, the poet has transferred the name of 'lion' to Achilles. Similes are useful in prose as well as in verse, but must be sparingly used, for they are poetical. They are to be employed in the same way as metaphors, from which they differ only in the point just mentioned.

Examples of simile

The following are examples of the simile. Androtion said of Idrieus [when the latter came out of prison] that he was 'like curs let off the chain—they fly at you and bite'; so Idrieus, freed from his bonds, was savage. Theodamas, again, said that Archidamus was 'like Euxenus—

minus his knowledge of geometry'; this is a proportional simile, and the other way round we have Euxenus as an Archidamus *plus* his knowledge of geometry [—each of them being an ignoramus]. In the *Republic* of Plato [5. 469 E] those who strip the dead are compared to curs 'that bite the stones thrown at them, but do not molest the thrower'; and there is the simile [*Republic* 6. 488 A] in which the people of Athens are likened to 'the captain of a ship, who is strong but a little deaf'; and the one [cf. *ibid.* 10. 601 B] about the verses of poets, which are likened to persons who have the bloom of youth without beauty of features—when the bloom has passed, the charm is gone, and similarly with verses when resolved into prose. Pericles likened the Samians [after alleged benefits from Athens] to children who take the sweetmeat and keep on crying; and the Boeotians to oaks, 'for as oak is shattered by oak [in a storm], so the Boeotians are ruining one another by their civil strife.' Demosthenes said that the Athenian people were like sea-sick passengers on board ship. And Democrates likened the political orators to 'nurses who gobble the bonbon themselves, while they slobber the children with kisses.' Again, Antisthenes said that the meagre Cephisodotus was 'like frankincense'—because 'he gives pleasure by wasting away.' All these comparisons may be expressed either as similes or as metaphors; those that do well as metaphors can obviously be turned into good similes; and you can turn the similes into metaphors by omitting the words of comparison. But the 'proportional' metaphor [or simile] must always be capable of reciprocal transference, and to either of its co-ordinate terms. For instance, if a bowl is the 'shield of Dionysus,' then a shield may fittingly be called the 'bowl of Ares.' [The proportion is: As the shield is to Ares, so is the wine-bowl (a shallow disk) to Dionysus. Two co-ordinate terms (for things of the same class) are *shield* and *bowl*; and the other two, Ares and

1407a

Dionysus. If the criss-cross transference cannot be made (this being the test), then the metaphor or simile is not good.]

Purity

3. 5. [STYLISTIC PURITY; UNDER FIVE HEADS.] Such, then, are the component elements of language. The foundation of good style is correct idiom; and this purity of language depends upon five things. (1) First, the correct use of connective words [particles and the like], and the arrangement of them in the natural sequence which some of them require. Thus, for example, μέν (as in ἐγὼ μέν) requires δέ (as in ὁ δέ) to follow in correlation. The answering particle must be brought in before the one it echoes is forgotten; no long dependent clause should intervene, nor should another connective appear, before the answering one required; at least this is seldom proper. Take, for example: 'But I, as soon as he had told me (for Cleon came both begging and insisting), set out accompanied by them.' Here many connectives are introduced before the word required to complete the sense of 'But I'; if there is a long interval before 'set out,' the sentence is obscure. One element, then, of an excellent style is the right use of connectives [—the right arrangement and connection of words and clauses.] (2) The second is the use of specific words, rather than [vague] general terms. (3) The third is the avoidance of ambiguous language; unless, indeed, you really prefer to be ambiguous—as do those who have nothing to say, but pretend that they have something in mind. Writers of this sort will put the thing into verse, as Empedocles did. With his long circumlocutions he imposes on us, and listeners are affected as the crowd is affected by diviners; when the diviners deliver their ambiguous utterances, the crowd nods assent. [So Croesus (Herodotus 1. 53, 91) acquiesced in the utterance of the oracle]:

1. Connectives

2. Specific terms

3. Avoidance of ambiguity

Croesus by crossing the Halys will ruin a mighty empire.

Diviners employ these general terms because thereby they are less likely to be mistaken in the event; just as we are more likely to guess right in the game of 'Odd or even?' if we say 'even' or 'odd' than if we guess at the actual number. So it is safer to say that a thing *will be* than to state *when*; and that is why the soothsayers will not supply their predictions with a date. All ambiguities have the same effect—vagueness; and hence, save when we aim at some such effect, ambiguity is to be avoided. (4) The fourth thing [on which purity of style depends is gender]; we must observe the classification of name-words by Protagoras into masculine, feminine, and neuter, and, here too, must make form correctly answer to form. Thus: 'Having come and spoken [=feminine participles], she went her way.' (5) The fifth thing is number; multitude, fewness [? = duality], and unity, must be correctly expressed. [The concords, for example, between plural noun and plural verb, must be preserved.] Thus: 'Having come [=plural participle], they struck me.'

1407b

4. Gender

5. Number

It is a general rule that a composition should be easy to read or—which is the same thing—easy to deliver. Such will not be the case where we have many connectives and clauses, or where punctuation is hard, as it is in the writings of Heraclitus. And a task it is to punctuate this writer, when you cannot tell whether a given word belongs with what precedes or what comes after it. Take, for example, the beginning of his treatise, where he says: 'Although this divine reason exists ever witless are men concerning it.' Here you cannot tell whether 'ever' should go with 'exists' or with 'witless are men.' Further, a solecism is produced by the want of agreement if you annex to a pair of terms a third term which does not fit them both. With a sound and a color, for instance, the word 'seeing' should not be used; 'perceive' will apply to both. Obscurity also results if you do not state your meaning

Pauses and punctuation

Zeugma

Suspended meaning

at the outset, when you intend to insert a number of details; for instance, if you say: 'I intended, after telling him this and that, and so forth, to go my way'—instead of: 'I intended to speak to him and go, and then this or that came up, and so forth.'

Impressiveness (dignity)

3. 6. [IMPRESSIVENESS; UNDER SIX HEADS.] We now turn to impressiveness of style. The following rules will help to secure it. (1) Describe an object instead of naming it; saying, for instance, not 'circle,' but 'a plane figure at all points equidistant from the centre.' If you aim at conciseness, you must do the reverse, using the name instead of the description. And if you have to mention anything foul or indecent [cf. 3. 2, p. 189], use the name when the description is objectionable, and the description when the trouble is in the name. (2) Use metaphors and epithets for vividness, being careful to avoid a poetical effect. (3) Use the plural for the singular, as do the poets—who say:

To harbors Achaean,

though only one harbor is meant; and [Euripides, *Iphigenia in Tauris* 727]:

Here the many-leaved folds of the tablet,

[though all that is meant is a letter.] (4) Avoid linking up two words with one article—use the article with each; thus: τῆς γυναικὸς τῆς ἡμετέρας. But in concise writing do so link them: τῆς ἡμετέρας γυναικός. (5) Use connecting particles; or, for the concise style, omit them, while yet avoiding disjunction; thus, respectively: 'Having gone and spoken,' and 'Having gone, I spoke.' (6) Another useful device is that of Antimachus—to describe a thing in terms of what it is not; Antimachus employs the method in describing Teumessus:

1408ᵃ

There is a wind-swept hill, not large . . .

[And so on. This line is but a memorandum for a longer passage (now lost) in his *Thebaid.* Compare St. Paul's use of negative expressions in his praise of charity (1 Cor. 13); so also the description of a paradise, in the Old English *Phoenix* (lines 14–20, translated by Cook): 'There neither rain, nor snow, nor breath of frost, nor blaze of fire, nor downpour of hail, nor fall of hoar-frost, nor heat of sun, nor ever-during cold, nor warm weather, nor winter shower, works aught of harm; but unscathed and flourishing the plain ever abides.'] This mode of amplification has no limit. It may be applied either to the good qualities or the bad—whichever way suits your turn—which your subject does not possess. By this method of deprivation the poets form negative epithets such as 'stringless' and 'lyreless'—'*stringless* melody,' '*lyreless* melody.' The device is effective in proportional metaphors [cf. 3. 4, p. 193], as when the blast of a trumpet is called a 'lyreless melody.'

3. 7. [Propriety.] We turn to propriety. Your language will be appropriate, if it expresses (1) emotion and (2) character, and if it is (3) in proportion with the subject. By proportion is meant that weighty matters shall not be treated in a slipshod way, nor trivial matters in a solemn way; nor should ornamental epithets be attached to commonplace nouns, or the effect will be comic, as in the poetry of Cleophon. He used phrases as absurd as it would be to say 'O Lady Fig-tree!'

Appropriate language

1. Proportion

For emotion, if the subject be wanton outrage, your language will be that of anger; if you speak of impiety or filth, use the language of aversion and reluctance even to discuss them; if of praiseworthy deeds, the language of admiration; if of piteous things, that of dejection; and similarly for the other emotional states. The appropriateness of your language to the emotion will make people believe in your facts. In their souls they infer, illegiti-

2. Emotion

mately, that you are telling the truth, because they, in a like situation, would be moved in the same way as you are; accordingly, even when the facts are not as the speaker says, the audience think he is right. Indeed, they are always in sympathy with an emotional speaker even when there is nothing in what he says; and that is why many an orator tries to stun the audience with sound and fury.

3. Dramatic characterization

But, further, this display of the facts through these external signs will make your style appropriate to character [to the persons of your story], since each class of men, each type of disposition, has a language suited to it. Under 'class' I distinguish differences of age, as boy, man, or old man; of sex, as man or woman; of nationality, as Spartan or Thessalian. Under 'dispositions' I refer to those habits only which determine the character of a man's life—for not every habit does this. Accordingly, if the speaker uses the words which belong to a type of life, he will reproduce its character; for a rustic will not say the same things as an educated man, nor talk in the same way. (To a certain extent an audience will be impressed by a device which speech-writers use to nauseous excess: 'Who does not know . . .?' 'We all know . . . ' The hearer, ashamed to be ignorant, agrees to the fact, so as to have his part in the common knowledge.)

1408b

Seasonable use of stylistic devices

There is an opportune use, and an inopportune, for all these rules of style. A corrective for every excess is the time-worn trick of self-criticism while you are speaking; the audience thinks that the style is right since the speaker evidently knows what he is doing. Further, it is best not to keep all the proportions going at once, or the hearer will not be deceived. [—He will see your artfulness, and be on his guard.] I mean, for instance, if your words are harsh, it is better not to make your voice harsh, too, and your features harsh, and have everything else in keeping. If you do, each several detail is seen to be an artifice; whereas, if you keep one proportion, and disregard another, you achieve your end, yet the art is not detected. (Of course, if mild words are uttered in a harsh voice, or harsh words in a mild voice, the result is unconvincing.) Compound words, fairly plentiful epithets, and strange words best suit an emotional speaker; an angry man will be excused for calling a wrong 'heaven-high' or 'colossal.' [The second (*pelōrion*) is a 'strange' or 'rare' word.] And we accept such language, once a speaker has his audience in hand, and has thoroughly roused them with praise or blame to love or anger. This is done by Isocrates at the end of his *Panegyricus* [186]: 'O the name and the fame!' And similarly [*ibid.* 96], 'in that they stood fast.' Men actually use such language when they are roused to enthusiasm, so they obviously will accept it from a speaker, once they are in a like state of emotion. That is why it was found fitting in poetry, for poetry is a thing inspired. This style, then, should be used thus [i.e., for legitimate emotion], or else ironically, after the fashion of Gorgias and of the passages [238 D, 241 E] in the *Phaedrus* of Plato.

Rhythm

3. 8. [PROSE RHYTHM.] The pattern [*schema*] of the diction should be neither metrical nor devoid of rhythm. A metrical structure makes the hearer distrustful by its manifest artifice, and at the same time distracts his attention, making him watch for the recurrence of the beat. Just so the children anticipate the answer to the herald's cry, 'Whóm does the freédman choóse for his ádvocate,' bawling out 'Cléon!' On the other hand, if the style has no rhythm, it is unconfined; and it should have some limit (though not the limitations of metre), or the effect will be vague and unpleasing, as the indefinite always is. Now it is number that limits all things, and for the pattern of prose, number means rhythm, of which metres are so many sections. Accordingly, prose should be rhythmical,

but not metrical, or we shall have, not prose, but verse. Its rhythm, however, must not be too precise—must be carried so far and no farther.

The rhythm of epic poetry

Of the various rhythms, the heroic has dignity, but lacks the cadence of the spoken language. The iambic is the characteristic rhythm of people as they talk, so that in ordinary conversation iambic feet recur more often than any others; but in a speech we need dignity, and the hearer must be stirred from his usual self. The trochaic rhythm, again, is too much akin to the comic dance, as may be seen in tetrameter verse, for the rhythm of tetrameters is light and tripping.

Iambic rhythm

Trochaic

1409a

The paeon

There remains the paeon, which speakers began to use in the time of Thrasymachus, though none of them could define it. Now this third rhythm, the paeon, is closely allied to the other two we have mentioned. [That is, it is allied to the dactyl or spondee (—⏑⏑ or ——) and to the iamb or trochee (⏑— or —⏑).] Its ratio is 3:2, while the ratio of one of them [dactyl or spondee] is 1:1, and that of the other [iamb or trochee] is 2:1. Between these last two ratios [$\frac{1}{1}$ and $\frac{2}{1}$] comes the ratio of $1\frac{1}{2}:1$ [$=\frac{3}{2}$]; and this represents the paeon. [Each of the other two has a ratio, then, properly considered, while the paeon has not. They are in the strict sense metrical; it is not, though it has much in common with them.] In prose, accordingly, the other two kinds of rhythm must be discarded, partly for the reasons given [in the paragraph before this], and partly because they are strictly metrical; and the paeon must be adopted, since from this alone of the rhythms no definite metre arises, and since it therefore least of all attracts notice. At present the same type of paeon is used at the beginning as at the end of a sentence; but the end ought to differ from the beginning. There are, however, two opposite types of paeon, one of which is suitable at the beginning of a sentence, where indeed it is actually used; this is the type which consists of a long syllable followed by three short ones:

– ⏑ ⏑ ⏑ – ⏑ ⏑⏑
Δαλογενὲς |εἴτε Λυκί|αν
(O Delos-born, or if perchance Lycia [thou callest thy birthplace]).

Or:

– ⏑ ⏑ ⏑ – ⏑ ⏑ ⏑
Χρυσεοκό|μα Ἕκατε |παῖ Διός
(Golden-haired Archer, Child of Zeus!)

The other type, conversely, begins with three short syllables, and ends with a long one:

⏑ ⏑ ⏑ – ⏑ ⏑ ⏑ – ⏑ ⏑ ⏑ – ⏑ ⏑ ⏑ –
μετὰ δὲ γᾶν |ὕδατά τ' ὠκ|εανὸν ἠ|φάνισε νύξ
(After earth and its waters, night blotted out ocean).

This type of paeon makes a definite close. To end on a short syllable, with the consequent lack of finality, would give the effect of a rhythm curtailed. Rather, a long syllable must be used for the break. That the sentence is over should be clear, not because of the scribe, or his mark of punctuation, but from the rhythm alone.

We have now seen that the language of prose should be well-cadenced, and not unrhythmical; have seen which rhythms will give it this quality; and have seen how these should be disposed. [It has not, perhaps, been made clear enough in this chapter how rhythms other than that of the paeon enter into the language of prose: the basic rhythm of this is iambic, and the main artistic variation the paeon. The occasional use of compound words and epithets (3. 7, p. 199) would bring in other rhythms; see also, for example, the φήμην δὲ καὶ μνήμην ('name and fame'—*ibid.*) of Isocrates, which Aristotle approves, though possibly on grounds other than those of the rhythm (– – ⏑ – – –). With Aristotle's chapter, compare Dionysius of Halicarnassus, *On Literary Composition*, ed. Roberts, pp. 254–7.]

Construction of periods (sentences)

3. 9. [THE PERIOD AND ITS MEMBERS.] The style necessarily is either running [loose, strung-out], the whole made one only by a connecting word between part and part—like the preludes in dithyrambs; or compact [periodic], returning upon itself—like strophe and antistrophe in the elder poets. The running style is the ancient [original] one; for example: 'This is the setting forth of the inquiry of Herodotus of Thurii' [Herodotus 1. 1]. In early times it was used by every one; not many use it now. By a 'running' style I mean one that has no stopping-places in it before the subject under discussion comes itself to an end. It fails to satisfy us, because it has no limit; every one likes to have the end of a thing within view. So is it with men in a race: they gasp and collapse at the goal; so long as they see it before them they can keep up their effort. Such, then, is the loose kind of style.

Running or loose style

Compact or periodic style

The compact is that style which is in periods; and by a period I mean a sentence that has in itself a beginning and an end, and can be taken in as a whole at a glance. Such a style is pleasing, and easy to follow. It gives satisfaction because it is just the reverse of indefinite; the hearer constantly feels that he has got something—that he is reaching some conclusion. To foresee nothing, to accomplish nothing, is very unpleasant. The style is easy to follow, because it is easily recollected; and this because language in periods has number, and number is of all things the easiest to recall. [Periodic language has a symmetrical structure, the parts of which are seen to be in a measured, and measurable, succession; we count these subconsciously and hence recollect the better.] That is why every one remembers verse better than casual prose. Verse has number—*is* verse through its measurement by number. Further, the end of the period must coincide with the sense; there must be no awkward break between them. Take, for example, the iambic passage of Sophocles [—really from the *Meleager* of Euripides]:

1409ᵇ

Lo, this is Calydon [;] of Pelops' land . . .

By not making the right pause, you may reverse the meaning. Here, by not pausing, one might take Calydon to be in the Peloponnesus.

Formation of the period

A period may be composed of several members, or it may be simple. The period of several members is a sentence complete in itself, divided into parts, and easily uttered at a single breath—as a whole, that is, and not with a breath at a point of division. A member [colon, clause] is one of the two parts of such a period. By a simple period I mean one that has but a single member [colon, clause]. The members, like the periods, should be neither curt nor long. If a member is too short, it often trips up the hearer; he is mentally hurrying on to complete the measure, having his own notion where it will end; if he is suddenly pulled up by a pause of the speaker, he is sure to stumble, as it were, from the check. When the members are too long, they give the hearer a sense of being left behind—just as people who walk beyond the turning-point before turning leave their companions behind. Much the same is true of periods; if you make them too long, they grow into a speech, or something like a dithyrambic prelude. The result is expressed by the jeer of Democritus of Chios at Melanippides for writing preludes instead of dithyrambic stanzas:

Its members

> A man contrives ill for himself when ill he contrives for another;
> A long-winded prelude does harm to us all—but harms, above all, the preluder.

These verses [parodying Hesiod, *Works and Days* 265, 266] apply as well to long-winded users of membered periods. On the other hand, when the members are altogether too short, the result is no period at all, and the listener is sent headlong.

The periodic style in which the sentence is divided into

Simple division of members

Antithetical members

1410a

members is of two kinds. The members are either (1) simply divided, or (2) antithetical. Thus, (1) divided: 'I have often wondered at the conveners of national assemblies, and the founders of athletic contests' [—from Isocrates, *Panegyricus* 1]. When the style is (2) antithetical, in each of the two members (*a*) an opposite is balanced by an opposite, or (*b*) two opposites are linked by the same word. For example [cf. *ibid.* 35, 36]: 'They served both parties—both those who stayed behind and those who came with them; for the latter they acquired additional territory larger than that at home, and to the former they left land enough at home.' Here the contrasted terms are 'staying behind' and 'coming with them,' and 'enough' and 'larger.' So [cf. *ibid.* 41]: 'Both to those who want to have money, and to those who wish to enjoy it'; where the contrast is between enjoyment and acquisition. Again [cf. *ibid.* 48]: 'It often happens in such enterprises that the prudent fail, and the fools succeed.' Or [*ibid.* 72]: 'They immediately received the crown of valor, and soon won command of the sea.' Or [*ibid.* 89]: 'To sail through the mainland and march through the sea, by bridging the Hellespont and digging through Athos.' Or [cf. *ibid.* 105]: 'By nature citizens, by law bereft of their city.' Or [*ibid.* 149]: 'Some of them perished in misery, others were saved in disgrace.' Or [cf. *ibid.* 181]: 'In our private households keeping foreign servants, as a public measure letting thousands of our allies live in foreign slavery.' Or [cf. *ibid.* 186]: 'To enjoy in life, or bequeath at death.' Take, again, what some one said in court of Peitholaus and Lycophron: 'These fellows while at home used to sell you; now they are here, they've had to buy you.' All these passages have the structure described above. This kind of style is pleasing, because things are best known by opposition, and are all the better known when the opposites are put side by side; and is pleasing also because of its resemblance to logic—

for the method of refutation [of the refutative syllogism] is the juxtaposition of contrary conclusions.

Such, then, is the nature of *antithesis*. *Parisosis* [parallel structure] is having the two members of a period equal in length. And *paromoeosis* [parallelism of sound] is having similar words at the extremes of the two members; this similarity must occur either at the beginnings or at the ends of the members. If at the beginnings, the likeness must always be between whole words; if at the ends, it must be in the final syllables, or in the same word repeated with different inflections, or simply in the same word repeated. Thus, with similar words at the beginnings [Aristophanes, frag. 649, Kock]:

Parisosis

Paromoeosis

ἀγρὸν γὰρ ἔλαβεν ἀργὸν παρ' αὐτοῦ
(Tilth he took, tilled not, from him).

Or [*Iliad* 9.526]:

δωρητοί τ' ἐπέλοντο παράρρητοί τ' ἐπέεσσιν.

With the similarity at the ends:

οὐκ ᾠήθησαν αὐτὸν παιδίον τετοκέναι
ἀλλ' αὐτοῦ αἴτιον γεγονέναι

(They did not presume him the father,
but the cause of the child's being, rather).

Or:

ἐν πλείσταις δὲ φροντίσι καὶ ἐν ἐλαχίσταις ἐλπίσιν.

Or, with inflections of the same word:

ἄξιος δὲ σταθῆναι χαλκοῦς, οὐκ ἄξιος ὢν χαλκοῦ;
(Worthy a statue of copper, and he himself not worth a copper?)

Or, with repetition of the same word:

σὺ δ' αὐτὸν καὶ ζῶντα ἔλεγες κακῶς καὶ νῦν γράφεις κακῶς

(Of him, while he lived, you spoke ill, and, now he is dead, you write ill [—that is, slandered him while alive, and wrote a miserable panegyric on him when he died]).

Or, with resemblance in one syllable:

τί ἂν ἔπαθες δεινόν, εἰ ἄνδρ' εἶδες ἀργόν;

(Would it be very shocking, had you seen a man idling?)

1410ᵇ

It is possible in one and the same sentence to have all these figures together—*antithesis, parison* [equality of members], and *homoeoteleuton* [similarity of endings]. The possible beginnings of periods have been rather fully enumerated in the *Theodectea* [? a parallel work of Aristotle to Book 3 of the *Rhetoric*]. There are also false antitheses, as in the verse of Epicharmus:

Now on a time within their halls I was;
But on a time beneath their roof was I.

Clever sayings

3. 10. [Lively Sayings.] We may now regard the questions above as settled, and must take up the question how to devise lively and popular sayings. Of course, the actual invention of these is a matter of natural talent or long practice; the affair of this treatise is to explain them. Let us proceed by enumerating them in full. And we may start from the principle that we all take a natural pleasure in learning easily; so, since words stand for things, those words are most pleasing that give us fresh knowledge. Now strange words leave us in the dark; and current words [with the things they stand for] we know already. Accordingly, it is metaphor that is in the highest degree instructive and pleasing. When Homer calls old age 'stubble' [—'but natheless I ween one might see from the stubble what the grain has been' (*Odyssey* 14. 213–4)], he makes us learn, gives us a new concept, by means of the common genus; since both things [old age and stubble]

The pleasure of learning

fall under the genus 'withered.' And the similes of the poets do the same, so that, if they are well-made, they have a lively effect. The simile, as we said before [3. 4, p. 192], is a metaphor, differing from it only in that the simile adds the phrase of comparison, which makes it longer, and hence less pleasing. Nor does it, like the metaphor, say 'this *is* that'; and hence the mind of the hearer does not have to seek the resemblance. [The simile being longer, using more words, you do not learn the same thing so rapidly from it as from the metaphor; and, being explicit (saying 'this is *like* that'), does not bring, as does the metaphor, the easy and pleasant operation of finding the resemblance—which is implicit in the metaphor.] It follows, then, for style and reasoning [enthymemes] alike, that in order to be lively they must give us rapid information. Consequently, we are not highly gratified by enthymemes that are obvious—and 'obvious' means absolutely plain to every one, not demanding a bit of mental inquiry—nor by those which, when stated, we do not understand. What we like are those that convey information as fast as they are stated—so long as we did not have the knowledge in advance—or that our minds lag only a little behind [cf. 2. 23, p. 172]. With these latter two kinds there is some process of learning; from the former two we learn nothing either instantly or soon. In respect to the meaning, then, such are the qualities an audience likes in the argument [enthymemes]. In respect to the style in which the argument is put, what they like in the arrangement is antithesis and balance; as [Isocrates, *Philippus* 73]: 'Deeming the peace that is shared by all the rest to be a war upon their own private interests'—where war is contrasted with peace. What they like in the diction is metaphor—metaphors not far-fetched, for such are hard to grasp, nor obvious [trite], for such leave no impression. And, finally, they like words that set an event before their eyes; for they must see the thing occurring

Style and substance

Lively substance

Lively style

now, not hear of it as in the future. In style, accordingly, the speaker must aim at these three points: Metaphor, Antithesis, Actuality.

Metaphor

1411[a]

Striking examples of it

Metaphors are of four kinds [see *Poetics* 21]; of these the best-liked are the proportional. For example: Pericles [in his *Funeral Oration*; cf. 1. 7, p. 43] said that the young men who had fallen in the war had vanished from their city 'as if the spring were taken out of the year.' Leptines, in allusion to Sparta, told the Athenians that he would not let them stand by and see Greece 'lose one of her eyes' [—the other eye being Athens]. When Chares [still in command of hired troops] was urgent to have his accounts approved for his part in the Olynthiac war, Cephisodotus said with indignation: 'He wants his account to be settled while his hands are at the people's throat!' On another occasion Cephisodotus urged the Athenians to hurry a force to Euboea, and said they must go 'with the decree of Miltiades for supplies' [—alluding to some rapid action of this commander]. When the Athenians made a truce with Epidaurus and the adjacent sea-board, Iphicrates said in vexation that they had 'thrown away their traveling-money for the war.' [Without the truce, Epidaurus could have been plundered for the maintenance of the war against Sparta.] Peitholaus called the galley Paralus 'the people's bludgeon,' and the town of Sestos [which commanded the trade of the Black Sea through the Hellespont] 'the granary of the Peiraeus.' Pericles bade his countrymen get rid of Aegina, 'that eyesore of the Peiraeus.' And Moerocles said he was 'no more a crook than the very respectable Mr. So-and-So'—naming his man; for So-and-So was 'a crook at an annual rate of 33 $\frac{1}{3}$ per cent.,' he himself 'only at 10.' Then there is the iambic line of Anaxandrides [? uttered by the Herald of King Aegyptus in a comedy on the Danaides] about the daughters who put off getting married:

> Methinks the maidens' marriage-bonds are overdue.

Polyeuctus said of a palsied man named Speusippus: 'He cannot keep quiet, though fate has shackled him in the pillory of disease.' Cephisodotus called the fleet 'painted millstones' [—from their grinding effect upon tributary states]. Diogenes the Cynic called the taverns [of Athens—with their orgies] 'Attic mess-rooms' [—alluding to the frugal public meals of Sparta]. Aesion said of Athens: 'They have emptied the town into Sicily' [—drained it for the Sicilian expedition]; the diction is metaphorical, and also puts the event before our eyes. And Aesion, again: 'Till all Greece shouted aloud'; this, too, in its way a metaphor, puts the thing directly before us. Cephisodotus bade the Athenians take care not to hold too many 'scrambles' [—to avoid turning their assemblies into mobs]; Isocrates [*Philippus* 12] used the same figure for the tumult at the great festivals. Another example occurs in the *Funeral Oration* [? of Lysias]: 'Well may Greece cut off her hair at the tomb of those who have fallen at Salamis [? rather, 'Aegospotami'], where her freedom and their valor are buried in one grave.' Had the speaker here merely said, 'It is right to weep while their valor is buried,' it would be a metaphor, and would place the action before one's eyes; but when he couples 'their valor' with 'her freedom,' we have a certain antithesis as well [—so that the passage illustrates all three qualities of lively diction]. 'The course of my words,' said Iphicrates, 'lies right through the middle of Chares' deeds'; this is a proportional metaphor, and the phrase 'through the middle' puts the thing before our eyes. So the expression 'to call in one danger to save us from another' is a metaphor, and likewise vivid. In defending Chabrias, Lycoleon said: 'Unawed even by yon statue of bronze which there intercedes for him.' [The speaker points to the statue of Chabrias' victory; it represents the victor awaiting attack in a posture suggestive (*now*, for the ends of the speech) of kneeling.] This

1411b

was a metaphor for the time being, not permanent, but vivid; only while Chabrias is in danger can the statue be said to intercede for him; the lifeless monument of his service to the State becomes animate. 'In every way practising littleness of mind' [Isocrates, *Panegyricus* 151]; this is a metaphor [from species to genus—cf. *Poetics* 21], for *practising* is a species of *increasing*. [Study or practice implies (is one sort of) increasing or promoting, commonly of some good; in the example, the liveliness of style consists in the unexpected turn of 'promoting' something unworthy.] Again [a proportional metaphor—author unidentified]: 'God kindled reason to be a light in the soul'; both reason and light make things clear. So [Isocrates, *Panegyricus* 171]: 'For we do not put an end to our wars, but only postpone them'; both postponement [in the ordinary sense] and the sort of peace in question are things of the future. [The metaphor, then, is from species to species, under a common genus; cf. *Poetics* 21.] So also to say [cf. Isocrates, *Panegyricus* 180]: 'This treaty is a trophy far nobler than those set up on battlefields; for they record some minor gain, some single issue; but it records the happy outcome of the war.' Both trophy and treaty are signs of victory [—species of a genus]. So again [author uncertain]: 'States pay a heavy reckoning [for their misdeeds] in the census of mankind'; a reckoning is a species of legal damage [—the metaphor is from species to genus].

3. 11. [Means to Liveliness Further Considered. The chapter continues the discussion of clever, lively, pointed sayings, which (so far as diction, rather than substance, is concerned) gain their quality through Antithesis, Metaphor (especially the proportional kind), and Actuality (putting a thing before the eyes). But the chapter adds something on the use of devices that were not in the programme announced in 3. 10 (p. 208).]

Actuality

We have said that liveliness is secured by the use of proportional metaphor, and by putting things directly before the eyes of the audience. But we have still to explain what is meant by setting things 'before the eyes,' and how this is to be effected. What I mean is, using expressions that show things in a state of activity. It is a metaphor, indeed, to say [with Simonides] that a good man is 'four-square,' since both the good man and the square are perfect [—are two species of a genus]; but the metaphor suggests no activity. There is, on the other hand, a sense of activity in the expression [of Isocrates, *Philippus* 10], 'with his vigor fully blooming'; and similarly in [*ibid.* 127], 'thou, roaming as free as a sacred bull.' So also [cf. Euripides, *Iphigenia at Aulis* 80]:

> Thereat the Greeks updarting to their feet.

Lifelike activity—Homeric

'Updarting,' a metaphor, conveys activity as well, for the word suggests rapid motion. So Homer constantly uses the device of metaphor to make lifeless things alive, and in every case gains his admirable effect by representing them as active; thus in the following passages:

> Downward again to the plain went rolling the boulder *remorseless* [cf. *Odyssey* 11. 598 (on Sisyphus)].
>
> The [bitter] arrow *flew* [cf. *Iliad* 13. 587].
>
> [The arrow] *yearning* to fly to its mark [*ibid.* 4. 126].
>
> [Of the spears, many . . .]
> Stuck fast in the earth, still *panting* to sate themselves with his flesh [*ibid.* 11. 574].
>
> And the spear-point, *quivering eagerly*, rushed through his breast [*ibid.* 15. 542].

1412a

In all these examples the objects are invested with life, and thereby give an effect of activity; 'shameless' behavior, 'quivering with eagerness,' and so on, are all of them forms of activity. And the poet has attached these concepts to the objects by means of proportional metaphors: as the stone is to Sisyphus, so is the shameless man to his victim. In his much-admired similes, too, Homer treats inanimate objects in the same way:

> [Waves . . .]
> Arched over, foam-crested, some vanward, more following after;
> [So the Trojans . . . (*Iliad* 15. 798–800)].

He makes everything live and move; and movement is activity.

The eye for resemblance

Metaphors, as we have said [3. 10, p. 207], should be drawn from objects that are related to the object in question, but not obviously related; [in rhetoric] as in philosophy the adept will perceive resemblances even in things that are far apart. Thus [the philosopher] Archytas said that an arbitrator and an altar were the same, since both are a refuge for the injured. One might say that an anchor and a hook aloft were the same, for in a way they *are* the same, the difference being that one holds from below and the other from above. And to talk of cities as 'put on a level' [cf. Isocrates, *Philippus* 40] is to identify two things that are far apart, the equality of surfaces and equality in political strength.

Deceptive surprise

Now liveliness through the use of metaphor is for the most part gained when there is an added element of surprise [deception]; the hearer, who expected something quite different, is all the more aware, from the contrast, that he has learned something. His mind seems to say: 'True enough!—and I never thought of it.' So with terse sayings [apophthegms]; their liveliness comes from the indirect statement of the intended meaning, as in the saying of Stesichorus [cf. 2. 21, p. 152]: 'The cicalas will chirp to themselves on the ground.' [This means: The enemy will destroy all the trees. When we see the veiled meaning, we are conscious of our success in learning.]

Learning through surprise

Well-devised riddles are pleasant for the same reason—the solution is an act of learning; and they are expressed metaphorically, too. Similarly with what Theodorus [the rhetorician] terms 'novelties of expression.' We have this 'novelty' when there is an element of surprise, and as Theodorus says, the thought turns out otherwise than we expected; like the jests found in comic writers, that are produced by substitutions in words. The alterations may affect but a single letter. The principle is that of deception, and the trick is used in verse as well as in prose. The listener anticipates one thing, and hears another; thus [possibly an instance given by Theodorus]:

> So minced he along, his feet being shod with—chilblains.

Here X thought that Y would say 'sandals.' In this sort of thing, the point ought to be clear the instant the words are uttered. Jokes arising from changes in the letters of a word [alterations within the word or phrase, as opposed to the substitution of one word for another] depend upon a twist of pronunciation that makes a word mean something else. An example given by Theodorus is the joke on Nicon the harpist, Θρᾷττ' εἶ σύ ['You Thracian strumpet!'], where the speaker makes as if to say θράττεις σύ ['You strum it'], and deceives the listener by saying something else. When the point is caught, the hearer likes it; if he did not know the harpist to be a Thracian, he would, of course, see no point in the thing. Another example [? from Theodorus] is: βούλει αὐτὸν πέρσαι. [This joke never has been explained; it may well depend upon some twist in the pronunciation of the last syllable.] Both examples demand suitable enunciation; and so do pointed sayings like the two following: 'To the Athenians the ἀρχή [command] of the sea was *not* the ἀρχή [beginning] of their woes, since they profited by it'; or the reverse, from Isocrates [cf. *Philippus* 61; *De Pace* 101]: *1412*[b]

'Their ἀρχή [command] *was* to the city the ἀρχή [beginning] of their woes.' In both cases the unexpected thing is the thing that is uttered, and the hearer accepts it as right. There would be nothing clever in saying that ἀρχή was ἀρχή; but Isocrates does not so intend it—he varies the meaning; and similarly in the negative statement the speaker varies the meaning. In all such cases, the merit of the pun, or of the metaphor, depends upon its being apposite. For example: 'Baring [a man's name] is past bearing.' Here we have a pun through the use of a negative; but it is apposite only if the man is unpleasant. Again:

Do not be more strange [ξένος] than, Strange [Ξένος], you must.

In other words, do not be more of the very thing [word, name, thing] you are than you can help. Or this: 'Our stranger must not always be a stranger'; here again the word ξένος is taken in two senses. Of the same sort is the much-admired line of Anaxandrides:

> Well is it to die before we have done aught worthy of
> death;

for this is equivalent to saying, 'It is a worthy thing to die without being worthy to die,' or 'It is worthy to die when one is not worthy of death'—that is, when your deeds are worthy of another return than death.

In all these examples the form of expression is the same; but the more concise and antithetical the saying, the better it pleases, for the reason that, by the contrast, one learns the more, and, by the conciseness, learns with the greater speed. Further, there should always be some personal application, or special merit of expression, if the saying is to ring true, and not to be tame—two requisites that are not always conjoined. Thus 'A man should die void of all offence' is true but tame, and so is 'A worthy man should wed a worthy woman.' But if we conjoin the two requisites, then a lively saying appears: 'It is worthy to die when one is not worthy of death.' The more excellences you combine, the livelier is the effect of the saying; for example, when the words are metaphorical, and the metaphor is of the right kind, and there is antithesis with balanced structure, and a sense of activity as well.

Similes

Effective similes, too, as we have said [3. 4, 10; pp. 192, 207], are, in their way, always metaphors [of the right kind], since, like the proportional metaphor, they always involve two relations. Thus, a *shield* (we say) is 'the bowl of Ares,' and a *bow* is 'the chordless lyre.' A *1413a* metaphor thus put is not 'simple'; the metaphor is 'simple' when they call the *bow* 'a lyre,' or the *shield* 'a bowl.' And we have the simile, too, that is 'simple'; as when they liken a flute-player to a monkey, or a short-sighted man to a sputtering lamp (since both keep winking). Success is attained when the simile is a [proportional] metaphor [converted]; for you can say that the shield 'is like' the bowl of Ares, or that a ruin 'is like' a building in rags. Or you may say that Niceratus is 'a Philoctetes stung by Pratys'—to use the simile of Thrasymachus when he saw Niceratus, still unkempt and unwashed after his defeat by Pratys in the competition of rhapsodes. [See the tale of Philoctetes, once stung by a serpent, and now just able to crawl, in the play of like name by Sophocles.] It is here that poets fail worst if they fail; and here that they please best if they succeed—that is, when the terms of their simile chime:

> Like parsley-stems his legs curl beneath him;

or:

> Just like Philammon boxing with his punch-ball.

Expressions like these are all similes, and that similes are metaphors has been often enough stated.

Proverbs

Proverbs, too, are metaphors; they are metaphors from one species to another [cf. *Poetics* 21]. A man, for example, in the hope of gain brings something home that later results in loss: 'The Carpathian and his hare!' says he; for both he and the Carpathian have had the experience described. [A Carpathian brought a hare to his island, and her offspring overran it.]

Hyperbole

We have now with some fulness explained how liveliness is secured, and the reason why lively sayings have their effect. It may be added that successful hyperboles are metaphors; as, for example, the one about the man with the black eye: 'You would have taken him for a basket of mulberries.' The black eye has the purple color; the exaggeration lies in the quantity of fruit. If you employ a word of comparison (saying, '*Like* this or that'), you have, in effect, a hyperbole, the difference lying only in the formula. Thus:

> *Just like* Philammon boxing with his punch-ball.

In effect: You would have thought him to be Philammon fighting with his punch-ball.
So also:

> *Like* parsley-stems his legs curl beneath him.

In effect: You would have thought he had, not legs, but stems of parsley, so curly were they. Hyperboles are characteristic of youngsters; they betray vehemence. And so they are used, above all, by men in an angry passion [as Achilles in *Iliad* 9. 385, 388–90]:

> Nay, not if he offered me gifts as the sand and the dust for number . . .
> And the daughter of Agamemnon Atreides I never will wed,
> Nay, not if in beauty she vied with Aphrodite the golden,
> And equaled Athena in skill.

1413ᵇ

(The Attic orators are particularly given to using hyperbole.) We see that it is unsuited to an elderly speaker.

3. 12. [Propriety of Style Resumed; Concluding Observations.] We must not fail to notice that each kind of rhetoric has its own appropriate style. The style of written prose is not the same as that of controversial speaking; nor, in the latter, is the style of public discussion the same as that of the law-courts. A knowledge of both the written and the spoken style is required. Debate demands the ability to utter pure Greek; while a command of the written style will save you from the fate of those who do not know how to write—that is, from being forced to hold your peace when there is something you wish to impart to the public.

Each kind of rhetoric has its own style

The written [literary] style is the more finished; the controversial is far better adapted to dramatic delivery, whether for the kind of speaking that reflects character, or the emotional kind. We see why actors try to find plays in the oratorical style, and poets seek for actors who can deliver such plays. Yet the poets who write to be read have their vogue, too; so Chaeremon, who is as finished as a professional speech-writer, and so, among dithyrambic poets, Licymnius. On comparison, speeches of the literary men sound thin in the actual contests; while those of the orators sound well, but look crude when you have them in your hands—and the reason is that their place is in a contest. For that they are fitted; so if you rob them of dramatic delivery, the dramatic devices in them fail to operate aright, and hence appear silly. Such devices as *asyndeta* [parallel expressions without connectives] and repetition of the same word, which are rightly enough censured in the literary style, have their place in the controversial style when a speaker uses them for their dramatic effect. But, if you repeat, you must also vary the repetition, in order to pave the way, as it were, to dramatic delivery; for example: 'There is the villain who duped you; there is he who quite beguiled you; there is he who had in hand utterly to betray you.' In the *Old*

The literary style and the spoken

Men's Passion of Anaxandrides, the actor Philemon used to do the like when he spoke the lines containing 'Rhadamanthus and Palamedes,' and similarly in the prologue to *The Pious Ones* when he repeated the 'I.' [Anaxandrides in composing the repetition had so varied the wording that the actor could vary the tone and emphasis. Compare the repetition of 'Et Tartuffe?' and its variation 'Le pauvre homme!'—each phrase occurring four times—in Molière's *Le Tartuffe* 1. 5.] Indeed, if such passages are not dramatically rendered, it becomes a case of 'the man who carried a rafter.' [That is, the speaker reminds one of a man who 'had swallowed a poker.'] So, too, with *asyndeta*; for example: 'I came; I met him; I implored him.' The passage must be made dramatic, not uttered as one idea, with unvarying sentiment and tone. And *asyndeta* have this further property of making it seem that a number of statements have been made in the time required for one. As the use of the conjunction turns a number of statements into one, just so the omission of connecting words does the opposite, turning a single statement into many. Asyndeton, therefore, serves to amplify an idea; thus: 'I came; I talked with him; I made my entreaty!'—so many facts, it seems; 'he disregarded all I said.' This is the effect that Homer aims at in the lines [*Iliad* 2. 671–3]:

1414a

> Nireus, again, from Syme . . .
> Nireus, son of Aglaia . . .
> Nireus, the comeliest man. . . .

If a good many things are said about a person, his name will have to be mentioned pretty often: accordingly, if his name is often mentioned, one has the impression that a good deal has been said about him. By the use of this fallacy, Homer, who mentions Nireus only in this single passage, makes him important, and has preserved his memory, though in the rest of the poem he says never a word more about him.

For popular speaking, we see, the style is in every way comparable to the painting of scenery in large. The greater the crowd, the more distant is the point of view; so that, in the speech and sketch alike, minute touches are superfluous, and blur the effect. The forensic style is more elaborate in detail; still more so the style intended for a single judge. With but one judge, the value of rhetorical artifice is at the lowest. He gets a better view of the matter as a whole, seeing what is relevant and what is off the point; thus, there being no actual contest, his judgment is uncontaminated. The same speakers, therefore, do not shine in all these kinds of style at once. Thus finish in detail has least scope where there is most room for dramatic delivery; and in this latter there is most play for the voice—above all, for a strong one. The style of epideictic speeches [panegyrics and the like] is the most literary, since it is meant to be read; next to it comes the style of forensic speaking.

To make further distinctions—to say that the style should be 'pleasant' or 'magnificent'—is needless. Why these particular qualities rather than 'restraint,' or 'liberality,' or any other excellence of character you please? Obviously, if our definition of excellence in style [3. 2, p. 185] was sound, the style will be rendered 'pleasant' by the means we have discussed. Why else should it be 'clear,' and 'not mean,' but 'appropriate'? If it is prolix, it will not be clear; nor yet if it is too compressed. Plainly, now, the midway is befitting. And the means we have discussed will make the style give pleasure: the happy blending of customary with unusual terms, and rhythm, and the persuasiveness that comes from appropriate feeling.

Herewith we conclude our discussion of style, both in its general bearing upon all the kinds of rhetoric, and in its special applications to each of them. We have yet to deal with Arrangement.

The two parts of a speech

3. 13. [ARRANGEMENT, OR *TAXIS*.] A speech has two parts. Necessarily, you state your case, and you prove it. Thus we cannot state a case and omit to prove it, or prove a case without first stating it; one who proves must have something to prove, and one who advances a statement does so for the sake of proving it. In Rhetoric we must call these two processes, respectively, Statement and Argument (which would correspond to the distinction in Dialectic between a Problem and its Demonstration).

Faulty current distinctions

The current division is absurd; surely 'Narration' of the facts is a part of the forensic speech alone. In an epideictic speech, or in a political, how can there be a 'Narration' like the one so called? How a 'Refutation' of our opponent, or an 'Epilogue to the Argument'? In political speaking, again, there can be a 'Proem,' a 'Comparison' of arguments, and a 'Recapitulation,' only when there are two conflicting policies; in that case, you often have accusation and defence, too, but not in so far as the speech is deliberative. Nor is the 'Epilogue' always a part of the forensic speech; it is needless, for example, when the speech is short, or if the facts are easy to keep in mind; an epilogue serves to reduce the apparent length of your speech.

1414[b]

Well, then, the indispensable constituents are simply the Statement and the ensuing Argument. These are the essential elements of a speech; at most, the parts cannot exceed four—Proem, Statement, Argument, and Epilogue. 'Refutation' of the opponent falls under the head of the arguments; and since a 'Comparison' of both sides is an enlargement of your own case, it too appertains to this head. The speaker who so augments his case does it in order to prove something. But the Prologue has no such function; nor yet the Epilogue; these only aid the memory. Accordingly, if you begin making such distinctions as are current, you will end with Theodorus and his school, differentiating 'Narration' proper from 'Post-'

and 'Pre-narration,' and 'Refutation' from 'Ultimate Refutation.' When you coin a term, it ought to mark a real species, and a specific difference; otherwise you get empty, frivolous verbiage like the terms invented by Licymnius in his *Art of Rhetoric*—'Accessory Argumentation,' 'Deviation,' 'Ramification.'

3. 14. [THE PROEM OR INTRODUCTION.] The Proem is the beginning of a speech; it answers to the prologue in poetry, or to the prelude in music for the flute. All three are beginnings, and, as it were, pave the way for what follows. Thus the musical prelude is like the proem in ceremonial [epideictic] speeches. A flutist will take some brilliant passage that he can play, and using this for a prelude, will link it on to the opening notes of his theme; just so should the author proceed in an epideictic speech. He should begin with whatever he likes to say, and then strike up his theme with a connecting link. It is precisely what they all do; for illustration take the proem to the *Helen* of Isocrates—there is no inner bond between the disputatious dialecticians [with whom he begins] and Helen. Meanwhile, even if you stray far from your point, it is better so—not to have the whole speech in a single vein.

Proem

Proems of ceremonial speeches

The ordinary proem for epideictic speeches is a bit of praise or blame [cf. 1. 3, pp. 17–20]. So Gorgias begins his *Olympic Oration* [speech at the Olympic games]: 'You deserve admiration far and wide, Men of Greece'—where he praises those who instituted the great festivals. Isocrates, on the other hand [*Panegyricus* 1–2], censures them for bestowing honors on athletic prowess, but giving no prize at all to men who succeed in the things of the mind. One may also start off on the note of advice; for example: 'We ought all to honor men who are good, so *I* will praise Aristides.' Or thus: 'We should honor those men neither famous nor bad, men of unrecognized merit—such a man as Alexander the son of Priam'; the speaker [see 2. 23, pp. 161, 163; 2. 24, pp. 175–6] is giving advice. Or, again, the epideictic speaker may use a proem from the law-courts; that is, he may appeal to the hearers for indulgence if his subject shall seem strange, or difficult, or hackneyed. So Choerilus [at the beginning of his poem on the wars with Darius and Xerxes begs indulgence for a subject that has often been treated]:

1415a

> But now, when the field has long since been apportioned . . .

Thus the proems of epideictic speeches will be drawn from the topics of praise, blame, persuasion, dissuasion, and appeals to the hearer's indulgence. And the entrance to your speech must be alien or akin to your theme [—as you choose (or perhaps according to the greater or less need of variety in the speech)].

Proems of forensic speeches

As for the proems of forensic speeches, you must assume that they have the same function as the prologue of a drama and the proem of an epic poem. The dithyrambic prelude answers to the epideictic proem, thus [in the dithyramb (of unknown authorship)]:

> For thee—for thy gifts, for thy spoils of war;

but in tales and epic poems the proem gives a hint at the plot, so that we may promptly know what the story is about, and our minds not be left hanging—since the indefinite is bewildering. So when the teller puts the gist of the action into your hand, as it were, he enables you with this hold to follow the story. So we have:

> Sing, goddess, the Wrath . . . [*Iliad* 1. 1 ff.]
>
> Tell me, Muse, of that Man . . . [*Odyssey* 1. 1 ff.]
>
> Guide me through another tale, how from the land of Asia
> There came a great War into Europe . . . [The appeal to the Muse in Choerilus' poem mentioned above.]

So, too, in Tragedy. The poets make matters clear about the play; if not, like Euripides, at the very outset, yet somewhere in the earlier part ['prologue,' in a very loose sense], like Sophocles:

My sire was Polybus . . . [*Oedipus Rex* 774 ff.]

And so in Comedy as well.

The real function of the Proem

This, then, is the superlative function of the proem, this its distinctive task: to make clear the end and object of your work. And hence, if your matter is plain and short, a proem really should not be employed.

Casual functions

Other kinds of proem are used, but they are all in the nature of antidotes; they lack the distinctive function. [They are remedies against the defects of the speaker, or of his audience or his subject, or against the strength of his opponent.] These proems have their source in (1) the speaker, (2) the audience, (3) the subject, and (4) the opposition. Those that concern (1) the speaker or (4) his opponent have to do with removing or exciting prejudice.

Arousing or allaying prejudice

But here we note a difference between one who is defending a position and one who is attacking it. The defendant will deal with prejudice at the beginning; the accuser will reserve such effort for the close of the speech. Nor is the reason for this obscure. When a defendant is about to present his case, he must dislodge whatever stands in his way, and so any prejudice against him must be removed at the outset. But if prejudice is to be excited, this should be done at the close, for then what you say will be better remembered.

The appeal to the audience

Appeals (2) to the hearer aim at securing his good will, or at arousing his anger; sometimes at engaging his attention, or, on occasion, at diverting it—since engaging it is not always an advantage, and for that reason a speaker will often try to set his audience laughing.

You may use each and all of these means, if you like, in your proem, with a view to making your audience receptive, and withal give an impression of yourself as a good and just man, for good character always commands more attention. Men pay attention to things of importance, to their own interests, to anything wonderful, to anything pleasant; and hence you must give the impression that your speech has to do with the like. If you wish to divert their attention, make them think that the matter is trifling—in no way concerns them—is displeasing.

1415[b]

Capturing, or diverting, the hearer's attention

But we must not forget that such things are, every one of them, extraneous to a speech. They are for the audience, an audience that is weak enough to accept utterances beside the point; and if audiences were not what they are, there would be no need of any proem beyond a summary statement of the matter in question; thus the body of your speech would have a head as well. And further, if the hearer's attention must be caught, this may have to be done in all parts of the speech; the interest throughout is more relaxed than just when you begin to listen. So it is absurd to prescribe that the thing should be done at the outset, when every one listens with most attention. At any point in the speech, therefore, when occasion demands, it is proper to say: 'Now I draw your attention to this, which concerns you as much as it does me'; or:

> I'll tell you that, the like of which you ne'er before

heard—for terror, or for wonder. This is doing as Prodicus said: 'When the audience gets drowsy,' to 'slip in for them a bit of the fifty-drachma course.' [Prodicus' cheapest, and his most expensive, lectures are referred to by Plato (*Cratylus* 384 B).]

It is plain that such tricks are devised, not for the impartial hearer, but for hearers as they are; in preambles of all sorts a man will try to excite prejudice or to dispel misgivings. [Thus the Guard who has caught Antigone burying the body, and who is afraid to reveal the fact to Creon, says to him (Sophocles, *Antigone* 223–36)]:

> My liege, I will not say that I come [breathless] from eagerness [speed]. . . . [My mind was holding much discourse with me: . . . 'If Creon shall learn this from another, will you not smart for it?' (Etc., etc.)]

[Take, again, the speech of Thoas to Iphigenia (Euripides, *Iph. in Tauris* 1162):]

> Why all this [novel] preface?

[Both the Guard and Iphigenia reckon with a hearer far from impartial.] Preambles are used by those whose case is, or looks, bad; they find it better to dwell on anything but the case itself. That is why slaves [when they are taxed with an offence] do not answer the questions put to them, but beat about the bush in a long proem.

The means of arousing the good will of your hearer, and of exciting, severally, his other emotions, have already been explained [2. 1–11, pp. 90–131]. It is finely said [by Odysseus in his prayer to Athena (*Odyssey* 6. 327)]:

> And may, when I come, the Phaeacians receive me
> with friendship and pity.

These are the two emotions we should chiefly aim at.

Proems in ceremonial speaking

In the proem of an epideictic speech we should make the hearer feel that our note of praise includes him, and applies either to himself, or his family, or his manner of life—or somehow touches him. As Socrates rightly says in his *Funeral Oration* [cf. 1. 9, p. 51], 'It is not hard to praise the Athenians at Athens, but is hard at Sparta.'

In deliberative speaking

Proems in political [deliberative] speaking are drawn from the materials used in the forensic proem; but, by the very nature of political speaking, proems are here least in order. The subject to be discussed is already known; the facts of it, then, need no introduction. Still, the speaker may, at the beginning, have something to say on personal grounds, or because of his opponents; or because the matter is taken less seriously, or more, than he wishes. Thus one may have to excite or remove prejudice, or to magnify or diminish the importance of the facts; either of these aims may call for a proem. Or the aim may be that of adornment; you may use a proem for fear that without

1416a one the speech may appear slipshod. Gorgias' *Eulogy of Elis* may so appear, for without even working his elbows —with no preliminary sparring at all—he starts right out with 'Elis, fortunate city!'

Prejudice
Defence against it

3. 15. [Prejudice.] In dealing with prejudice, (1) one procedure is the use of those arguments with which you would clear yourself of any injurious suspicion, no matter if the suspicion has not been uttered. This procedure, then, is of a general sort. (2) Another way is an open counter on definite issues; you either deny the alleged fact; or you deny that it has hurt any one, or hurt a particular person, or hurt him as much as he says; or you deny that what you did was unfair, or very unfair; or you say that it was not disgraceful, or not much out of the way. The dispute always turns on some such point. Thus Iphicrates, in reply to Nausicrates, admitted that he had done what the latter alleged, and had done Nausicrates harm, but denied having done him injustice. Or, admitting the wrong, you may balance matters by saying that, if your act was harmful, at all events it was honorable; or that, if it caused pain, nevertheless it did good; or strike some other balance. (3) Another way is to urge that the thing was a mistake, or a mischance, or unavoidable. Thus Sophocles said that he was not trembling, as his slanderer alleged, in order to make the jury think him an old man, but because he could not help it—his eighty years were not of his choosing. Or you may balance your deed with your professed motive, and say that you intended no harm, but to do thus and so; or that you did not wish

to do what is slanderously alleged against you—the damage was quite accidental: 'An abominable man indeed I should be, had I deliberately worked for this result.' (4) Another way presents itself, if your traducer is or has been, either directly or through his associates, involved in a like suspicion. (5) There is another, if the calumny against you would involve persons who are admittedly innocent of the charge. The argument runs like this: If X must be thought an adulterer because his appearance is sleek, then Y must be an adulterer, too. (6) Another, if your accuser, or some one else, has traduced other persons, or if, without express calumny, these persons have been suspected, as you are now, and yet have been proved innocent. (7) Another is to meet calumny with calumny; thus: 'How monstrous to rely on the statements of this man, when you cannot rely upon *him*.' (8) There is another when a verdict has already been given. So with the reply of Euripides in the case over the exchange of properties, when Hygiaenon accused him of impiety, saying that the poet had encouraged perjury in the line [*Hippolytus* 612 (Hippolytus speaking)]:

> My tongue hath sworn—no oath is on my soul.

Euripides said: 'My accuser himself is at fault in referring a decision from the Dionysiac contests to the law-court. In the theatre I have already answered for the words, or will do so if he wishes to arraign me there.' (9) Another way is to denounce calumny—to show what an evil it is, and in particular how it raises false issues, and implies a distrust in the merits of one's case.

(1) The argument from presumptive signs is available for accuser and accused alike. Thus in the *Teucer* [of Sophocles] Odysseus says that Teucer is closely allied to Priam, since his mother Hesione was Priam's sister. [The inference is that Teucer has been friendly to the Trojans.] Teucer replies that his father was Telamon, an

1416[b]

Methods of accusation

enemy of Priam, and that he himself had not betrayed the Grecian spies [on his secret expedition with them in Troy]. (2) Another way, available for the accuser, is to praise at great length some trifling merit of the accused, and then to put a great slur upon him concisely; or to list a number of his merits, and then condemn him for one bad quality that bears heavily on the case. Such is the method of the most artful and unscrupulous speakers; they try to damage a man through his merits, by mixing these up with evil. (3) There is another way, available for both traducer and apologist. Since the same act may be done from various motives, the traducer must aim to disparage it by arguing from the worse construction, and the apologist to defend it by arguing from the better. Take, for example, the question [cf. 2. 23, p. 168; *Iliad* 2. 242–7]. Why did Diomede choose Odysseus as his companion in arms? One disputant would argue: 'Diomede thought Odysseus the bravest of the heroes.' And the other: 'Such was not the motive. He chose Odysseus as the only hero so worthless that he could not rival Diomede.'

Narration

3. 16. [NARRATION.] So much for the treatment of prejudice. We turn to the subject of Narration.

In epideictic speeches

In an epideictic speech, Narration is not continuous, but intermittent. Some account there must be of the actions that give rise to the speech, for the speech consists of two elements. One of these, namely the actions, is not supplied by the speaker's art, for of the actions he is in no way the author. The other is supplied by his art; and this element is the proof (where such proof is required) that the actions were performed, or the exposition of their quality, or of their magnitude—or even the setting forth of all these things. The reason why it is sometimes undesirable to make the narration continuous, and exhaustive, is that the exposition thus becomes hard to recollect.

Accordingly, it is well to make a selection from the facts —from some of your hero's deeds to show that he is brave, from others that he is wise or just. A speech thus devised will be simple as compared with the former, which is involved and profuse. Now, among the deeds you must recall, there are, on the one hand, those that are generally known; being well-known facts, then, for the mass of people they need no rehearsal. They need none, for instance, if your aim is the praise of Achilles; since every one knows the deeds of the hero, it only remains to employ them. On the other hand, if your theme is the praise of Critias, you must tell what he did, since his deeds are not a matter of common knowledge. [Lacuna in the text? . . .]

At present there is an absurd demand that the narration should be 'rapid.' It reminds one of the baker who asked if he was to make the bread hard or soft. 'What!' said the customer, 'can't you make it just right?' So here. The narration must not be over-long, just as the proem must not be over-long, nor yet the arguments. Here, too, then, the right thing is neither rapidity nor brevity, but the proper mean. And the mean consists in saying just so much as will make matters plain—enough to make your hearer believe that an act has occurred, or that a man has caused harm to another, or done him wrong, or *1417a* that affairs have the importance you would have people attach to them. If you are the opposing speaker, you must do the reverse.

Narration in attacking

Incidentally you may narrate whatever tends to your own credit, or to the discredit of the other side; for example: 'Meanwhile I kept reminding him of his duty, and urged him not to abandon his children. But he answered me that, wherever he might be, there he would have other children.' Say this was the answer of the mutinous Egyptians as recorded by Herodotus [2. 30]. Or add anything else that will please your judges.

Narration in defence

The defence needs less narration. Here you have to contend that the act did not occur, or that it did no harm, or that it was not unjust, or that it had not the importance alleged. So you must not waste time on a fact you admit, unless your story will bear on the contention that, granted the act, it was no injustice, or the like. Further, speak briefly of events as past and gone, except where representing them as present will excite pity and indignation. For an example, see the story told to Alcinous as retold to Penelope in sixty lines. [Homer has Odysseus tell the long story of his wanderings to Alcinous in Books 9–12 of the *Odyssey*—and the reader then has the facts; Odysseus later retells the story to Penelope in *Odyssey* 23. 264–84, 310–43 (55 lines).] Another instance is the summary of the Epic Cycle by Phayllus, and another the Prologue to [Euripides'] *Oeneus*.

Ethos in the Narration

The narration should depict character; and it will do so if we know what imparts character [*ethos*]. One thing that will give this quality is the revelation of moral purpose; for the quality of the *ethos* is determined by the quality of the purpose revealed, and the quality of this purpose is determined by its end. Thus mathematical discourses exhibit no moral character, for they reveal no moral purpose; there is no question in them of pursuing or avoiding an end or object. On the other hand, Socratic dialogues do exhibit character, since they discuss such questions [of choice and purpose]. Other things that impart character are the traits that belong to each type; thus: 'Still talking, on he went'—which reveals the type of blusterer and boor. And, in narrating, do not speak as if from the intellect—after the fashion of the day; let the words come as if from a moral purpose: 'This I willed; aye, it was my natural choice; nay, though it profited me nothing, even so it was better.' This way of speaking reveals the man of virtue, while the other would indicate discretion; the man of discretion shows himself in his pursuit of advantage, the good man in his pursuit of what is noble. When a choice may appear incredible, then add the reason for it, as does Sophocles in an example in *Antigone* [911–2]. Here Antigone says that she had cared more for her brother [Polyneices] than she ever would care for a husband or children; for, if these were to perish, they might be replaced:

> But now my mother and my father are departed,
> No brother's life can bud for me again.

If you can add no such reason, at any rate say you are aware that your statement is hard to believe: 'But such is my nature—though men will believe in no motives save those of self-interest.'

The emotions in Narration

1417[b]

And in narrating employ the traits of emotion. Use the symptoms familiar to all, and any special signs of emotion in the defendant or his adversary. For example: 'With a scowl, he left me'; or—as Aeschines described Cratylus—'hissing, and working his fists.' These touches carry conviction; the hearer knows them, and, to him, they evince the truth of what he does *not* know. Many similar touches are to be got from Homer [—for example, after Penelope reminds the nurse Eurycleia of the lost Odysseus (*Odyssey* 19. 361)]:

> So she spake; but the old woman buried her face in her hands.

It is the right touch: people beginning to weep put their hands to their eyes.

Bearing of the speaker

Present yourself from the outset in a distinctive light, so that the audience may regard you as a person of this sort, your opponent as of that; only do not betray your design. It is easy to give the right impression; observe the demeanor of those who bring news. We cannot tell what the news is about, yet we make some surmise from the messenger's bearing. —You should distribute narration throughout the speech; sometimes there should be none at all at the beginning.

Narration in Deliberative speaking

In Deliberative speaking there is least room for narration, since no one can 'narrate' what is yet to be. Here, if there is narration at all, it must be of the past, and its object to remind your audience of what happened in the past, with a view to better plans for the future. It may be used in condemning people, or in approving them; but whenever you do that, you are dropping the function of adviser. If, in advising, you tell something your hearer does not believe, you must vouch for its truth, at once explain why it is credible, and array such statements as may win him. Thus in the *Oedipus* of Carcinus, when [Oedipus] is trying to learn what became of her son, Jocasta at each inquiry avouches the truth of her story. [? She gives a reason why it is true, and counsels Oedipus to desist from the search.] The Haemon of Sophocles does the like. [In *Antigone* 683 ff. Haemon makes a speech of advice (=deliberative oratory) to his father, Creon. He says (=narration) there have been murmurs among the people against Creon's condemnation of Antigone; since this statement will appear unlikely to Creon, Haemon vouches for the truth of it, and explains: people are afraid openly to object, but he himself has had private opportunity to hear the murmurs. He then vouches again, and proceeds to marshal reasons that should appeal to Creon (*Antigone* 700–23): 'Such is the darkling rumor that spreads in secret. For me, my father, no treasure is so precious as thy welfare. What, indeed, is a nobler ornament for children than that a father's good name should flourish?' Etc.]

3. 17. [THE ARGUMENTS AND THEIR ORDER. This chapter takes up the third of the four divisions of a speech mentioned in chap. 13 (p. 220).]

Your arguments should have the effect of demonstrations; and, as there are four possible issues in a dispute, your attempt at demonstration must directly bear upon the issue that really is in dispute. Thus, if the point is (1) that an act was not committed, then your primary concern at the trial is to show just that. If the point is (2) that the act did no harm, there is the thing you are to prove; and similarly with the issues (3) that the harm was less than is alleged, or (4) that the act was justified; whichever (2, 3, or 4) is the point, that is your primary concern, and as much your concern as if the issue were (1) whether or not the act was committed. But bear in mind that this first issue [—Was the act committed?] is, of the four, the only one in which it can be true that either the defendant or the accuser is necessarily a rogue. Here ignorance cannot be pleaded, as it might be if the parties were disputing whether the act was justified or not. In the first case, then, proofs that your adversary must be a rogue may be used, but not in the others.

The Argument (or Proofs)

In Forensic speaking

In Epideictic speaking, where the main thing is to show that a man's deeds were noble and of service, your chief means will be amplification. [Your Argument will magnify (or, seldom, minify) his deeds.] The facts themselves must be taken on trust; proof of them is given but rarely—when a deed seems incredible, or when it has been ascribed to some other man.

The Argument in speeches of display

In Deliberative speaking, you may contend (1) that a certain thing cannot be done; or, granted that the thing urged by the opposition can be done, you may contend (2) that it is unjust, or (3) that it will do no good, or (4) that it has not the importance the opposition gives it. Note any false statements your opponent makes in matters apart from the issue; they can be made to seem proofs that his major statements are false. Argument from examples is best-suited to Deliberative speaking; argument by enthymeme is more characteristic of Forensic speaking. Deliberative speaking is concerned with the future,

In Deliberative speaking

1418a

to which the speaker must find parallels [as 'examples'] in events that are past. Forensic speaking has to do with matters of fact—now true or untrue, and necessarily so; here strict proof is more feasible, since the past cannot change. But the enthymemes should not be given in an unbroken string; interweave them with different matter, or your arguments will damage each other's effect. There is a limit to the length of each series:

In Forensic speaking

Friend, lo, you have said *as much* as a wise man would say.

[Menelaus, commending the youth Pisistratus (*Odyssey* 4. 204), puts it 'as much as,'] not 'such things as.' Nor should you try to argue [find enthymemes] on every point; otherwise you will be doing just as some in philosophy do, who by syllogistic process reach conclusions more familiar and obvious than the premises from which they are drawn. And avoid using the enthymeme when you are trying to stir an emotion, for it will either dispel the emotion or itself be futile; simultaneous motions of the soul tend to efface each other, and, if not mutually destroyed, are mutually weakened. Nor, again, should you resort to an enthymeme in a passage where your aim is to depict character; demonstration is devoid of both character [*ethos*] and moral purpose. Maxims, however, should be employed in the proofs; here their use has an ethical value, as it has in narration: 'All the same I let him have it, though well I knew the maxim, "Trust no man."' If your aim is emotional, put it thus: 'And I have no regrets, wronged though I have been.—"His the gain, mine the justice."'

Deliberative and Forensic speaking compared

Deliberative speaking is a more difficult task than Forensic; and naturally so, since the Argument has to do with the future. The Forensic speaker argues about the past, which is already known—'even to the diviners,' as Epimenides of Crete said; and he did not use divination 'concerning the future, but only concerning dark things in the past.' Moreover, Forensic arguments have a basis in the law; and, given a starting-point, you can more easily find your proof. And again, Deliberative speaking offers few opportunities to pause for attacks on the adversary, discourse about oneself, or the excitation of feeling; there is least chance of all for such things in deliberative speaking, so long as you keep to that. You must be in difficulty before you do as the Athenian orators and Isocrates. In deliberative speeches, even, Isocrates attacks, for example, the Lacedaemonians in his *Panegyricus* [110–4], and Chares in his speech on the Alliance [*De Pace* 27].

Epideictic speaking

In an Epideictic speech you should interweave the argument with bits of eulogy, as Isocrates does; he is always bringing some one in for casual praise. And this is what Gorgias meant when he said that in speaking he never was at a loss for matter; if his subject is Achilles, he praises Peleus, then Aeacus, then Zeus [father, then grandfather, then great-grandfather]; in like manner, if his subject is courage, he says it does this and that, or is like this or that, and so on.

Argument and moral character

If you have proofs of your case, then use them, and speak from moral character [use moral suasion] as well; if you have nothing for enthymemes, then rely upon moral suasion alone. After all, it is more in keeping with true worth to reveal yourself as a man of probity than as sharp in argument. Refutative enthymemes are better-liked than demonstrative; the refutative process always makes the conclusion more striking, for setting opposites side by side renders their opposition more distinct.

1418b

Refutation a part of the Argument

A 'Refutation of your Opponent' is no separate division of the speech [3. 13, p. 220]; it belongs to the Argument. You are to break down his arguments, partly by objection, partly by counter-syllogism. In Deliberative speaking, as well as in court, if you are the first speaker you should first present your own arguments, and then meet the opposing arguments by direct refutation or by pulling

Its place

them to pieces in advance. If, however, the opposition has many proofs of its case, then begin with these, as Callistratus did in the Messenian assembly. First of all he demolished the arguments they were going to use against him, and then he presented his own. If your turn comes later, and especially if the opposing arguments have been well received, you will have to deal first with them, by the method of refutation and counter-syllogism; for, as the mind of the hearer rejects a man against whom it has taken a prejudice, just so it refuses an argument if the opposing speaker has made a good impression. You should therefore make room in the minds of the audience for the argument you are going to offer; and this will be done if you demolish the one that has pleased them. So combat it—every point in it, or the chief, or the successful, or the vulnerable points, and thus establish credit for your own arguments. [Thus Hecuba (Euripides, *Troades* 969–71) replies to Helen, who shifts the blame for her own behavior to (among others) a 'goddess':]

> Now, first, I will defend the goddesses,
> [And will convict *her* of a slanderous tongue.]
> Never, I ween, would Hera, [or Pallas the Maiden . . .]

Here the speaker fastens right off on the other's silliest point.

So much for the Arguments [persuasion by proofs]. Let us turn to *ethos*. [The distinction (still under the head of Argument; cf. 3. 13, p. 220) is between convincing the audience by process of reason and convincing them by your character (cf. 3. 17, p. 234). Here the treatment of *ethos* concerns the character of the person speaking (cf. also 1. 2, p. 8), and may be called subjective; for the treatment of character on the more objective side, in relation to the audience, see 2. 12–17, pp. 131–40, and in relation to persons represented, see 3. 7, pp. 197–9.]

There are things which, if you say them of yourself, will bring you dislike, or will be tedious, or will arouse contradiction; and things which, if you say them of another, will make you appear abusive or ill-bred. Such things, if said, should be put into the mouth of a third person. This is the method of Isocrates in the *Philippus* and in the *Antidosis.* [In *Philippus* 4–7 the author says that friends who have heard one of his unpublished compositions have been struck with its truth and value. In *Antidosis* 132–9, 141–9, he quotes utterances against popular tendencies, and in praise of his own writings, that would seem invidious if they came from the author himself in the first person.] Such is the method, too, of Archilochus in satire; thus, in his lampoon [on Lycambes and his daughter], he represents the father himself as saying of the daughter:

Persuasion through the *ethos* of the speaker

What to quote

> Think not, vow not, that aught can never be, [etc.]

And he makes Charon the builder spokesman in the lampoon beginning:

> Not for the wealth of Gyges.

So with Sophocles [*Antigone* 688–700]. Haemon pleads with his father in behalf of Antigone in the words of others: ['Such words as would offend thine ear. . . . "No woman," they say, "ever merited her doom less." ']

Further [—still with a view to *ethos,* moral suasion], sometimes you should convert your enthymemes into maxims; for instance [? cf. Isocrates, *Archidamus* 50]: 'Men of sense must agree in time of success; thus their gains will be greatest.' Put this in the form of an enthymeme, and you have: 'If men ought to reach an agreement at the time when agreements are most helpful and gainful, then they ought to reach an agreement in time of success.'

Ethical maxims

3. 18. [THE ARGUMENT, CONTINUED. In following this subject, the chapter goes into the subdivisions of Interrogation, Reply to Interrogation, and persuasion by ridicule.]

1419a

Interrogating your opponent

As for Interrogation, (1) the best time to use it is just when your opponent has made such an admission that, if you put one more question, the absurdity is complete. Thus Pericles questioned Lampon [the soothsayer] about the mode of celebrating the rites of the Saviour-Goddess [Demeter]. Lampon declared that no uninitiated person could be told of them. Pericles then asked: 'Do you yourself know them?' 'Yes,' said Lampon. Indeed!' said Pericles; 'How can you, when you are n't initiated?'

A second chance is (2) when one premise to a conclusion is obviously true, and you see that your opponent must admit the truth of the other as soon as the question is put. Simply ask him about this one premise; do not add a question about the one that is obvious. But state the conclusion. Thus [cf. Plato, *Apology* 27 c], when Meletus denied that Socrates believed in the existence of gods, Socrates asked: 'Do I say there is something like a *daemon*?' Meletus said 'Yes.' Then Socrates asked: 'Are not *daemons* either children of gods or in some way divine?' When Meletus answered 'Yes,' Socrates replied: 'Well, then, is there any one who thinks there are children of gods, but denies the existence of gods?'

A third chance is (3) when you are about to show that your opponent contradicts either himself or what people believe. A fourth is (4) when he cannot meet your question save by an equivocal answer. If he answers evasively, 'Yes and no,' or 'Partly yes, and partly no,' or 'In one sense yes, in another sense no,' the audience thinks he is caught, and applauds.

In situations other than these you had best not attempt interrogation; for if your opponent gets in an objection, you will seem to have been defeated. You cannot go on asking a string of questions—an audience lacks the power to follow. For the same reason you should make your [interrogatory] enthymemes as compact as may be.

In replying, you should meet (1) ambiguous questions by a reasonable definition of terms, and not answer curtly. In meeting (2) questions that involve you in a seeming contradiction, you must explain the difficulty at the outset of your reply, before your opponent has put the next question or drawn his conclusion. It is not hard to foresee the drift of his argument.—We may assume, however, that this point, and the means of refutation in general, have been made clear in the *Topics* [8].

Reply to Interrogation

Again, when your opponent in drawing his conclusion shapes it as a question, you must add the reason for your answer. Thus when Sophocles was asked by Peisander if he had voted like the rest of the Board of Safety to set up the 'Four Hundred,' he said 'Yes.' 'What!' said Peisander; 'did you not think it an evil course?' 'Yes,' was the reply. 'And so *you* did this evil?' 'Yes,' answered Sophocles, 'for there was nothing better to do.' So, too, the Lacedaemonian, when he was being examined for his conduct as ephor, was asked whether he thought that his fellow-ephors had been justly put to death. 'Yes,' he said. 'Well,' said the other, 'did not you act in concert with them?' 'Yes,' was his reply. 'Well then,' asked his opponent, 'would not *you* too be justly put to death?' 'Not at all,' said he; '*they* acted so because they were bribed; *I* acted, not for money, but from conviction.' It is a mistake, then, to ask any more questions after the conclusion is drawn, or to put the conclusion itself in the form of a question, unless the balance of truth is much in your favor.

1419b

As for the means to laughter: these are thought to be of some value in controversy. Gorgias said that we must ruin our opponent's earnestness with our jocularity, and his jocularity with our earnestness. His saying was right. The forms of the laughable have been classified in the *Poetics*. [This is not true of the *Poetics* in its present condition; see, rather, the *Tractatus Coislinianus* (cf. note

The use of the ludicrous

on p. 66.)] Some of the forms befit a gentleman, and some do not; irony befits him more than does buffoonery. The jests of the ironical man are at his own expense; the buffoon excites laughter at others.

Epilogue or Conclusion

3. 19. [The Epilogue.] The Epilogue is made up of four elements. (1) You must render the audience well-disposed to yourself, and ill-disposed to your opponent; (2) you must magnify and depreciate [make whatever favors your case seem more important and whatever favors his case seem less]; (3) you must put the audience into the right state of emotion; and (4) you must refresh their memories.

The last ethical impression

When at length you have shown the truth of your case, and the falsity of your opponent's, it is in the natural order of things that (1) you should commend yourself, censure him, and drive the difference home. In doing this, you must aim at one of two things. You must reveal yourself as a good man, and him as a bad one, in this particular case, or yourself as a good man, and him as a bad man, absolutely. How you are to present men in either light—the *topoi*, that is, which you are to employ in representing them as good, and as bad—this has already been discussed [1. 9, pp. 46–55; cf. 3. 17, pp. 236–7].

Final magnifying and minifying

And again, now that the facts have been established, the next step (2) naturally is to magnify or depreciate [to increase or diminish their alleged importance]. The facts must be admitted before one can discuss their importance; if bodies are to increase, they must be in existence. The means of magnifying and depreciation, the *topoi*, have already been set forth [1. 7, pp. 34–44; 2. 19, p. 146].

Appeal to the emotions

This done, and now that the nature of the facts, and their importance, are alike clear, the next thing (3) is to make the audience feel the right emotions—pity, indignation, anger, hatred, envy, emulation, antagonism, [or whatever the case requires]. The *topoi* for these, too, have been previously discussed [2. 1–11, pp. 90–131].

Recapitulation

All that remains, then, is (4) to recapitulate what has been said. Here you may properly do what some wrongly advise doing in the earlier parts of the speech; they bid you reiterate your points so that the audience may learn them well. Now what you should do in your introduction is to state the subject, so that the issue to be judged may be perfectly clear; whereas in the Epilogue you should give a summary review of your proofs. In this review, you begin by noting that you have done what you undertook to do. So then you must state what you have said, and why you have said it. One way of doing this is by a comparison of your opponent's argument with your own; and here you may contrast what he said and you said on the same point, or not do it point by point. Thus: 'My opponent said this, and I that, on this point, and my reasons were these.' Or ironically: 'Of course he said this, *1420a* and I said that'; or, 'How content he would have been to prove all this instead of merely proving that!' Or put it as a question: 'What has not been proved?' or, 'What *has* my opponent proved?' Your recapitulation, then, may take this form of direct contrast; or you may follow the natural order, that of the arguments as they were given, first taking your own, and then separately, if you like, *1420b* those of your opponent.

Aristotle's peroration

You may in fitting style close your speech with an asyndeton; it will mark off the Epilogue as a true peroration. 'I have done; you all have heard; you have the facts; give your judgment.'

A LIST OF USEFUL BOOKS FOR REFERENCE

ARISTOTLE. *Aristotelis Graece ex Recensione Immanuelis Bekkeri.* Edidit Academia Regia Borussica. Berlin, 1831. [The *Rhetoric* occupies in vol. 2 the pages, columns, and lines 1354ª 1–1420ᵇ 4.]

———. *The Works of Aristotle*, translated into English under the editorship of J. A. Smith and W. D. Ross [latterly under the editorship of Ross]. 11 vols. Oxford, 1908–31. [Volume 11 contains, besides Forster's translation of *De Rhetorica ad Alexandrum*, Roberts' translation of the *Rhetoric* and Bywater's of the *Poetics*; for these two items, see also below.]

———. *Aristotelis Ars Rhetorica.* Edidit Adolphus Roemer. Vol. 1 of *Rhetores Graeci* ex Recognitione Leonardi Spengel. Leipzig, 1885.

———. *The Rhetoric of Aristotle*, with a Commentary, by . . . Edward Meredith Cope; revised and edited . . . by John Edwin Sandys. 3 vols. Cambridge, 1877.

———. *The Rhetoric of Aristotle*, a Translation by Richard Claverhouse Jebb; . . . edited with an Introduction and with supplementary Notes by John Edwin Sandys. Cambridge, 1909.

———. *Rhetorica* [translated] by W. Rhys Roberts. In vol. 11 of *The Works of Aristotle*, translated into English under the editorship of W. D. Ross. Oxford, 1924.

———. *The Rhetoric of Aristotle*, translated, with an Analysis and critical Notes, by J. E. C. Welldon. London, 1886.

———. *Aristotle on the Art of Poetry;* a revised Text, with critical Introduction, Translation, and Commentary, by Ingram Bywater. Oxford, 1909.

———. *Aristotle on the Art of Poetry;* an amplified Version, with supplementary Illustrations, for Students of English. By Lane Cooper. New York (Harcourt, Brace and Company); first issued in Boston, 1913.

PLATO. *Phaedrus.* In *The Dialogues of Plato*, translated into English . . . by B. Jowett, third edition, 1 (1892). 431–89. [Jowett's Introduction to this dialogue is, in an essential point, quite misleading; he has not grasped the unity of the whole.]

———. *Gorgias.* In Jowett's translation, as above, 2 (1892). 325–421.

DEMOSTHENES. *The Public Orations*, translated by Arthur Wallace Pickard-Cambridge. 2 vols. Oxford, 1912.

ISOCRATES. With an English Translation by George Norlin. 2 vols. In the Loeb Classical Library. London, 1928–9.

DEMETRIUS. *On Style;* with an English Translation by W. Rhys Roberts. In the Loeb Classical Library. London, 1927.

DIONYSIUS OF HALICARNASSUS. *The Three Literary Letters;* . . . Greek Text, . . . English Translation, . . . Notes, by W. Rhys Roberts. Cambridge, 1901.

———. *On Literary Composition;* being the Greek Text of the *De Compositione Verborum;* edited with Introduction, Translation, Notes, . . . by W. Rhys Roberts. London, 1910.

'LONGINUS.' *On the Sublime;* the Greek Text . . . with Introduction, Translation, Facsimiles, and Appendices, by W. Rhys Roberts. Second edition. Cambridge, 1907.

CICERO. *Oratory and Orators*, translated by John Selby Watson. (*De Oratore*, or *On the Character of the Orator; Brutus*, or *Remarks on eminent Orators.*) In Harper's Classical Library, New York, 1850.

———. *De Oratore, Orator*, and *Brutus*. [Text, and translation by Charles Stattaford and E. W. Sutton.] In preparation. Loeb Classical Library.

ANONYMOUS. *Rhetorica ad Herennium.* [Of this work, which is listed under the supposititious writings of Cicero, there is a German translation by Karl Kuchtner, Munich, 1911. The unprinted English translation by Harry Caplan he expects in due time to publish.]

QUINTILIAN. *The Institutio Oratoria* . . . with an English Translation by H. E. Butler. 4 vols. In the Loeb Classical Library. London, 1921–2.

———. *Institutes of Oratory; or Education of an Orator;* . . . literally translated . . . by . . . John Selby Watson. 2 vols. In Bohn's Classical Library. London, 1882.

BLASS, FRIEDRICH. *Die Attische Beredsamkeit.* Second edition. 3 vols. Leipzig, 1887–8.

CHAIGNET, ANTELME ÉDOUARD. *La Rhétorique et son Histoire.* Paris, 1888.

COOPER, LANE. *An Aristotelian Theory of Comedy;* with an Adaptation of the *Poetics* and a Translation of the '*Tractatus Coislinianus.*' New York, 1922.

———. *Theories of Style, with especial Reference to Prose Composition; Essays, Excerpts, and Translations;* arranged and adapted. New York, 1907. [Includes a Bibliography of 10 pp., and (pp. 52–96) Welldon's translation of Aristotle's *Rhetoric*, Book 3, chapters 1–12.]

Cope, Edward Meredith. *An Introduction to Aristotle's Rhetoric,* with Analysis, Notes, and Appendices. London and Cambridge, 1867.

Jebb, Richard Claverhouse. *The Attic Orators from Antiphon to Isaeus.* 2 vols. London, 1876.

Navarre, Octave. *Essai sur la Rhétorique Grecque avant Aristote.* Paris, 1900.

Norden, Eduard. *Die Antike Kunstprosa vom vi. Jahrhundert v. Chr. bis in die Zeit der Renaissance.* 2 vols. Leipzig, 1898.

Roberts, W. Rhys. *Aristotle on Public Speaking.* In the *Fortnightly Review.* 122=116 (Aug. 1, 1924). 201–10.

———. *Greek Rhetoric and Literary Criticism.* Vol. 53 of *Our Debt to Greece and Rome,* edited by Hadzsits and Robinson. New York, 1928.

Volkmann, Richard; Hammer, Caspar; Gleditsch, H. *Rhetorik und Metrik der Griechen und Römer.* In *Handbuch der Klassischen Altertumswissenschaft,* hgb. v. Iwan von Müller. Munich, 1901.

INDEX

References are to the Introduction (pp. xvii-xxxv) and the translation of the *Rhetoric* (pp. 1–241). Arabic page-numbers printed italic refer to proper names and titles not supplied by the Greek text.